The Divine Blueprint

Roadmap for the New Millennium

by

Robert Perala

with

Tony Stubbs

Author of An Ascension Handbook

UNITED LIGHT PUBLISHING
CAMPBELL, CA USA

The Divine Blueprint: Roadmap for the New Millennium
by
Robert Perala
with Tony Stubbs

Published in 1998

00 99 98   0 9 8 7 6 5 4 3 2 1

Published by
UNITED LIGHT PUBLISHING
PO BOX 112467
CAMPBELL, CA 95011
VOICE MAIL: (408) 792-3333
FAX: (408) 370-3818
E-MAIL: rperala@unitedlight.com
INTERNET: www.unitedlight.com

Cover design and photographic illustration by Glen Wexler

Author's cover photo by Tim Coleman

Library of Congress Cataloging in Publication Data

    Perala, Robert, 1955–

       The divine blueprint : roadmap for the new millennium
Perala with Tony Stubbs
      p.   cm.
Includes bibliographical references
ISBN 0-9663130-7-0
1. Alien abduction–United States. 2. Spiritual life–Miscellanea.
3. Perala, Robert, 1955– , I. Stubbs, Tony, 1947– ,   II. Title
BF2050.P45   1998
001.942—DC21

                         98–8123
                           CIP

ISBN 0-9663130-7-0

Printed in the USA

Contents

Dedication

This book is dedicated to my Mother and Father for their love, support, and guidance that continues even to this day from the other side.

Till we meet again ....

Acknowledgments

I would like to take this opportunity to thank the following people:

Tony Stubbs for his invaluable insight, wisdom, and contribution, for without him, this book would not have been the same. If you are looking for assistance in writing and publishing, you can contact him through the publisher or see Resources.

My family, Dennie and Ross DeLong, Chrissy, Yvette, Rick, Kayla and Connor.

My son, Christian, who is the light of my life.

To Christian's mother, Toni, and her husband, Mark.

Gina Lake and Theodore, for their insight and contributions of *The Extraterrestrial Vision* and *ET Contact*.

Randolph Winters, for his outstanding sharing of *The Pleiadian Mission*.

Dannion Brinkley, whose love, compassion, and service to us have changed our lives and paved the way to a beautiful future.

Bettie Eadie, for showing us that there is no death, but only transformation.

Drunvalo Melchizedek, a pioneer who opened me up to the vast cosmic wisdom I so yearned for all my life.

Paula Peterson and EA, whose counseling and wisdom have been invaluable.

Gregg Braden, whose contributions with *Awakening to Zero Point* and *Walking Between The Worlds* have informed and fascinated us.

Tricia McCannon, dear friend and soul mate.

Dr. Angela Brown-Miller, whose deep friendship has been a constant source of support.

Sheldan Nidle, who has contributed wonderful insight and information with his book, *You Are Becoming a Galactic Human*.

Clarissa Bernhardt, for helping me take the first step into the unknown.

Robert and Anita Gerard, for their insights and assistance.

Bep and Floyd Jordon, whose love and support have been boundless.

Ruth Lowery, for saving me in Egypt and for loving and supporting me unconditionally.

Standing Elk and the Yanktown Sioux, my brothers in spirit.

Teri Weiss of Power Places Tours, for taking us to magical England.

Jim Downey, for introducing me to the ways and magic of "radio-land."

To Jane Hofstetter for the gracious gifts of her artwork.

Pam, who has touched my soul and shown me the essence of love.

Sir Paul McCartney, George Harrison, Ringo Starr, and Yoko Ono, whose art, music, and message have been a constant inspiration to me.

Louise Harrison, for enlightening me on the deep ecological concerns on our planet.

And in memory of John Lennon, whose pioneering spirit has touched my soul, and of Linda McCartney, artist and photographer, and beloved wife of Paul.

In memory of Princess Diana; as one great light leaves, it causes all the other lights to focus on the values they set forth.

In memory of Bev Geiger, my best friend, who always stood by me. Till we meet again ....

To Master Jesus, my guides, and members of the Spiritual Hierarchy for their constant unconditional love, support, and teaching.

And finally, in memory of my mother and father, my life-givers and way-showers, for their love, support, and guidance that continues even to this day from the other side.

Preface

Planet Earth, a place of love, hope, and wonder. It is here we come to learn about life, living and creation. It is this wondrous mission we take on so we can grow and expand our awareness of who we are and how great we can be.

Let me extend my deepest, heartfelt thanks to each and everyone of you for choosing *The Divine Blueprint: Roadmap for the New Millennium*. It is my greatest honor that I share these precious words with you.

It is a most personal story, and here I bare my soul to all. To some who have known me all my life, this may certainly come as a shock, while to others, they will know all too well that these mystic musings are etched on their soul as well. There is a common thread that brings us all together. We are all seeking the same thing: a sense of connectedness, a sense of hope, a place where the heart calls home.

Man's quest to understand how he is connected to the universe has continued since the beginning of time, and it is through my research and experiments in consciousness, spirituality, and the esoteric that I have found the fascinating components of the Divine Blueprint.

The source of my work includes twenty years of research into the esoteric, metaphysics, the mystery schools, and the Bible in addition to my expeditions in foreign countries, and of course, my "nighttime visitors." My audiences are a little awestruck when they find out about my visitors; semi-transparent men and women who look just like you and I, who perhaps have simply benefited from greater time and greater knowledge. Only on a few occasions have they identified themselves as coming from Earth's future, or more aptly put, the Pleiades, a cluster of seven stars the Bible calls the Seven Sisters.

The visitors would materialize in my house in the middle of the night as luminous, full-bodied apparitions and impart telepathic and visual concepts, potential scenarios, and objectives for Earth's present and future. It was in these visitations that I later realized that the apparitions were, in fact, extraterrestrial. In this "secret school," I was being prepared to fulfill an agreement I made before my birth.

I had agreed to be part of an extraordinary process and thus have chosen to pave the way for a new expression. Sharing a relationship with extraterrestrials is not as strange as people might think. It is simply a matter of changing one's belief system and refocusing one's intent. It will be now and in the new millennium that we will learn more freely how and why contact is a reality.

On my tours and public appearances, some have said that I am a pioneer ahead of my time. There is some truth in this, but the old adage may well apply: "nothing ventured, nothing gained."

We are at the crossroads at this time in Earth's history and we must choose between continuing as we have or embracing the fact that we are not alone in the universe. It may astonish many to see our extraterrestrial neighbors become a reality in our lifetime.

The Divine Blueprint is not an ancient document or a scroll from a cave near the Dead Sea. It is not etched on an ancient wall in Peru or a tablet buried under the sands of Egypt. Nor is it a secret handed down in the Native American oral tradition. While these all hold pieces of the Divine Blueprint, it is, in fact, the search on the part of you and I for our divinity within the overall purposes and life path of our soul, our soul group, mankind in general, and the Creator.

As we come to understand our own divine spark, we fill in our blueprint with all of the choices and decisions we make along the way. If we choose wisely, then we can reap the rewards of all our endeavors and in turn share them again with others.

I have written this book with my dear friend, Tony Stubbs, and I want to thank him, for without his insight and wisdom, this book would not have been the same. We share some of the timeless wisdom of the ancients as well as hope for, and insight into, the future. Tony was simply invaluable to this project and it was obvious to both of us that Spirit brought us together to present this wonderful work. When Tony and I first started *The Divine Blueprint*, we were literally exploding with ideas, and we knew that spirit supported us because it was all so easy and we really felt in the flow.

I want to personally thank each and everyone of you for investing in yourself. For when you invest in yourself, you invest in all of us. And this, my friend, is where the healing begins. Now let's enjoy the adventure together.

Blessings,
Robert Perala

Chapter 1

Angels in Spacesuits

A Close Encounter of the Scary Kind

I T WAS DECEMBER 26, 1977, and I was at Heavenly Valley, deep in the Sierra Nevada Mountains near Lake Tahoe on the California-Nevada border. My parents, sister, her husband and I were in our cabin in the heart of ski country. They took the two bedrooms upstairs and I slept on a sofabed downstairs.

Tonight was the night I'd chosen to conduct an experiment. It all began when I'd read a book about UFOs and ETs, called *The Edge of Reality* by J. Allen Hynek, a U.S. government UFO expert, and Jacques Vallee. In a magazine article, I'd also read that thoughts are real and once released from the mind, have a reality of their own. The mind transmits them like a radio or TV antenna does, and off they go into the universe, mingling with everyone else's thoughts, waiting to be picked up by whatever is out there. So, I reasoned, if I wanted to contact any beings out there, all I had to do was transmit a powerful and clear thought out into the universe.

The second part of the equation is attitude and intent. The only way this will work is if you earnestly want to be of service to humanity and the planet. Given that that's how I felt, I hoped that someone would pick up my message and show up on my doorstep. I still had a lot to learn about discernment and being careful about what you wish for.

I opened a window and breathed in the crisp night air. The cabin was remote so no artificial lights interfered with my night vision. Tiny rags of cloud scudded across the night sky. A crescent moon stuck one horn above the mountain skyline as it began its ascent to join the millions of stars punctuating the pitch black sky. The idea of getting away to this remote paradise had seemed perfect. It was just the right time and place for some quiet metaphysical work. But the universe was about to present me with an experience that would change the course of my life forever.

I lit a candle and began with a prayer for divine guidance and protection. With my palms out, I raised my hands to the crystal clear night sky and began breathing and drinking in the energy. I knew that everything is energy and everything is Spirit and that energy is the matrix by which all thoughts and entities travel, so it made sense to try to merge thought and travel this way. I don't know how I knew to do this; it came from a deep level of knowing. I concentrated on reaching those who might await my sincere request and then said aloud for emphasis, "If anyone is out there, I'm here and would like to meet you."

I hadn't known what to expect. Maybe a ship would land in the back yard and cosmonauts would step out and say, "Robert, we love you. Do you have any questions?" or an angel in full dress wings would appear. An hour or so had passed and nothing had happened. Finally, I went to bed, wondering if anyone had heard me. A little discouraged, I grumbled, "No one listens to you when you're twenty-two years old. It would be a miracle if anyone out there was listening." Then, I fell into a deep sleep. Little did I know that my call had been heard ... and would be answered that very same night.

BOOM! I am awakened by a sound like the shriek of a hurricane's wind. I open my eyes to see the room filled with iridescent blue flashes bouncing off the walls and ceiling. None of this registers yet on my unsuspecting mind as it is pulled from a deep sleep.

I sit up to look around for the source of the blue flashes, and what I see turns my blood cold. Three huge figures stand at the foot of my bed. Seven to eight feet tall, these things are wearing some kind of silvery suits, the source of the blue flashes. Miniature lightning arcs off them, from short spikes of a couple of inches into thin air to giant sparks clear across the room that bounced off the walls and furniture. The suits have black visors so I see no faces. Their gloves are made of the same shiny material. Iridescent waves of blues, greens, and purples wash over the suits and as each wave passes, the lightning sparks intensify.

I'm frozen in panic. Wild thoughts rush through my head. My parents and sister upstairs. Are they okay? Why can't they hear this deafening sound. It's like a freight train hammering through the house. What's happened to them? I try to shout to them but there's no air in my lungs.

I take a deep breath and just as I'm about to scream, I'm pushed flat on the bed and wrapped in a blue cloud that paralyzes every muscle

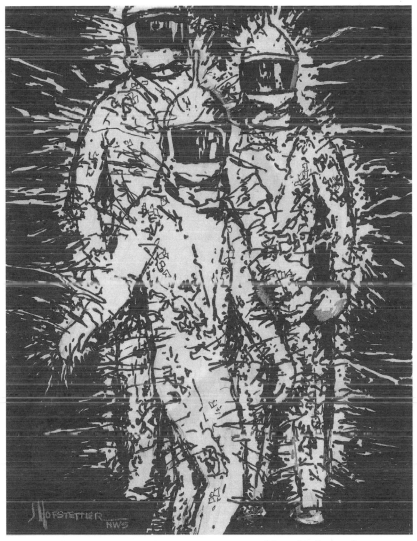

My "angels in spacesuits" [Drawing courtesy of Jane Hofstetter]

in my body. My panic increases even more and as I struggle even harder, I feel a burning on my neck, shoulders, and chest. The more I fight the blue cloud, the more it burns. Suddenly I understand that if I don't struggle, it won't hurt, so I lie still.

The blue cloud begins to move with me inside it, frozen and helpless. Waves of panic hit me again as every cell in my body erupts in terror. As the blue cloud nears the wall, a white tunnel opens up and swallows the cloud with me in it. As I enter the tunnel, the blue cloud disappears and with a whooshing sound, I hurtle feet first through the tunnel. Sparkles of iridescent blue, green, indigo, and violet light play around me as I'm propelled at breakneck speed to God knows where.

The whooshing stops and I am in some kind of room about 30 feet across. The only thing in the room is a huge diamond-shaped object about ten feet high, hovering just above the floor. Diffuse light illuminates the walls, which appear to be of some blue-gray material.

My whole attention is drawn to the diamond object and somehow I know that it is "reading" everything about me—my thoughts, feelings, life experiences. I am an open book to this thing but I seem to have no objections. In fact, I have no thoughts, no feelings, no physical sensations at all. All my senses are numb. However, I have a vague impression of a being in the room watching me, like a scientist studying an experiment. I am aware that I am naked, of being observed by something not of this world, but nothing registers in my mind. I simply stand before the hovering device, somehow magnetized to it.

Abruptly, I am back in the tunnel again, hurtling feet first, surrounded by the same light show and whooshing sound. I still haven't learned and I continue to struggle mentally and physically, and the burning sensation intensifies. My mind is able to manage, *Oh God, please help me. Save me.*

As if on cue, the sound stops and I'm back in the house, hovering over my bed, once more encased by the blue cloud. The cloud lowers me to the bed and slowly dissipates, leaving me lying on top of the bed. The three figures are still in the room, electrical storms still raging round them. Suddenly they are gone. No fading out, just gone. The room is deathly quiet.

My senses are magnified. I hear the ticking of a clock in the next room. I have the sense of being able to see in a full circle, like I know what's behind me in the room. And the smell! Oh, the smell, like a tomb is opened that's been sealed for a thousand years—the stale smell of dead air. I lie on the bed, exhausted and confused as my mind tries to make sense of all this. What the hell just happened? I wonder, and then I pass out.

I come to and crawl across the floor to the bathroom. I look in the mirror and cry out in horror at what I see. Someone else is looking out at me. Wild, panic-stricken eyes ringed with dark circles peer out of a deathly white face. His upper body is sunburned, and his hair and shoulders are covered in some honey-colored gooey stuff. It takes a full minute of staring at this apparition in the mirror for my overloaded mind to realize ... it's me!

As I clean up, the questions flood in on me. Is this what insanity feels like? What had happened? Who or what were those beings? Would they come back? Where did that tunnel lead? Why hadn't my family heard all the commotion? All questions and no answers. The answers would come, however, but it would be almost two decades before the pieces came together.

The odd thing is that after I returned from the abduction, my copy of the book by Hynek and Vallee had vanished and I never saw it again. I still wonder to this day if the ETs took it.

I returned home, excited because for the first time in my life I was to live alone, in a sweet little cottage apartment in Los Gatos, about 40 miles south of San Francisco.

The Tahoe incident had left me with a lot of questions and emotions that were new to me. It also changed me; I could now see colors around people. I first discovered this when I noticed that my hands glowed when I looked at them. I also discovered weird things around me, like small spheres floating through the air in my apartment. Had these been there all along, simply unnoticed, or was I now attracting weird things to me because of Tahoe? And what had *really* happened up there, anyway?

A small part of me reasoned that this might have been an encounter with angels or whatever, but my rational mind wanted to dismiss it as hallucination. Was it a psychic vision? Were they physical beings? Or had it just been a bad dream? And what about the sunburn and the gooey stuff? All questions and no answers.

Another odd thing: I felt compelled to read the Bible, something I rarely did at that time. But I thought that if those beings had been angels, at least I ought to read up on them. I even went to the church down the street thinking that *they* should have some answers if anyone would.

About half a dozen women were in the church, plus a guy who looked like the head honcho. I approached him. "Excuse me, your ... er ... your holiness."

"You can call me Pastor Joe," he replied, smiling.

"Okay, Pastor Joe, I think I've seen an angel. Well, three, actually."

"Really! What did they look like?" he asked, intrigued.

"Let me show you." I pulled a sketch out of my pocket and handed it to him.

He looked at the crude drawing I'd made: spacesuit, visor, antenna, and all. His smile changed to a frown, then horror as his mouth uttered only guttural sounds. Finally, he looked up at me, crumpled the paper, and said, "That ain't Jesus!"

"I know that. I never said it was. I said I thought it was an angel."

"Are you trying to be funny, kid?" he asked, visibly agitated.

"No. Honestly, I really saw three of these things in silver spacesuits, visors, antenna, mittens, and glowing like the sun."

Pastor Jim motioned me over closer to him. "Come 'ere, kid." He placed me so that two women were behind me and he was in front of me. "Now!" he commanded the two women.

Together, all three pounced on me, wrestling me to the ground. With my arms locked behind me and one cheek pressed against the cold floor, I heard the pastor scream his lungs out, "DEMON, BE GONE! LEAVE IN THE NAME OF OUR LORD, JESUS CHRIST!"

He went on using every name he could think of for Satan, convinced that I was possessed. As I lay on the floor, I saw a young woman about ten feet away in exactly the same position as myself, only she was facing me and talking in a strange language that sounded like Swedish, although I'd never heard anyone speak in tongues before. I came to my senses and said to myself, *these folks are crazier than I am. I've got to get out of here NOW.*

I'd been struggling against the two women, so I relaxed. They relaxed, too, just enough for me to jump up and free myself from their grip. I spun around to face the minister, who was now red in the face from his battle with the Evil One. Pointing to the girl on the floor, I shouted, "You shouldn't be praying for me. You should be praying for her. That's not even English!"

I bolted down the aisle into the clean, fresh air outside. As I paused to take a deep breath, I looked back at the church and had to laugh at the sign that said: ANGELS ARE REAL.

Next I went to a metaphysical bookstore in Los Gatos, where I found *Alien Meetings* by Brad Steiger, a popular paperback that was selling well at the time. In a chapter synchronistically called "Angels in Spacesuits," Brad talked about a woman, Clarissa Bernhardt, who had an experience with extraterrestrials whom she called "space brothers." I was riveted. Standing in the bookstore, I read the entire chapter and then bought the book. She described these beings as seven to eight feet tall in silver spacesuits—*exactly as I had seen them!*

Clarissa's account restored what little sanity I had left. At last! I was so relieved that, even if I was crazy, at least I wasn't alone. But if it *was* real, maybe those entities up at Tahoe really had been ETs. Fortunately, Clarissa lived close by and her number was in the book, so I called and talked for a long time with her husband. He agreed that I had probably had a similar experience. Suddenly he asked, "Can you be here at three tomorrow afternoon?"

"Yes. Yes. Most definitely, I'll be there," I said, not wanting to sound too eager but probably failing.

I met Clarissa the following day at her apartment clubhouse, a beautiful, modern wooden building surrounded by trees. It was deserted, all the other tenants presumably at work. Clarissa was a tall, beautiful woman with long blonde hair and a calm, reassuring air about her. I immediately felt in safe hands.

We began by discussing the various kinds of "close encounters," the phrase popularized by J. Allen Hynek. Then Clarissa explained that she was a trance medium, or channel. She told me that she could bring in entities and let them speak through her.

"I'm not sure that I want to meet them again so soon," I protested, the terror of Tahoe still fresh.

"Don't worry," she laughed. "I'll just be speaking for them. You won't actually meet them."

"Okay." I relaxed, full of curiosity about the channeling process. I arranged the pocket tape recorder I'd brought with me on the table between us.

She closed her eyes and took a few deep breaths. "The space brothers are here in this room with us. They're telling me that they're from the star system Arcturus and that they're scientists. They know you and are related to you."

"Related to me?" I scoffed. This was all new to me and I was having a hard time accepting the fact that I was related to creatures from outer space. I looked furtively around the room, just in case they were about to drag me off again.

"They want to tell you why they are here, and to remind you that you invited them in the first place," Clarissa continued.

"What?" I said, completely forgetting that I had put out the call to the universe that night at Tahoe. It would be fourteen years before that particular memory would come back to me.

"They came here to let you know—" There was a loud click as the tape recorder switched itself off. It can't be, I thought, it's a fresh tape and new batteries. I jabbed the RECORD button several times but nothing happened.

"It won't work," Clarissa said. "This is for your ears and memory only, so listen carefully. They want me to tell you that, yes, they are real, and that you're about to begin a new phase of your life, a new journey into the spiritual realm. You are to make a commitment to yourself to learn everything you can about metaphysics and spiritual matters and about mankind's role in the universe. It is important that you accept that this encounter really happened and that you take heed of it, because it is your life's work to perform this service and share what you know with many, many people around the planet."

"Really?" I asked, full of doubt. This was heady stuff for a 22-year-old. It would be another 15 years before I would stop being a "closet mystic" and go public. But I knew none of this back then.

"Do you have any questions for them?" Clarissa asked.

I shook my head. My poor overloaded mind was numb. Clarissa took a deep breath to come out of trance and the tape recorder mysteriously began to work again. Unfortunately it recorded only her breathing.

I grabbed the machine, thanked Clarissa, and left. All the way home, I was four feet off the ground. I simply couldn't believe what was happening to me. I was excited, scared, thrilled, and panicky all at the same time. I really did have a close encounter. It really had happened. I was delighted that it was true yet, at the same time, I was terrified that it was true. I raced home, rewound the tape, and sat down to listen.

"They came here to let you know ..." and then nothing. I sat on the grass outside my apartment, still dazed. My world had been turned upside down. I was now an abductee with a mission.

A few days later, I had dinner with my parents and sister who lived close by in Saratoga. I had gone over in my mind a hundred times whether to tell them about this turn of events and had decided that tonight would be the perfect occasion. Once we'd eaten and were relaxing around the dinner table, I cleared my throat and said solemnly, "There's something I have to tell you."

My mother and father leaned forward, apprehension in their faces. "What is it, son?" my mother asked, not sure she wanted to hear what was coming.

"Well," I began, "when you discover something about yourself that makes a great change in your life, you can hide it only so long. Eventually you have to accept it and face the world with it. So I have to tell you that I ... er ...." I stumbled, searching for the words.

"Are you telling us that you're g... g...?" my father asked, unable to complete the word.

I took a deep breath and blurted out, "I've been abducted by aliens!"

"Thank God," my father roared. "Is that all?"

"What do you mean, 'is that all?' "

"Well, son, I thought you were going to tell us you're gay, but you've only been abducted by a bunch of ETs," he replied, visibly relaxing.

"That's wonderful," my mother exclaimed, laughing and crying at the same time.

I was dumbstruck. My big secret was out of the bag, but this was not the reaction I'd expected. I'd been waiting for something along the lines of "you're crazy and should get some professional help." Instead my parents were jumping for joy. My mother summed it all up with, "That's the most wonderful thing that could have happened to you. We're all gonna be famous. We're all gonna be rich!

And that's how it all started. Looking back on it all, once we stopped laughing, we all looked at each other and were pretty scared. No one in our family had ever been abducted before. My sister asked whether we should call the police—that's how naïve we were.

Now that my secret was out, little did I know that this fantastic experience would launch me into lifelong research into metaphysics, spirituality, the mystery schools, UFOs, ETs, and alien abduction. You name it, I wanted to study it. Consulting with psychologists, I found that they knew little about abductions and considered them more myth than scientific fact. Hypnotherapists just kept asking all kinds of questions, such as, "Tell me about the burning sensation."

Slowly, we would put the pieces together, but in those days, we had more questions than answers.

Chapter 2

Mystics, Magic, and Metaphysics

The Rocky Road to Enlightenment

MY MOTHER COUNTED AMONG her friends a woman named Selma. She had known Selma since 1965 through a women's group of female aviators. My mother was drawn to Selma, a teacher of metaphysics and extraterrestrial wisdom. In the hope of shedding some light on my abduction experience, my mother had arranged a meeting with her.

Selma was a portly woman, short in stature but big in personality. A real firecracker, she was full of energy and very much alive for her 65 years. Even though it was early spring, the afternoon sun was hot, and I was glad to be in the cool darkness of Selma's house. It was jammed with spiritual artifacts from around the world, with more books and manuscripts than I'd ever seen together in one place.

Into metaphysics all her life, Selma was in regular contact with a group of beings called ascended masters, advanced non-physical entities who worked tirelessly with the energies on our planet to spread love and light, and dispel fear and negativity. Each of Selma's thousands of sessions with them had been transcribed, which accounted for the stacks of manuscripts on every flat surface.

"ETs are in constant contact with humanity," she told me, "and have been since life began on this planet. They have shaped, molded, and influenced our civilizations and they even engineered our DNA. I think you should meet my son. He's extremely gifted and has been in telepathic contact with ETs and the masters."

My mind reeled. Until a few months ago, ETs were just a theoretical possibility. Now I was in ET headquarters. Clarissa had told me that my mission was to gather and disseminate information from and about ETs and that I would meet many people who would help me in this quest. Her prediction was coming true, and very quickly.

Surrounded by decades of Selma's research, I was exhilarated, breathless, and eager to begin working with her and her son.

Selma asked if I would like to attend one of their regular meetings, warning me that I would need her son's permission first. After a lengthy telephone "interview" with him, I was accepted. The need to get his approval made the group seem even more mysterious, exclusive, and prestigious. The fact that not everyone was accepted really boosted my young ego and I looked forward to the first meeting.

There were about 45 others there, a fascinating mix of professional people from every field, united by one thing: an insatiable curiosity about the higher dimensions. Those meetings went a long way toward satisfying our curiosity. Typically, Selma would relay the latest information she had received from her son and her guides, and then we would discuss it. Topics ranged from the story of creation, how the universe worked, what role the Creator played, and the nature of our relationship to the Creator and creation.

As the newest member of the group, I was a neophyte in a mystery school. I studied hard to catch up but even so, I left most of those meetings understanding little of the esoteric complexities. What thrilled me was being on the inside track to the cosmic wisdom that I'd yearned for all my life.

A few months after joining the group, I attended the wedding of two of the members and would finally get to meet Selma's son who was to conduct the ceremony. Until then, he'd been just a mysterious figure in the background. Having heard repeatedly that he was a special blessed being who radiated divinity, I was instantly attracted to him; it was like meeting up with an old friend after a long absence. He was bright, charming, witty, and ebullient. I was captivated. His most noticeable features were his piercing blue eyes and perfectly groomed hair, like a TV evangelist. His eyes and charismatic glow made him seem older than his 26 years, and sometimes much younger.

Two years rolled by during which time I progressed steadily as a sales executive in my father's company, Royal Optical sunglasses and fashion accessories. I also courted and married Toni, a beautiful brunette with an infectious sense of humor that matched mine. We had a wonderful time setting up home together. She had been raised in Arizona in a conservative Christian environment so my involvement with the group caused problems almost from the beginning. I would come home from the meetings bubbling with the latest revelation from the cosmos, eager to discuss it with Toni. Instead, I was met with, "How can you do this? Don't you know that channeling is dangerous, Robert?"

For two years, we stuck it out, but things became more and more tense. Even the birth of our son, Christian, didn't help bridge the growing chasm between us. For the sake of our sanity, Toni and I agreed to divorce. Now I could focus all my passion on the group, which I did with abandon. In hindsight, however, Toni's cautionary words of wisdom would prove to be right on the mark.

For the next five years, my life ran like clockwork. I sold sunglasses by day and studied with the group by night. By 1987, however, disillusionment had set in. I was restless for different kinds of information and new types of experiences, so I withdrew from the group and threw myself into Life.

Working major accounts like Macy's and Nordstroms took me into a world of BMWs, foreign trips to buy and sell *haute couture* fashion accessories, scantily-clad swimsuit models, and a healthy number of unclad models, too. My father and I sponsored numerous sporting events with our line of sport sunglasses, Ski Optiks. This took me around the world to ski slopes, auto racing circuits, and beaches to mingle with the jet-set. I had become the ultimate yuppie while striving to exemplify some of the qualities of my hero, Paul McCartney—charming, witty, heartfelt, and a total blast!

Flipped, Flopped, and Failed

The lavish good life came to an end, however, when my father sold the company at the end of 1989. For the first time, I faced, at the age of 35, going out into the world and finding a job. Now the product I was selling was me and though I had no trouble getting jobs, keeping them was another matter. I had gone from being a big fish in my father's pond for 18 years to being a minnow in a cold, hostile ocean where things much higher up in the food chain lurked. I suffered several painful bites and wounds along the way. I joined a light aircraft service company as a partner and ended up cleaning exhaust soot off airplane fuselages. How the mighty had fallen—from playboy executive to soot scrubber!

My life fell apart and I drifted without a rudder. That didn't matter, however, because even if I'd had a rudder, I had no course to steer. Why had this happened? I asked repeatedly. Has it all come down to this meaningless existence? Is this all there is?

Around Christmas, 1991, a ray of sunshine beamed through my clouds of self-pity in the form of a book on how to change your life. I inhaled every word and that book became my constant companion. I would even rest it on the steering wheel while driving. On January 6, 1992, I didn't even see the car that had stopped in front of me. I rear-ended it at great speed and totaled both cars. The irony of the situation was that I was driving to my insurance agent to reinstate my lapsed car insurance. The gods must have had a good laugh at my expense.

Battered and bruised emotionally and physically, no car, feeling like the world's biggest idiot, I was cleaned out financially. Could it get much worse? Could anything else go wrong? Was there any way out?

In an act of final desperation, I began to pray: "Please show me my purpose. Show me my mission. I don't care what it is; I just want to know. I want to be of service. Please show me a direction."

How often I've heard the scenario that you screw your life up so badly that you can't get out, and you surrender to a higher power. Then things begin to turn around, but first you must surrender. And your guides can't just march into your life and begin to rearrange it without being asked—you have to ask for their intervention. Well, I asked, and they answered.

The first clue in the Robert Recovery Program took the form of a psychic at a local metaphysical fair I attended a few days later.

"Your guides are telling me something," she began.

"My guides?"

"Oh, yes. They're standing right behind you. They say they've been trying to contact you for a long time but you weren't listening."

This was news to me. After all the heady esoteric years with the group, I hadn't learned the basic spiritual survival skills like communicating with your guides. Apparently, we each come into this life with two or three guides who drop hints and ideas into our minds to help us along the path and stay focused on our mission. They nudge us toward people, places, and events that are important to our soul's intended purpose during this incarnation. All we have to do is listen. After years of looking to the stars for guidance, it was as close to me as my own thoughts and had been right in front of me all this time, if only I'd known where to look.

"They're telling me," the psychic continued, "that it's very simple. Just write your name and phone number on a piece of paper, along with, 'Come and hear me talk.' Then put this on the bulletin boards of metaphysical bookstores and people will come."

Yeah, right, I thought. Forget the hundreds of resumes, the dozens of interviews, and all those crummy jobs. It's so simple. Like people will really flock to hear a completely unknown speaker. Is that the best these guides could come up with? I hoped not.

Over the next few months, something amazing happened. Visitors began to appear—ghostly apparitions who would float around my bedroom, talking to me, coaching me on a wide variety of topics. They told me telepathically that they were here in answer to my call.

My ghostly friends schooled me on subjects like ascension, the scenario in which the energy making up planet Earth and all her inhabitants is steadily increasing in frequency. Apparently, we are slowly leaving the third dimension, headed ultimately for the fifth. One night, they told me that, in the near future, we and the planet would begin to glow as our auras became brighter and brighter. All we have to do is to drop the base emotions like fear, anger, greed, and jealousy from our lives. Simple, right? That's why ascension won't be an overnight process!

Apparently, this is happening according to some vast cosmic timetable and has nothing to do with our local calendar that puts so much stock in the new millennium. It has been planned for eons and planet Earth is currently blessed by the presence of the largest gathering ever of ascended masters, angels, archangels, and ETs from every corner of the galaxy. They are here to observe, help, guide, and generally do whatever they can.

My "night school" became just as real as my daytime activities, and a whole lot more important. With my final desperate act of praying for guidance, the doldrums would prove to be over. It was the summer of 1992. I had hit rock bottom at the age of 36, but I was beginning to bounce back.

Many years of learning and studying were beginning to pay off when I realized I had a powerful message to share. Maybe people really would come to hear me talk. I organized my material into a lecture format I called "The Extraterrestrials Are Here." I put together a flyer and sent it to MUFON (Mutual UFO Network), an organization that researches UFO sightings and contacts. After a lengthy phone call with Virgil Staff, state director of MUFON, I was invited to speak the very next month at the Divine Science Church in San Jose.

The day of my public debut came. When I got to the meeting hall, my heart stopped. Over 250 people jammed the hall to hear me. Oh, God, what have I done now. I must have been crazy; 250 seasoned UFO buffs and me, an upstart neophyte giving his first talk.

I sat down in the back row and scrunched down, glad that no one knew who I was.

"Hope this Perala fella's good," the heavy-set guy next to me said, gruffly. "We've had some real doozies lately."

"I sure hope so, too," I gulped. "I'm dying to hear this."

"Ladies and gentlemen, this afternoon we have a brand new speaker on the UFO circuit. Please welcome Robert Perala."

As the audience applauded, everything slowed down. The walk from the back of the room to the podium seemed to take hours. I stepped onto the podium, took a deep breath, and turned round to see 250 faces locked onto mine.

"Good afternoon, ladies and gentlemen. My name is Robert Perala, and I have a very personal story to tell you. In 1977, I was abducted ..."

I concluded over an hour later, and as one body, the audience rose to its feet to reward me with a one-minute standing ovation. The space brothers had been right 15 years ago. The psychic had been right. The apparitions were right. I had finally found my purpose. I had arrived.

After my talk, a member of the audience approached me. "That was wonderful. Look, we're having a meeting next month. Would you come and tell us the same story? Oh, and we'll pay you to do it."

Thus my career as a public speaker was launched. Bookstores, churches, colleges, meeting halls—I would speak anywhere that people would gather to hear my story. Soon I was a guest on radio shows, then television. Later I would host my own radio and TV shows. I loved the speaker circuit panels, where I rubbed shoulders with the likes of Pulitzer Prize winner John Mack; astronaut Brian O'Leary; Whitley Strieber; and crop circle king, Colin Andrews. Mystics, magic and metaphysics became my everyday life. I would get calls from all over the world with invitations to be a telephone guest on talk shows.

The apparitions had been right. I was slipping into my soul mission: a messenger with a message that people wanted to hear. But I wasn't telling them anything new. I was simply reawakening ancient memories that lie deep within all of us—the Divine Blueprint.

Chapter 3

Auras, Abductions, and Apparitions

I n March, 1992, I attended a gathering in Redwood City at the home of Nancy Worthington, a dedicated lightworker, famous for her soirées that usually featured a notable speaker. The speaker that night, Art Martin, intrigued me from the start. In his early fifties, he was of medium height and build, and had a fascinating face, full of character.

Art was an "etheric surgeon," meaning that he worked on people's auras, the cocoon of subtle energy that surrounds every living thing, from a blade of grass to you and I. Art saw this energy very clearly and made a living out of "tuning it up" by removing old, stuck energy patterns such as addictions and obsessions, or "evicting" unwanted energy that rightfully belongs to someone else, or somewhere else. The technique he used was called Neuro/ Cellular Repatterning.

If you had just come out of a poor relationship, for example, and the break up had been messy, the other person's energy could be stuck in your aura, meaning that the break wasn't clean. The anger and bitterness would continue, and neither party could begin healing and getting on with their lives. In such cases, Art would remove the energy by sending it back to the other person, dissipating it, or "giving it back to the universe," as he called it.

Art also had the ability to "read" your aura, that is, decode the memories held as energy patterns, and tell you things about yourself that you might have forgotten. As the featured speaker that night, Art was there to demonstrate his healing arts on a few volunteers

Before his demonstration, he approached me. "Do you know that you have an implant?"

Interesting icebreaker, I thought. How do I respond to that? I knew vaguely that an implant was like a tiny transmitter/receiver and could be either good news or bad, depending on who or what was on the other end. Or it could just be for tracking purposes, much like we tag animals and birds to see where they go and to find them again. Part of me was irritated that a perfect stranger could know so much about me but I asked, "Tell me about it. How bad is it?"

"It's not really bad, but it should come off," he replied. "You've had an encounter, haven't you? With something very unusual. A physical encounter."

Shocked that all this should be so visible in my aura, I said, "Yes, but it was a long time ago."

"That doesn't matter. It's in the aura forever. Interesting. I see it was an extraterrestrial abduction."

Suddenly, I had a stunning revelation. "Do you think there's a connection? Was the implant put there during that experience?"

Art nodded and smiled. "Do you want a private session so that we can go into this in more detail?"

We arranged the details and Art went to prepare for his demonstration. How could he possibly know all that? And just what's been happening with this thing for the past 15 years? Questions turned cartwheels in my mind for the rest of the evening.

In all, seven volunteers occupied Art's massage table to have their auras cleaned, fluffed, decoded, and tuned up. Art slowly moved his hands over the person, sensing and reading energy in the aura. Occasionally, he would ask a question like, "How much do you love yourself?" or, "Do you think your parents love you?" If he saw something that shouldn't be there, he would ask the person's permission and then clap his hands over the energy to break it up. Then he would scoop it up in his hands and lift it up high, as though casting it to the sky. As he did this, he would ask the person to repeat an affirmation like, "I'm learning to love myself more deeply, more completely. As my divine right, I am claiming that now."

All the volunteers reported feeling lighter or clearer immediately. Art explained that the real changes would be felt over a longer period.

Art came to my house a few days later for our session. He went through the same procedure with me. He then asked, "So, are you ready for the implant to be removed?"

"I don't know. Give me more time to think about it." If I'd lived with the thing for 15 years, what's a few more days? "But tell me more about it."

"Okay. It's on the back of your neck."

I reached back to feel it, but there was nothing there.

"You won't be able to feel it," he said. "It's in your aura. It's etheric. It acts kind of like a beacon to higher dimensional beings and they're drawn to it."

"Who are these beings?"

Art took a deep breath, closed his eyes, and went deeper into trance. After a few moments, he simply said, "Arcturans. They're beings from Arcturus, a star system. They're explorers and very intelligent. They've been involved with Earth and humanity for a long time."

"What do they want with me?"

"They're related to you," he replied.

"Were they the ones who abducted me?" I asked, putting two and two together. Clarissa, the psychic, I went to fourteen years earlier had used almost exactly the same words.

"I'll bet you have nighttime visitors, too, don't you?"

"Yeah, that's right."

"Tell me, do you have trouble focusing on things?" Art asked.

"Why?"

"If you do, it may be the implant. It ought to come off sometime but for now, how about we work on your relationship with your parents?"

It would actually be ten sessions later before we tackled the implant. In the meantime, we'd work on issues like self-love, relationships with my parents, ex-wife, various women that had been or still were in my life, childhood events, and so on. Before we got to that tenth session, I would meet someone else who would also be instrumental in my life.

The week after Art's appearance at Nancy Worthington's, I met Peggy McConnell, a fascinating woman who, out of the blue, told me, "You have an implant, you know."

My God, can everyone see this thing? I thought. It'll be the supermarket checkout clerk next! "Really. Where is it?" I asked, feigning surprise.

"Just here, on the back of your neck." She pointed to the exact same place that Art had.

"Do you know Art Martin?" I asked, wondering if they were in cahoots.

"No, I don't think I do," Peggy said, shaking her head.

"So, tell me, what do you think it is?"

"You've had an encounter with something, haven't you? It's very prominent in your etheric field. Being this strong, it was definitely physical."

"That's amazing," I said. "Art said exactly the same thing. Is that bad, do you think?"

"No, not really. It seems to connect you with those who put it in. Probably just for tracking and monitoring. Occasionally, they use it to feed you ideas you think are your own."

Thoughts of alien mind control, automatons, and mindless zombies reeled through my head. No, they're interested in me and are studying me, but not controlling me. Then I wondered how I knew that.

"Should it come out?" I asked.

"I don't think so. Not just yet. Let's take a deeper look at it. Why don't you come to one of my workshops?"

I agreed and signed up for a private session with her. Her approach was similar to Art's but she concluded that the implant was benign and should probably be left alone.

At Peggy's meetings, we talked about things like integrating a more complete relationship with spirit guides, how the guides are here to learn more about the human experience, and that extraterrestrials are also here to learn more about us. Through implants, they study their human subjects, their thoughts, emotions, choices.

I learned that there are three kinds of implant: etheric (which exists in a higher dimension), organic (growing in your body with your other organs), and physical (like a computer chip, often placed in the nasal cavity).

The researcher in me was excited and fascinated with all of this, but another part was confused, even anxious. Why had those extraterrestrials "tagged" me 15 years ago, and how had they been using it? Was I "bugged" and had they been spying on me all this time? Was this a massive invasion of my privacy? Could they listen in on conversations? Did the bug pick up thoughts and emotions? What had they transmitted to me? Were my thoughts my own or theirs? Had they influenced any major decisions, and if so, to their advantage or mine?

I decided to leave the implant alone for now. During the tenth session with Art, I would change my mind but for a very different reason.

That session began with Art saying, "I want you to go back to the actual abduction experience."

I relived the details while Art held one hand on my shoulder and one on my knee. When I was deeply in the memory, Art said, "This is extraordinary. You seem to have called to these ETs. Somehow you learned how to transmit out into space, and they responded. It looks like you were conducting some kind of experiment."

"My God, you're right!" I shouted. "I did. I'd just read about sending thoughts out to the universe." Jumping up, I said, "I called them and they came." I was excited. The abduction didn't just happen to me. I initiated it! Fifteen years of being a victim abductee fell away, replaced by awe at my own powers and abilities. I could hardly contain myself. I ran around the room shouting, "I did it!"

But that wasn't the only surprise Art had for me during that session. "Did you know that you'd met them earlier, before the abduction? You also had an encounter in April of that year. I want you to go back to that time."

Art put me into a light trance and took me back to April, 1977. I felt a strong rushing motion and saw a lot of flashing lights. Art read the energy that lit up in my aura. "The implant was actually put on you at this time and once it was there, it was easier for them to return in December. That would account for the very powerful nature of the experience. They know you. You are one of them!"

This was very disturbing because it echoed what Clarissa had told me back in 1977.

"They've been watching you all this time, monitoring your experiences. As you grow in understanding, they grow. It's like you're part of their team, a part that's come to Earth," Art continued.

My response was a mixture of surprise and acceptance. I reasoned that our whole Earth experience would be a waste of time if it wasn't looked over and recorded by someone other than our little ego-selves—whether it was a Christian God or an extraterrestrial. Rather than feel invaded or violated, I was excited to be part of some grand experiment. I'd always wanted to make contact with otherworldly beings and I'd just found out I'd been in contact all my life.

With all the excitement, what was I to do about the implant: leave it or heave it? Without it, I would communicate better with my ghostly friends, more able to control my dealings with them, and have improved clarity. I gave Art permission to take the thing out.

As he reached to the back of my neck, I tensed and had to consciously relax. Art took the implant between his fingers and slowly removed it with the care of a bomb disposal expert. I felt a pulling sensation and began to drift off into a kind of sleep.

"Stay with me, Robert. Stay awake," Art urged. He clapped his hands around it to break up the energy. "There, it's gone," he announced proudly. I felt light-headed and floaty. After Art left, I went to bed and slept for hours.

As the days went by, I began to think more clearly and my communication with the apparitions did, in fact, improve. This was important for what was going to happen next in my life.

(To contact Art Martin, see the Resources section.)

Chapter 4

My Pals, the Pleiadians

They Made Me a Messenger

I WAS UPSTAIRS IN my bedroom taking a catnap around seven in the evening while Art saw a client downstairs. I was in that delightful twilight state—half awake, half asleep—when you're in both worlds.

Suddenly, out of nowhere a tall, beautiful woman appears in my bedroom doorway. She is dressed in a snug-fitting, white jumpsuit with a shimmering, iridescent mother-of-pearl sheen and a blue sash around her chest. Her hair is done up in a turban, also with a matching blue sash. Her energy is very feminine and she puts out a slight glow.

I sit up on my bed, startled and stunned. I open and close my eyes but she's still there. She is not a purely psychic phenomenon. If I can see her with my eyes open and closed, she must be real. My mind's feeble attempts to sort all this out are washed away by a wave of serene calmness emanating from her. It is so thick that I can almost touch it.

"Don't worry," she says. "All is well. Be still. I only have a moment."

Her lips don't move. Ideas flood into my mind. "The thoughts you are having are mine," she says in my mind.

The visitor's penetrating blue eyes hold mine unwaveringly and I sense, rather than see, a stream of iridescent energy coming from behind her, over her head, toward me. I have never felt such overwhelming love and compassion in my life as wave after wave of ecstasy wash over me. I am in danger of losing my grip on reality and falling into a bliss state when the thought stream starts again.

I am from the star system you call the Seven Sisters or the Pleiades, and I have a message for you, I hear in my mind. I receive the clear knowing that she is from an ancient, ancient culture and that I am one of them. Her thought patterns feel strangely familiar, like hearing someone talk in a language you learned a long time ago but had forgotten.

My role is to nurture, assist, and bring about remembrance.

The word "remembrance" echoes in my mind. Why? I wonder.

It was placed in your consciousness long ago as a wake-up trigger. It is the key to your memories of who you were before you began this cycle of Earth lives. You are one of us. She smiles with such warmth and radiance that I catch my breath. It feels like meeting a friend/lover/ mate after a long, long absence.

Welcome, I reply telepathically. *I've missed you.*

She smiles again and ancient memories flood into my conscious mind. The Pleiades star system, or Seven Sisters, is a star cluster with hundreds of planets, home to many different evolving species of which her race is one. This, too, is my stellar heritage.

We have been watching over you all your life and honor your commitment to your mission. I am here to remind you what that is and to ask if you are ready to begin in earnest. We have noted your diligence in tackling the issues of who you are, where you come from, why you're here, and where you're going. We will answer these questions for you in future visitations.

She has accurately assessed my burning desire, obsession even, to communicate with extraterrestrials. I have devoted my spiritual quest almost exclusively to this mission, intuitively knowing that it is related to my service to this planet and humanity. What I am learning now is that this intense desire had been built into my being before I'd been born into this lifetime. It wasn't just ego-driven curiosity.

Would you be willing to be part of a very wonderful experiment? To be a mouthpiece, a spokesman for us?

Again, inner knowing wells up in me. Earth is undergoing a great transformation and within one lifetime, a new humanity will emerge from who we are today. This process has been underway for several years and is accelerating. It will bring about a new expression where we will be aware of our truly magnificent identity and integrate with it. It has been predicted that toward the end times, we will have great visions of what the future holds for all of humanity and our beloved planet.

This new expression calls for humanity to integrate its stellar heritage, the cosmic wisdom of countless civilizations throughout the galaxy. And we will discover our deeply-rooted connection with those of other civilizations. This wondrous process has been dubbed "ascension," and we are being prepared to bring forth this new expression. But in the midst of this vast scenario, doubts start to bubble up in me. *What does it mean to be a messenger? How will I accomplish this? Will I be up to the task?*

Don't worry, the visitor smiles. *We are helping you. Prepare yourself and we will bring the people to you. All you need do is take what you already know and what we will teach you. Organize it into lecture formats and be ready to deliver it.*

I'm blown away. This is exactly what the psychic at the metaphysical fair relayed to me from my guides. I form the question, *Are you one of my guides?*

She smiles and any doubts simply vanish. I telepath my wholehearted acceptance of the mission, mentally and emotionally, and deep down I remember making this very contract before coming to this planet. This is what my life is about.

I signal yes. And with that, the visitor promptly disappears.

I ran downstairs shouting to Art, "I found it! I found it!"

"Found what?" he asked calmly, familiar with my energetic outbursts by now.

"I've found my connection, my mission, the link I've been looking for. Didn't you see her? That tall Pleiadian woman?"

"No, but I guess you did," he said with a twinkle in his eye.

This was the beginning of my newest adventure. After the woman in white, I began seeing a series of apparitions who identified themselves as Pleiadian emissaries. They would simply appear in my bedroom at all hours of the night. They looked just like you and I, only a little taller. Semi-etheric, or slightly transparent, they could travel through physical objects. They didn't talk to me in words but communicated by giving me complete ideas.

The visitors told me that they possessed a greater knowledge than humans simply because their culture was much older. They stressed that I was not to see them as superior to humanity. They were here simply to educate us because our planet was entering a dramatic phase of its evolution, us along with it.

A Pleiadian female, typical of those apparitions that visited me
[Drawing courtesy of Jane Hofstetter]

In my lectures, I use the term "stellar heritage." Many people in this country proudly claim that they're, say, a quarter French, a quarter German, and one-half Irish. This is their earthly heritage, recorded in their DNA, honored in the very blood in their veins. But what if, at the soul level, we incarnate not just on Earth but on planets in other systems? That would mean that our full identity might include, say, Pleiadian, Sirian, and Arcturan energy and experiences. As we grow into a fuller knowledge of who we *really* are, we will be able to lay claim to the wisdom, depth, and creativity of our true identity.

My nocturnal visitors told me that for those who are ready, they will make themselves known now more than ever. They explained that there were planetary changes occurring. They explained cosmology, planetary physics, and light-body work. They said the planet was ascending, which means that it is reaching the end of a vast, long cycle and will be birthed into a much bigger picture. We will become much more aware of the Spiritual Hierarchy that has been working with this planet and with all the other entities involved. Every man, woman, and child will be a part of this ascension process.

Seeding the Big Windows

My Pleiadian visitors spent most of 1992 tutoring me on their agenda for planet Earth. Sitting on my bed with me, they would show me photographs, like in a photo album, and drawings of planetary gridwork and alignment, telepathically dropping concepts into my mind. They said that preparing humanity for ascension is a multi-stage process and that they are currently engaged in Stage One, which involves increasing the awareness of the population. They explained that they are "seeding the big windows of the planet." By "big windows," they meant the media TV, radio, newspapers, books, magazines, and movies, all of which deeply affect our conscious and subconscious minds. They are using the media to influence our belief systems and mass consciousness.

When I reflected on this, I realized that they are hard at work planting seeds in our subconscious minds to prepare us for their arrival. They use fictional metaphors to get in under our skepticism but even so, it will take some time for us to get used to the idea of a galaxy literally teeming with other inhabited planets.

Notice the TV ads by big businesses that use ETs and UFOs to sell products. Madison Avenue has decided that the viewing audience will not only accept these alien icons, but will warmly embrace them. Once one advertiser gets away with it, the others jump on the bandwagon to take advantage of the current popularity. A truck rental company has even painted up a truck with the words, WHAT REALLY HAPPENED AT ROSWELL?

I saw a billboard in southern California for a utility company featuring photography by Glen Wexler, the same artist who created the

Glen Wexler's photography used in a Department of Water and Power billboard [reproduced with permission]

cover for this book. Glen also kindly let me include another example of his images produced for advertising (see opposite).

Then we have the movies. Forgetting all the low budget B movies of the fifties and sixties which were a diversion from the Cold War, the man who legitimized the science fiction genre was Arthur C. Clarke with *2001* and *2010*. He opened the floodgates. Soon we had *E.T.,* and *Close Encounters of the Third Kind* from Steven Speilberg, *Star Wars* from George Lucas, and the *Star Trek* movies spun off from Gene Roddenberry's TV series, the two *Cocoon* movies, plus countless others.

Star Wars chronicles the epic war between the forces of good (the Alliance) and evil (the Empire) ruled by the Emperor, a Jedi knight who uses the mysterious Force to terrorize the galaxy. The good knight, Obi-Wan Kanobi, describes the force as "... what gives a Jedi his power. It is an energy field created by all living things. It surrounds us, permeates us, and binds the galaxy together."

The movies are about the ultimate battle to harness the Force, yet ironically, only a handful of people—the Jedi knights—even believe it exists. That George Lucas studied mythology under Joseph Campbell comes as no surprise. Campbell was, until his death, *the* authority on this planet's mythology and *Star Wars* contains just about every mythological component imaginable. Despite the impressive technology and special effects, it all boils down to the triumph of love over fear.

The major picture in late 1997 was *Contact*, based on Carl Sagan's book of the same name that portrays a very realistic scenario in which a

Glen Wexler's art in advertising [reproduced with permission]

coded message is received of plans for a device for interstellar travel. Jodie Foster plays Ellie Arroway, the selected traveler who finds herself elsewhere in the galaxy, face-to-face with an ancient race who actually inherited the travel technology from an even more ancient race, long since departed. Contact has been made. Interestingly, the traveler's experience lasts about 18 hours, yet less than one second of Earth time has passed.

The whole theme behind all of this ET/UFO coverage is to get us used to the idea, so that when contact is finally made, it will be a case not of, "Agghh, the aliens are coming!" but more like "their ships are bigger than the *Enterprise.*" And thanks to television, ETs come into our homes every night courtesy of *Star Trek: Next Generation, DS9,* and *Voyager.*

Of course, the granddaddy of them all, *The X-Files*, "pushes the envelope" of our beliefs. From abductions to cover-ups, from the secret world government to conscious computer programs, each week we are stretched a little more. Maybe the program and the 1998 movie are best summed up by the "I Want To Believe" poster in the main character's office.

Some episodes of *The X-Files* are scary because you can be sure that if the script writers have come up with those ideas, you know others already have. Personally, I think we need "belief stretching" if we are to be ready for contact.

So, the cowboy movies of the fifties and the low-grade sci-fi movies with bug-eyed monsters are replaced by lavish productions with thoughtful, meaningful scripts and masterful special effects. At any moment in time, at least one *Star Trek* episode is playing somewhere on this planet. Since our broadcasts are monitored, I'll bet our ET friends are patting themselves on the back. With a steady stream of Vulcans, Klingons, Romulans, Ferengi, Cardassians, and Bajorans coming through our living rooms every night, doesn't this make you feel as though you're being prepared for galactic citizenship?

For over three decades, Roddenbury's legacy has followed society's changing mores, nudging them along considerably. Good-bye to the white male macho era of Captain Kirk and hello to minorities and ETs in command. We now see ETs as complex individuals, living culturally rich lives and facing many of the same problems that we do on Earth. Thank you, Gene! And thank you, Pleiadians, for this incredibly rich "big window."

Where do these amazing scripts come from? In his book, *Cosmic Voyage*, Courtney Brown describes a technique he calls Scientific Remote Viewing (SRV), where he can project his consciousness to anywhere in the galaxy (and maybe beyond) and to any time period. In one SRV session, he visited a subject who was associated with writing scripts for *Star Trek* while the subject was dreaming. Courtney noticed that the subject's dreams were influenced by an information stream via a strange non-terrestrial device, possibly a relay station. Following the stream back to its source, Courtney found himself inside an alien craft where a small team was transmitting images and a plot for a possible *Star Trek* episode. The dreamer woke up with an entire storyline in mind. This is not mind control, Courtney emphasized, because the person was at full liberty to discard the dream.

If you're not into sci-fi TV programs, we still have *20/20, Primetime Live, 60 Minutes, Dateline, Oprah,* and *48 Hours.* They've all featured ET/UFO stories. And, of course, we also have the specialized weekly shows like *Sightings, The Unexplained,* and *Strange Universe.* To top it all, *Alien Autopsy* was reportedly Fox Network's most watched program in 1996.

Hollywood conducts regular polls to determine the kinds of movies that we want to see. In the most recent poll, the most popular topic was ancient wisdom. This shows that seeding the big windows really works.

The last five years of the old millennium have seen the most amazing phenomenon: the Internet. Anyone with a computer can now be in instant communication with any other computer user on the planet. Someone sees a UFO in Australia and within minutes, everyone in the world knows about it. A UFO is spotted over Phoenix, Arizona, and a few minutes later, over Belgium. The same one? Who knows, but without the Internet, it's doubtful that either site would find out about the other's sighting. In addition to the speedy flow of information, the Internet is also the new "town square" where everyone gathers to exchange gossip, discuss the year's harvest prospects, and complain about the weather. Never before in our history has anything like this been available.

The Pleiadian agenda also calls for the activation of anyone involved in accelerating awareness on this planet so that they can be more effective. The visitors said they were working with these folks one-on-one. They would be supported energetically with such changes as cellular restructuring and DNA repatterning to align them with their piece of the Divine Blueprint.

Another item on the Pleiadian list—the frequency and public nature of UFO sightings—is being stepped up. Clandestine sightings give way to events that cannot be ignored. Witness the famous Phoenix Triangle that hovered over the city for several hours in March, 1997. So many people flocked into the streets to view the phenomenon and so many TV crews captured footage of the UFO, that it was hard to brush the sighting off. The lame "official" explanation that it was actually caused by flares dropped from an Air National Guard aircraft didn't hold much water with the excited citizens of Phoenix.

Another technique used in raising planetary consciousness is to change public perception of abductions and ET contact so that those involved are no longer subject to ridicule or sanctions for going public with their stories. Such a relaxation means that far more people will come forward rather than suffer in silence or seek underground support groups. It's working: in the nineties, we are seeing abductees treated as celebrities on TV talk shows.

The Pleiadians' visits continued through the summer. They coached me in planetary physics, especially the magnetic grid that maintains the planet's alignment. The network of ley lines—those invisible lines of magnetic force that connect all the ancient sites such as Stonehenge, Silbury Hill, and Avebury in England—have a number of purposes. Some are internal to the planet's structure and others are external, relating to the planet's rotation and orbit round the sun. These lines are significantly decreasing in intensity, allowing the tectonic plates more latitude to move relative to each other. Already the planetary rotation has developed a slight wobble.

With almost no science classes in school, all of this was a foreign language to me and I would lie in bed wondering what I was supposed to do with all this information. It would be all of two years before I would meet people like Gregg Braden, author of *Awakening to Zero Point* and *Walking between the Worlds* (see Reading List), who would explain the same phenomena in scientific terms. The significance of receiving this information in 1992 was, in retrospect, to receive confirmation in 1995, a clever ploy on the part of the Pleiadians. And evidence abounds, as we'll see in later chapters, of the Earth's resonance, her collapsing magnetic fields, and the wandering magnetic north pole.

I was also told about future erratic weather patterns, again confirmed every time I watch the evening news. As the seasons begin to coalesce and reorganize themselves, we can expect much more violent weather patterns—the Divine Blueprint unfolding.

The Pleiadians' most sobering warning concerned a serious imbalance on the planet today. We have a proliferation of weapons such as nuclear bombs, chemical and biological warfare weapons, and top-secret energy beam devices. We have also developed tools like HAARP (High-energy Active Auroral Research Project) that scientists and the military plan to use to bombard the ionosphere with high energy beams. (The ionosphere is that charged layer of high atmosphere from 30 to 100 miles up that protects us and the planet from harmful gamma rays. It is also important to radio transmission because the transmitted signal bounces off the ionosphere to return to Earth.)

The potential of HAARP crystallizes the Pleiadians' concerns: the power to destroy all life on this planet in an instant in the hands of those without the responsibility to handle it. It's like giving a loaded gun to a five-year-old. Any worries we have about the ozone layer will seem trivial once HAARP starts to work on our atmosphere. We'll need triple digit sunblock factor if we lose the ionosphere—the planet's lifesaving sunscreen.

For the dissemination of knowledge about HAARP and many other "heads up" issues, we are indebted to the worldwide syndicated Art Bell radio show, *Coast to Coast* and website: www.artbell.com, which deal extensively with ET/UFO matters. A show in February, 1998, featured Dr. Nick Begich, co-author of *Angels Don't Play This HAARP* (see Reading List), who likened the HAARP situation to the time when the first atomic bomb was exploded. Scientists had no idea what would really happen but they went ahead and did it anyway. The same mentality is currently in control of HAARP, if anyone can really be said to "control" this doomsday weapon.

Interestingly, however, the Pleiadians worry less about sudden mass annihilation than they do about the slow, inexorable destruction of our planet's biosphere. The toxic waste we dump into the air, the oceans, and underground inevitably moves up the food chain until it lodges in our bodies, causing genetic defects, cancers, and birth abnormalities. So not only are we wiping out other forms of life, we are poisoning our own future. Those responsible are serving industry's greedy shareholders, and leaving a legacy to their children and grandchildren of an uninhabitable planet.

During that amazing summer of 1992, I was shown potential scenarios for planet Earth as she is birthed into the New Age:

The Earth is engulfed in a great light, a new form of energy that permeates the atmosphere, the Earth, and our bodies. The visitors confirm that this is an ancient prophesy foretold in many religions of the coming of a great light.

Light particles collide with atoms and change them in ways I can't understand. The body's cells absorb increasing amounts of light and our two-strand DNA mutates into a more complex 12-strand form as ancient, dormant strands reactivate, giving us powers that we can't even dream about yet.

As we enter the light, our frequency increases until we vibrate in a new expression, or dimension, of who we are. The light becomes so strong and compacted that it begins to block out the sun's light. The Earth's biosphere becomes so compressed that it gets dark and stays pitch black for three days, during which people go into some kind of hibernation. At the end of three days, many wake up to a new kind of light, diffuse, like it's coming from everywhere. But many wake up on a different planet that is pretty much like Earth.

In the first scenario, people are very different. They know more because they are telepathically linked to each other and to countless guides and teachers who are helping them. The Christ Consciousness energy returns, but not as a being as it did two thousand years ago. It's more like an energy moving through us, changing us and allowing more of our spirit to embody in our cells and our consciousness.

Some of those whose consciousness has been raised understand what's happening, but many do not. It is a time of confusion and those who know teach those who don't.

In the second scenario, in which people have not prepared to accept this light, they are taken to a world that is similar to Earth to continue learning and growing.

When will this all come about? Only time will tell but I got the impression of 2010 through 2012. But because it will happen simultaneously across the history of the planet, no soul who has ever lived here will miss out. (Time paradoxes really mess with your head and it's impossible to explain in words what was shown to me.) This may explain the Biblical reference to "the dead rising up." Any soul who has had an Earth life will ascend from one life or another.

Many human and ET teachers and communicators will guide and educate us about life after the momentous event. I also saw that many people will try to deny what's happening because their belief systems are not large enough to accommodate the events happening around them.

Another vision concerned the Biblical reference to "the stars falling from the heavens." Apparently, our planet will be relocated in space so we will see totally different constellations in the sky, which explains why the ancient prophets got confused. What they might have unknowingly seen was this relocation occurring.

The visitors would often sit on my bed and show me a kind of animated photo album that depicted the movement of the solar system through this vast cloud of light energy toward a star system called Lyra/Vega. This, they told me, is where our species originated countless millions of years ago. Our new location will bring us much closer to some kind of federation of populated star systems.

The Book of Revelation's reference to "heaven will manifest on earth" was shown to mean that the entire paradigm (the fundamental view of reality that governs every aspect of our lives) for humanity will change. We will embrace those dimensions or layers of existence that are currently not visible or accessible to us. Imagine that every television set on the planet can receive only one channel, even though thousands of channels are being broadcast. Then we all get new sets that receive these thousands of channels where we find and communicate with ETs, angels, the Spiritual Hierarchy, and so on.

These beings are already here, moving freely among us, but we can't see them. Several *Star Trek* story lines have featured beings that are slightly "out of phase" with the crew of the *Enterprise* or *Voyager* and are hence invisible to them. After the shift, we will not need a fancy chronaton particle beam or whatever to see them. We just will.

I had no idea what to make of all this. The visitors answered my puzzlement by saying that the future lay outside what my current picture of reality could accommodate, and not to worry. Other people were being given the same information, they told me, and when those folks started talking and channeling, these visions of mine would allow me to know how accurate the others were.

The visitors told me that all this information and much more had been "downloaded" into my aura and was now available on demand should I be asked a question. The information would also be released to my conscious mind at some point in the future.

It would be a full year before the visitors' predictions would come true of meeting others with the same information. Then, in 1996, I would hear Gregg Braden talk about "the zero point," and in 1998, I would read *Kirael: The Great Shift* by Fred Sterling; finally there was another name for the phenomenon in addition to ascension. (Chapter 13 explores the Great Shift in much more detail.)

I was told that my job wasn't to do anything directly about all of this, but merely to convey the information to whomever would listen. I was a messenger rather than an activist. Since then, I have faithfully incorporated all this information in my talks, as we'll see later.

As part of my mission, I even participated in my own big windows. For example, since 1993, I've hosted the TV show *Space Cities* on KMVT Channel 6 in Mountain View, California with producer Sloopy Barreau. The show explores the common ground between science and metaphysics. Also, I host *The Robert Perala Show* on KEST 1450 AM out of San Francisco which explores a wide range of metaphysical topics.

Being the recipient of all this information had a tremendous impact on me personally. Every encounter with my Pleiadian visitors stretched my pictures of reality. Even the very fact that the encounters were happening at all was a major stretch for me. That beings were coming into my house to tutor me was heady stuff, never mind what they had to say to me. So imagine my consternation being asked to go public as the messenger for a bunch of extraterrestrials.

Rather than feel "special" in any way, it deepened my sense of humility and awe in which I held creation. The more I learned about the magnificent universe I lived in and its awesome Creator, the more humble I became in my service to it.

Over and over, the Pleiadians stressed something that I've rarely heard from other speakers on the UFO/ET circuit: we will find our ET friends to be very much like us. Yes, there are greys, reptilians, ones that look like a giant preying mantis, and who knows what else, but the guys we'll be dealing with will look like you and I. The only difference is that their civilization is several million years older than ours, so they've had longer to evolve. They may be wiser, smarter, and more psychic, but that's about all. We should *not* put them on a pedestal and worship them, but neither should we fear them. Give us a million years and we'll be there too.

That summer held a fine balance between the nocturnal tuition and my daily dealings with my fellow human researchers, experimenters, and messengers. It became clear to me that many are called as messengers and we each have our piece of the overall Grand Message. And my piece, received over those 18 months, would fall into place, ready for my public debut at MUFON in July, 1993.

Little did I know that, even in childhood, the skills I would need to fulfill the mission of cosmic messenger were being built in and carefully woven into my emerging personality. In fact, many of the tools I would need in later years had been placed in my body and its neural circuitry before birth. It had proved to be an interesting childhood ....

Chapter 5

Secrets

The Boy Who Saw True

T WAS OCTOBER, 1967. I was 12. My mother and I were in our living room in La Jolla, California, with the Reverend John Henkins, a minister with the gift of psychic sight. Outside, the sounds of the ocean drifted in through the open patio door as my mother turned on the huge Victor tape recorder.

The minister began by asking for the protection of the Christ Light, and we waited to see which being would come in to help us with the session.

"Did Robert have a brother?" the Reverend asks my mother.

"Yes, but he only lived for three days, and that was several years before Robert was born," my mother replies, puzzled.

"The reason I asked is that he is here with us now. And he has been guiding Robert since he was born, helping him from the other side," the Reverend explains. "He has something he wants you to know: that Robert has a very special gift and that we should cultivate it. Robert is here with a very specific purpose and he will need that gift as he gets older."

After a pause, the Reverend continues, "I'm seeing Robert, older now, before many people, talking to them. They are listening eagerly to his message. His mission is that of a messenger. It's why he came here—to communicate with people. You do like talking to people, don't you, Robert?" he asks, turning to me. "Later in your life, you will be a messenger with a spiritual message, so your brother is asking me to tell you to study spiritual things so that you will be ready."

After the session, which lasted only a few minutes, the Reverend said to me, "You know, Robert, you remind me of a character in a book I once read, *The Boy Who Saw True*. You should read it sometime."

My mother had arranged the session because ever since I could remember, I'd seen people that others couldn't. At school, I routinely saw two people standing behind the teacher. They looked just like everyone else except that they were somehow not quite as solid as the teacher. In fact, when she would be writing on the board, she would walk right through them. That always made me giggle and she would say, "Robert, is there something you want to share with the class?"

"No, Miss Burlson. I'm sorry," was my usual answer. I tried to stifle more giggles as she continued to walk backwards and forwards through them.

I was often surrounded by my own entourage. They were here to tutor me and a constant stream of thoughts flowed through my mind, courtesy of my guides, often interfering with the thoughts my teacher would rather I had.

My mother listened to Reverend Henkins with rapt attention but didn't express any surprise. Instead, she just nodded in agreement. A psychic was sitting in our living room telling my mother that her 12-year-old son had come to the planet with a mission and was constantly accompanied by non-physical beings here to guide him, and she just nodded. What a mother.

Fortunately, she realized just how real and important all this was and took it very seriously. She never told me that I was just making it all up, the way most mothers would. She took it all in stride and shouldered the responsibility of fostering and developing the gift I'd come in with. But neither did she make the mistake that other mothers would of putting me on a pedestal and treating me like I was somehow "special." I was just her son, with a few quirks.

I was born in 1955 and my first five years had been completely normal. My first passions were building model airplanes and watching John Wayne movies. Of course, he faired better than the planes, which usually had a short maiden flight before crashing into a tree or nose-diving into the ground.

About the age of five, the apparitions started. I'd be lying in bed and would notice groups of men and women in my room talking to each other. I wasn't scared, however, because their arrival would herald a bath in the warmest, most delicious love I'd ever experienced. These visitors were almost solid but occasionally I would see a bright object shining through them. I watched them for hours, eavesdropping on their conversations. I could understand them plainly but I was never invited to join in. I really enjoyed their visits, more for that feeling of love than anything else.

After about a year of this, I remarked casually to my mother, "Do you know that we have visitors in the house at night? They were here again last night."

"No, there was no one here last night."

"Yes there were. They were up in my room. About six of them. Didn't you see them? Sometimes there's children, too, but not last night."

"What were they like? How often does this happen? How long do they stay?" Questions tumbled out of her.

"Well, it happens a lot. Maybe every week or so," I said.

"Hmm. Let me talk it over with your father."

That was the end of the matter. My father's response, of course, was only to be expected. "That's interesting. Now about that new product line I was telling you about ...."

My mother was a lot more involved and took me to specialists and counselors who had me stack up little blocks, group things together of the same color, and tell them what I saw in ink blots. After several sessions, they were baffled. I, too, was puzzled because I couldn't figure out what the big deal was. What I didn't know, of course, was that not everyone saw these beings or the colored lights around people's heads. To me, it was just normal.

Next, I was packed off to a hospital where my head was shaved and covered with little wires. I had no idea what an EEG was, but it sounded very important and everyone was very nice to me so I didn't mind too much. Except that their machine didn't work too well. They found nothing wrong and declared me a normal, healthy ten-year-old.

All this was beginning to affect my school life. With so many distractions in the classroom that the other kids didn't have, I was diagnosed with Attention Deficit Disorder. It was a crock, of course. I had normal attention; I just had a whole lot more to attend to than the other kids, something that parents of children with ADD might check out for themselves.

My teachers were very concerned at what I called "the lights" around people, and all those "invisible" people who talked incessantly among themselves without moving their mouths. But even at the age of ten, I knew I was overhearing their thoughts, some of which they were probably implanting in the minds of those they were guiding.

My experiences were quite normal to our housekeeper, Bep Tyhof, however. Bep was a short, stocky Dutch woman with crystal blue eyes. She was straight and honest as they come. Her thick Dutch accent did nothing to hide her sharp wit and feisty attitude. And was she psychic! She used to tell my mother that my visitors were real because, after all, she saw them, too.

With all this spookiness going on, it's no wonder my mother became very interested in metaphysics. Doctors were replaced with psychics and the paranormal became an everyday topic of family conversation. My mother even held seances, and all that moaning and chanting coming from our house scared the hell out of the neighbors.

However, I wanted to fit in so much that eventually I learned to keep quiet about the crowds of guides filling the classroom. Only my mother knew and she often joked that it was our secret. But with the hormonal ravages of puberty around age 13, the apparitions appeared less and less. With so much else pressing in on my life, such as my newfound fascination with girls, I soon forgot I'd ever had them, a memory that would not return for two decades.

I lived the life of a normal teenager: dating, learning to drive and, of course, listening to the Beatles. To me, they were the architects of the new age and they could do no wrong. They defined a new culture, one I couldn't wait to grow up in.

In 1968, when I was only twelve, my boyhood heroes went to see the Maharishi Yogi in Rishikesh, which is at the bottom of the Himalayas, where the Ganges meets the plains. John Lennon and George Harrison stayed in the ashram for four months, learning about God, cosmic consciousness, and meditation. When they returned to England, they said in a press conference that they had learned that thoughts were things and had the ability to travel. This got me thinking: if you send a thought into the universe, someone or something could hear that and might even respond to it. This struck me deeply and would stay with me for the rest of my life.

It wasn't just the Beatles' music that inspired me but also their role-model lifestyles. They gave an entire generation the okay to look at everything no matter how unconventional, and the Eastern flavor that colored their later music has influenced my own music even today. To me, Linda and Paul McCartney's relationship exemplified the ultimate love story: total trust, honesty, and integrity. I was profoundly upset when I heard of her death in April 1998 and deeply mourned the loss.

Paul is an activist for ecological and animal causes and I admire his commitment and contribution to our planet. The enormous debt of gratitude I owe to the "Four Lads from Liverpool" is repaid in some small measure by the opportunity to support DROP (Determined to Restore Our Planet), the ecological cause headed by my dear friend, Louise Harrison, George Harrison's sister.

If you're a Beatles fan and are concerned for Mother Earth, then please contact Louise and DROP (see the Resources section).

Chapter 6

Voices, Visitors, and Visions

Voices

"Hello and good evening. This is Mark Twain, and I'm here to tell you a few things about life."

This should be good, I thought. It was the summer of 1992 and I was at Nancy Worthington's to hear a channel named Caroline. Looking like anyone's next door neighbor, Ms. Average America was in some kind of trance and supposedly in touch with America's most illustrious author, Mark Twain. She had already explained that she had long been fascinated by the classics, and when she began channeling, she naturally sought out her favorite author in the higher dimensions.

This evening, Caroline had said her introductions and settled in to begin her trance. After about three minutes, she began talking with some weird inflection in her voice, like a fake southern drawl. After introducing itself as Mark Twain, the voice continued.

"Life is unpredictable and full of choices. And those choices can be difficult because you are forced to choose. And choosing isn't easy because it forces you to make choices.

"Writing is like talking, except that you're talking with a pen.

"Right now, I'm sitting on my back porch, smoking my corncob pipe and reflecting on my life."

This flow of banality went on for almost an hour, telling us nothing of significance or even interest, let alone sharing inner secrets of the universe with us. And we learned nothing of the life of this fascinating and enigmatic character who was one of Nikola Tesla's few close personal friends, a rare distinction indeed.

Afterwards, Nancy asked me, "Well, what did you think?"

"I don't know, Nancy. This channeling is a tricky business. Sometimes you don't know whether you're talking to St. Germain or chow mein!"

Nancy laughed, but it's true. Channeling is a subjective art, but there are some things to look for. Above all, the material should be helpful or insightful. Any observations or anecdotes should reveal more about life—who we are, and what we're doing here. It should be inspirational, using metaphors we might not hear every day, giving you the sense of "Wow, I hadn't thought about it like that before."

Caroline believed that she was channeling Mark Twain, but was it because she really *wanted* to believe it? Anyone who has read enough about a historical figure can patch enough together to put on a superficial performance, especially in front of people who are ignorant of the subject. So genuine channeling should inspire, educate, or entertain, preferably all three.

Even in a genuine channeling, you never *really* know who's on the line. Just because they're in a higher dimension doesn't mean that they're serving the Light. There are countless stories of negative entities who claim to be someone else and draw you in with some fine-sounding truths. Once you're hooked, they will slip in something negative or judgmental, immediately followed by another fine truth. Over time, you're slowly sucked into their point of view, which may *not* have your highest and best interest at heart.

Even some of the most prominent channels out there have fallen for this trick at one time or another. We humans, with our overgrown but fragile egos, are easy marks for a malevolent or just a plain mischievous entity who has a superior insight into the human psyche and how to manipulate it.

Many people experience thoughts or actually hear voices when there's no other physical person around. To avoid being labeled crazy, these unwitting eavesdroppers keep quiet. "Having bats in the belfry," "a screw loose," "not playing with a full deck," or "not having all your oars in the water" are some of the kinder expressions used to describe these people. In a country where conforming to the norm is paramount, these are labels most of us do not want.

Anyone who hears voices—or worse, talks back—has a definite mental illness according to the *Diagnostic and Statistical Manual of Mental Disorders (DSM–IV)*. Dissociative Trance Disorder is a diagnosis under category 300, "an alteration in the state of consciousness characterized by replacement of the customary sense of personal identity, attributed to the influence of a spirit, power, or deity." The DSM does, however, allow for this as part of a collective religious or cultural practice and is more lenient if the disorder does not result in distress. But watch out channelers; they've got your number.

Accepting that this happens, however, and that countless people *do* hear voices, where do they come from and what is the listener supposed to do about it? Is it your own mind, angels, God, or even the devil? Many murderers throughout history have claimed that "the voices told me to do it." So who are the voices, or the sources of all these thoughts you think are your own?

There are many sources, some benign and some not quite so benign. How does the average Joe or Jane tell the difference? Many people in my workshops ask me this. This what I tell them is that the possible sources include:

1. **External guides and entities.** Receiving these messages is often termed "channeling." Discernment is especially important because not all these non-physical critters have your highest or best interests at heart; often they have agendas of their own. More on this later.

2. **Your own higher self, soul, spirit, or whatever you want to call it.** You, as pure spirit/soul, decided to incarnate in this time/space in the physical body that you're wearing. You came in with a full agenda of what you wanted to learn and experience. You need to guide that ego of yours so that you will accomplish your agenda. You might implant thoughts and actually speak audibly, so audibly, in fact, that your ego can't possibly shrug it off as imagination.

3. **The inner churning of your mind and emotions.** These thoughts and feelings may be fear-based or lead to separation from others, and even cause harm to them if fear-based. These are definitely thoughts and voices *you do not want to listen to*.

4. **Dreams**, the invaluable source of inner wisdom, although some of the wisdom may be wrapped up in symbolism and hard to decode, but worth it if you have the time and patience.

Let's take a deeper look at this phenomenon we call "channeling."

Channeling

God's wisdom or the devil's trickery? It all depends on who you talk to. Many fundamentalists are convinced that unless the words are in the Bible or fall out of some preacher's mouth, then they are the evil urgings of the Lord of Darkness or his minions.

Most people reading this book, however, probably accept the validity of the phenomenon of channeling. Having attended countless channelings over many years, I can personally attest to their validity, *but with major reservations. By definition, no channel can ever be 100 percent accurate simply because he or she is human.*

Even if you're channeling the fount of cosmic wisdom itself, the words are filtered from higher dimensions down through your third-dimensional brain and are inevitably distorted and bound by your limited picture of reality. There is absolutely no way round this and no channel is immune. As long as you're physical, you are corrupting the information in some way, however slight.

The distortion may simply be the need to express non-linear, multidimensional concepts in a linear language. Or channels may "infect" the material with their own fear and limited view of reality. The worst scenario is that the channel isn't channeling at all but simply using the word "channeling" to convey his or her personal agenda. For example, if the channel is an investment broker by day and the purported entity tells you to invest through the channel's brokerage, run away as fast as you can.

Regardless of source, the main criterion for evaluating any material, channeled or otherwise, is whether it is open, expansive, inclusive, and love-based. Does it leave you feeling more empowered, with options and choices that you may not have thought about before? Does it provide you with new insights that expand your choices, or does it limit them? Is it closed, restrictive, exclusive, and fear-based? Are you being told what to do, how to behave, or what to think? Does the material embrace the good of all, or does it advocate acting in a way that will result in winners and losers? Does it lead you gently along the way with loving encouragement, or does it give you an easy way out, with little or no work on your part?

Ultimately, there is only one decision-maker in your life—your own spirit. Forget channels and entities who "lay it on the line," no matter how comforting it is to have some authoritative spook tell you how it is and what to do. Treat the information just like any other source, such as the advice of a friend. And don't think that just because a channel was accurate once before that he or she is being accurate today. Their contact with the higher dimensions can vary from day to day. Keep your discernment alive and well, actively weighing any channeled information.

Just because a channel seems to have a clear path open to a highly articulate entity doesn't mean that the entity had your highest and best interests in mind. There are many dark entities out there who want to keep you in the dark. The prospect of this planet ascending terrifies them because they believe that they'll lose their power. Just because they may be in the higher dimensions doesn't always mean that they are of the Light.

By now I must sound like the Ralph Nader of channeling. Good, maybe I am. So many charlatans out there are not only ripping people off with worthless information, but are actually doing them harm with false information. They give good, honest, legitimate channels a bad name. So, *caveat emptor!*

On the other hand, many people are endowed with great psychic gifts and are true channels. Thanks to one of these, Paula Peterson, I have had a long and fruitful relationship with EA, an extraterrestrial collective consciousness.

According to Paula, the word "channeling" has become the term widely used to describe an extraordinary aspect of our evolutionary awakening as spiritual beings. As the human race continues to achieve advanced levels of consciousness, we will witness a rise in unusual phenomena and supernatural abilities among human beings.

Channeling is a demonstration of opening specific biological circuitry within the brain, central nervous system, and human energy fields that generate pathways to altered states of awareness which allow access to other dimensions, other fields of consciousness, and heightened creativity.

How deeply an individual is able to consciously surrender to this process determines how deep or how expanded the channeling experience will be. The intention of the individual is of paramount importance. If the intent is to impress others, to sway them, to gain control, or to get attention, then it is highly likely that the channel will attract a source of information that has a similar agenda. This may play itself out with information or experiences that could be purposely misleading.

On the other hand, if the intent is to be of service to others, to personally grow in healthy ways from the experience, and to take mature responsibility for the process, then the channel will attract a much higher vibrational source that is also in true service to humanity.

Channeled information can be influenced by the thoughts, fears, and beliefs of the individual who is channeling. An authentic channel is one who can set aside his or her ego-based and beta brain-wave state personality to allow the uninhibited flow of communication or creative power from the source of inspiration. Some channels will close their eyes to create a deep trance state to achieve this level. Others seem to be able to keep their eyes open.

Channeling is a theta brain-wave state. Theta is the state that all children experience from birth through the very early stages of development. Theta is our most creative state of existence and is also the state in which we are able to see, hear, and interact with those in other dimensions such as angels, fairies, and the spirit forms of those who have died. Theta is the state of being fully inspired and connected to a Higher Power.

As children mature and become conditioned by the adults around them, the theta state eventually becomes squeezed into a brief stage that we experience as we move from the light sleep or trance states of alpha-wave to the deep sleep states of delta-wave.

The theta state of heightened creativity is the pathway to the divine, and bridge to other dimensions is the future of humankind. It has often been predicted that the new species of human being will be a theta state being, a being of supernatural abilities, extraordinary creativity and fully awakened with the inspiration of the Higher Power of Spirit.

Channeling as we now know it is only the beginning, a mere glimpse of the phenomenal and super human future to come.

EA, The Extraterrestrial from Future Earth

On many occasions, EA has spoken through Paula to counsel me on personal and business matters and to reveal insights about spiritual principles and how ETs operate within our reality.

On the subject of working with guides, for example, EA told me how they influence our dreams and drop thoughts into our minds just when we need them, and that we should learn to trust their guidance. EA has also worked with me to more easily interact with my guides and ETs, and told me that the inner goal of humanity is to become more telepathic, whether we know it or not. EA also told me that interacting with ETs is within the reach of anyone who is open enough to allow it. I was and so it happened.

EA (pronounced Ee-ah) is a collective consciousness consisting of extraterrestrial and highly-evolved, hybrid beings existing peacefully and creatively on future Earth. EA is not a name that they call themselves, but for communication with humans. They have chosen this representation to describe the consciousness that they are. Among some Earth tribes, EA is the name given to the living consciousness of Earth, similar to our use of the name Gaia. When the name EA is sung (eeeeeeeaaaaahh), the vibration of that tone activates and unites mind and heart, translated as "heart-mind," or to "think and create through the heart."

Intelligent beings from EA's future have traveled through time, visiting humanity at strategic intervals throughout human history. Their appearance has been described in some ancient historical accounts as that of gods or angels.

On future Earth, which is less than 500 years from now, EA exists as a unified race of all cultures, including extraterrestrials from other worlds. Future Earth is free from discrimination, disease and lack, war and pestilence, and from systems of currency and central government.

They focus on developing individual creativity for pure enjoyment and as a means of spiritual expression. They use their creative energy to be of service to one another, to create a world of peace and great beauty, and to assist developing races on other planets.

Because they are not limited by our linear concepts of time and space, they are able to project portions of their consciousness into our reality for interactive purposes. They specifically seek out human beings with highly sensitive central nervous systems (empathic), with evolved minds that are resilient enough to work with higher concepts transmitted from the future. Such highly sensitive human beings are trained as messengers and transmitters to bring enlightenment, inspiration and support for humanity during the great shift and ascension that is occurring on our planet at this time. Future transmissions can occur through channels, artists, musicians, visionaries, writers, inventors, healers, and humanitarians.

Since the consciousness of EA is from our future, they know that the changes we make in our behavior and attitudes today dramatically alter the world of tomorrow. Their mission is to assist us to avoid world calamities, destruction, and catastrophes. These prophesied events do not need to happen when we are able to transform our thinking and behavior in time.

EA's message has been consistent since their first contact with Paula in 1987. EA emphasizes the need to create greater personal happiness and wholeness, and to shift humanity's course onto a higher path by means of the following actions: 1) Achieve self-love; 2) Love Spirit-God; 3) Love, support and serve others; 4) Show kindness and respect towards each other and all living things; 5) Express your fullest creativity; 6) Find beauty everywhere you go and in everyone you see; 7) Treat your body like the spiritual temple that it is by caring for it and putting only the healthiest foods into it; 8) Play more, dance more, sing more, and laugh more; 9) Love, respect and commune with Mother Earth; 10) Pray; 11) Establish loving extraterrestrial communication and contact by practicing all of the above; 12) If you are impatient and want to communicate with extraterrestrial civilizations immediately, go swim with dolphins!

In EA's own words: "It doesn't matter to us whether or not you believe we really exist. What does matter to us is that you live your lives with greater love, enjoyment and creative fulfillment. What matters to us is that you treat each other and all of life with honor and respect. By accomplishing just these things, you transcend your present world conditions and set about establishing a new order of love and peace. You set about creating your future of brightness without needing to pass through a frightening stage of mass destruction and annihilation. Some day you will meet us face to face and it will be a glorious moment. But for now, focus on these things we share with you for, by doing so, you are preparing the way for our meeting. Until then, we thank you for allowing us to be of service to you in love."

I am very grateful to Paula and EA to have had my own personal extraterrestrial counselor. (See Resources for how to contact Paula.)

Visitors

In the spring of 1994, I was invited to give an all-day talk in a beautiful home in Aptos, California, overlooking the Pacific Ocean. As people arrived for breakfast, I couldn't help but appreciate all the interesting people I meet. Everybody was catching up on old friendships or creating new ones, but nothing could have prepared me for the gentleman I saw staring at me from the other side of the room. If there ever was anyone who stood out in a crowd, it was this guy. Once he'd caught my eye, he began to approach me and I bit my lip with apprehension. Who is he? — or what is he?

He walked slowly up to me and just stood, staring me full in the face with piercing deep blue eyes. What was I to think?

On a chain around his neck was some sort of symbol that looked like hieroglyphics. About six feet tall, he was smartly groomed, with long hair, and a fascinating characterful face.

Uncomfortable with the prolonged eye contact, I decided to break the ice. I extended my hand, "Hi, thanks for coming," I said.

He mumbled a quiet, "Hello."

What is this? I kept thinking. Some kind of weirdo, spacenut, a walk-in maybe? He's not from around here. People just don't stare into other people's eyes like that. And those eyes had me wonder who was home.

He spoke slowly, "It's good to be here."

"What's your name?" I asked.

He looked at me with a deadpan expression and said, "Please call me Isaac."

This guy had a vibration unlike anything I'd ever experienced. I was unsettled and asked him where he was from.

After a long pause, he replied, "Well, I ... er ... I'm from outside the Alpha Centauri system, outside the Kanga System, next to the three novas."

"Huh?" I stepped back in astonishment, expecting him to tell me he was from Ohio or somewhere.

My friend Harry walked over and whispered, "Who *is* this?"

"I don't know," I whispered back, "but don't spook it. I'm taking this pretty well, don't you think?"

"Tell me," I asked, "Why did you come to my lecture?"

"I've only been to two lectures before this but my little girl had brought home your flyer and I was curious about what you have to say about the Photon Belt and the Pleiadian and Sirian Councils. I was instructed by an angel, one of my guides, to help you in this work," he added nonchalantly.

"And which angel might that be?" I asked.

"A big one. A very big one."

A big angel? What the hell's going on here? Use your discernment here, Robert. Am I to buy this or what?

"Well, I hope this big angel is on our side," I joked.

"Let me show you something," he said.

He took out a stone that looked like a thirty-carat diamond, only a brilliant red. He put it up to my forehead and then ran it down my chest and then across. And then to my amazement, he began speaking in a language I'd never heard before. I've been around the planet and heard many, many different tongues, yet I heard no familiar word rhythms.

The room became quiet. I looked around to see everyone frozen, staring at the mystery man. What kind of guy walks into someone's house and begins speaking a language from another galaxy?

"What language is that?" I asked.

"Sirian."

The moment was broken by the hostess calling, "Robert, it's about time to start."

I introduced myself, and asked the 35 attendees to do the same. I began by reminding everyone that as children, we all had the gift of inner knowing and sight that we struggled so hard to reclaim as adults. We already had the gift but had temporarily misplaced it.

Then I recounted my "Angels in Spacesuits" story and asked how many people wanted a similar encounter with ETs, or with angels, fairies, or whatever.

There was a unanimous "Yes!"

I explained that the reason why most people don't see these things as a matter of routine is that their belief system simply can't allow for this stuff and so filters out images that are constantly received by the brain. Any enlargement of psychic sight must begin with enlargement of the belief system to allow for what you want to see. Rather than, "I'll believe it when I see it," we must switch to, "You'll see it when you believe it." This is also the title of a great book by Dr. Wayne Dyer, which I heartily recommend. But, of course, I pointed out, belief system growth must be preceded by a burning desire—the usual pattern of: Desire–Action–Accomplishment.

Next, I turned to Soul Infusion, the process by which more and more of your soul's energy infuses into your physical body's envelope. This starts with right relation to service—humility—and involves building your half of the bridge to your spirit. Your spirit has already built its half and waits patiently for you to catch up. I urged everyone present to examine their commitment to their own soul's purpose and its service to humanity.

Then I challenged the group on the source of their current beliefs. For example, many otherwise empowered people hesitate to walk under a ladder or are uneasy about Friday the 13th. These are irrational throwbacks from superstitions they inherited from parents and relatives. We are saddled by the limitations inherent in the belief systems we inherited, and even though we think we've dispelled them, they may still lurk in the dark corners of our minds.

I was fortunate in that my mother, the main source of my beliefs, raised me to believe that the non-physical world is every bit as real as the physical world in which most children play. There was never a time when I didn't fully accept its validity. Not only did I accept it fully, but I actively sought it out and interacted with it.

Going further, many metaphysicians accept that your belief system creates the very reality that you call your life. I noticed several people squirming a little at this. People can be uncomfortable with that kind of responsibility. We are eager to claim responsibility for the good stuff, but less eager to claim the negative stuff. There are no exceptions, however. *We create it all.*

Next, I turned to the subject of mystery schools. For me, they are not just the ancient learning institutions of the Egyptian or Mayan cultures, but the endowment of mankind's search for answers to age-old questions: who are we and why are we here? To me, *life* is a mystery school and by incarnating, we automatically enroll in it.

My father often told me, "Life is a mystery, son, and you've just got to accept that." Not good enough, I would think. My life is about throwing myself into the mystery and trying to dispel it. Many people waste an entire incarnation, not asking even the most basic questions, or if they do, they accept the superficial answers handed out by society.

If you accept the challenge of probing the furthest reaches of the mystery, life becomes a wonderful adventure. The so-called New Age movement is not so much a philosophy as it is a matter of taking responsibility for your own growth. Pagan rituals, shamanic practices, Eastern and Western thought and so on are all pieces of the Grand Puzzle. Part of the fun is getting up every day and trying to put the Divine Blueprint together.

People who find life boring and mundane haven't committed themselves to dispelling the mystery. I know many people who are practically dead at the age of forty because they've stopped searching, or they never started. Other people I know get up in the morning eager to throw themselves into the mystery. My friend Bev Geiger, for instance, just couldn't wait to start each new day and would often call me up and say, "Robert, guess what I've just learned!"

Your life is a novel that you write each day. What do you want your lead character to do today? Be a hero or heroine, or play a victim role? You get to choose.

The idea of life as a mystery school is a foundation of my work and I can spot "fellow students" a mile away. They are fascinated with life and therefore fascinating to be with. They are uplifting, charming, and are fully engaged with life as the ultimate adventure.

"Man shall not live by bread alone, but by the breath of spirit," admonishes the Bible. Well, spirit is all around us, beckoning us to join the search and offering so much in return if only we can break free of distorted beliefs.

It's sad that one of the fastest growing businesses today is video rental. Millions of people every night sit mesmerized by other people's lives instead of being fascinated by their own.

After the workshop, when people had drifted away, Isaac handed me a napkin with a drawing of a UFO, saying, "Here, keep it."

Despite the soft texture of the paper, it was incredibly detailed. Apparently he had dashed it off during my talk. I sat down and looked at it more carefully.

While I was studying the drawing, Isaac took the red diamond out again and held it in the palm of his hand. To my amazement, it began to glow a faint magenta. I was speechless; I'd never seen anything like it.

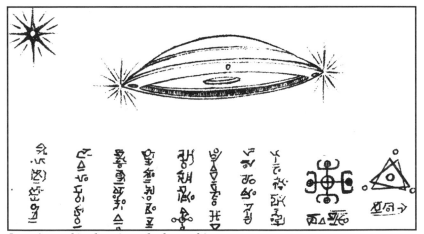

Isaac's napkin drawing of a beamship

"Isaac, how did you get here?" I asked, my researcher's curiosity getting the better of me.

"I came here in a beamship about thirty years ago, just like the one in the drawing. I walked into the body of a three year-old boy who was at the point of death. I am here simply as an observer. I want to invite you to visit me at my home. And you'll get to meet Mary, too."

I was too stunned to challenge or question this crazy confession. Part of me was a little apprehensive about being alone with this guy, but I wanted to hear more. His tale sounded feasible. He said that this had happened 30 years ago, but he actually looked much older.

Before he left, we arranged to meet a few days later.

A 13-year-old girl answered the door and ushered me in. "Hello, my name is Mary."

Her eyes captivated me. They were not the eyes of a young girl, but of someone far older who had seen far more of the universe than she should have at her age.

Her rosebud mouth was set in a white alabaster skin, with crystal clear, deep blue eyes that looked into your soul. Shoulder-length auburn hair framed the face of an angel. I suddenly became aware that I was staring at her, drawn into those eyes.

I entered the apartment and my eyes widened. I stared at the walls, not knowing what to make of them. They were covered with drawings and paintings—hieroglyphics, mathematical equations, and paintings of landscapes of other worlds.

I wanted to jump up and down at discovering this guy. At the same time, I stared blankly, a little off center.

"Hello, Robert," Isaac said, extending his hand as he entered the room.

I responded with a light handshake and a faintly mustered, "Hi."

"Do you want something to drink?" he asked.

"Just water, please." My head still reeled from the artwork on every wall. I felt uneasy but couldn't put my finger on why.

"What's this drawing?" I asked, pointing to the closest piece of art.

"That comes from a different galaxy where there are star clusters still waiting to be discovered. It's too far away."

"I see," I said lamely. Too much for my mind right now.

Isaac invited me to sit down, and as he sat, he sighed deeply, a sigh that spoke of weariness and confusion.

An example of Isaac's extraterrestrial writing

Pen and ink sketch showing Isaac's incredible attention to detail

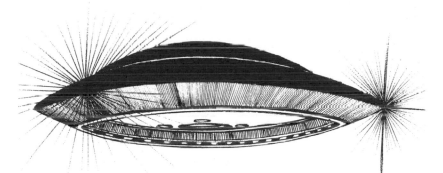

Isaac's external view of a beamship

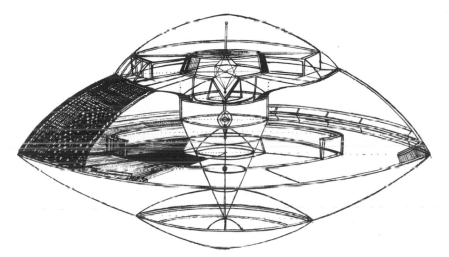

Isaac's cross-section view of a beamship

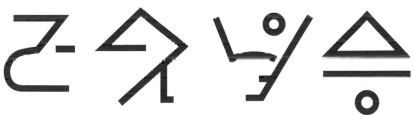

Detail from one of Isaac's drawings

A wave of compassion flowed through me. The words *a stranger in a strange land* went through my mind, from the novel about an extraterrestrial coming to Earth.

"Here, take a look at this," Isaac said.

It was obviously writing of some sort, but not of any civilization on this planet. "What is it?"

"This one's Sinarsh, this one's Sirian, this is Pleiadian. Shall I read it to you?"

I nodded and Isaac launched into a spiel that should have been unpronounceable. I was astonished to hear him read the writing as if it were a grocery list.

A 3 x 5 card, actual size, filled with Isaac's hieroglyphics, with inset detail below

Two more of Isaac's other-worldly written languages

"Interesting, eh? Would you like to look around?" Isaac asked.

There was more artwork than a gallery—lunar and Martian landscape scenes, drawings, spacecraft blueprints, strange vehicles whose purpose I could only guess, strange animals, horses with horns. When I moved in for a closer look, I saw that the drawings were actually made up not of shading with a pencil or charcoal, but of millions of microscopic lines woven together in intricate patterns.

I remembered the drawing on the napkin of the UFO and the fine cross-hatching. When I expressed my amazement at his attention to detail, Isaac said casually, "Keep them. They're yours."

We turned a corner into another room and Isaac opened a closet door. What I saw took my breath away and I almost lost my knees. Feeling faint, I grabbed onto a table to steady myself. Staring back at me was a painting of a face so ancient, wise, and powerful that it looked older than time itself. I began to lose myself in the eyes. They were drawing me in, like two whirlpools I was unable to resist. Fortunately, I was rescued by Isaac's voice.

"Isn't he beautiful! Mary painted him. This is her room."

The room was full of Mary's work, all of it beyond genius. Suddenly Mary bounded into the room and jumped up and down on the bed. "Isn't he great?" she asked with all the enthusiasm of a young girl.

"Who is he?" I asked, still holding onto the furniture.

"He's an Orion. I channeled him and he comes to me in my dreams. This is what he showed me he looks like. He comes to me often so I thought I'd do a painting of him. Do you want to see some more?" she asked sweetly.

"Yes, please, Mary."

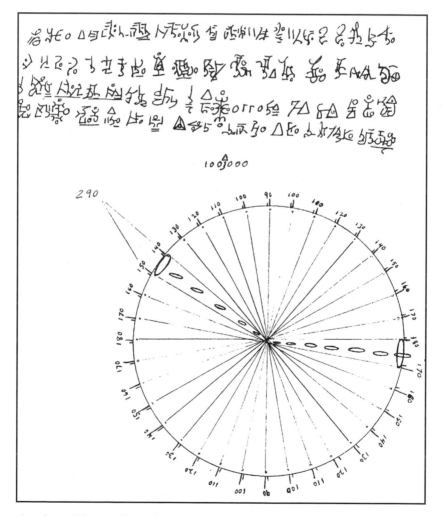

Another of Isaac's hieroglyphics, portraying a celestial stargate

She pulled out a portfolio with dozens of sketches and oils, mostly other-worldly beings and landscapes. I was amazed at her skill and motivation in painting these subjects.

Mary handed me a color sketch. "This is one of my friends who visits me in my dreams and teaches me."

"Teaches you what?" I asked.

"Oh, about what life is like on other planets. I'm from the same planet as him."

My amazement in this girl continued to spiral out of control. Not only was she a talented artist, her walls covered with other-worldly scenes, but she was so matter-of-fact about her ET heritage. She was as confident with other worlds as most girls are with their Barbie dolls. Her sweet naiveté blended so easily with the ancient wisdom of a shaman.

Isaac, too, was an odd blend. On the one hand, he was a genius with things like celestial physics and how the universe operated, yet in other ways, he could barely function. Some of his ideas were so off the wall that I thought he lived on that fine line between genius and madness. But underlying his outer shell, I saw something common to all living beings—the simple need to be loved and appreciated.

Appreciate him I did. And when he told me he was routinely in contact with ETs and other higher dimensional beings in the ships orbiting Earth, I saw an opportunity to gather information about something that was troubling me.

"Isaac," I begin, hesitantly, "my father is very sick and he's getting worse. He's been ill for about a year and doesn't seem to be getting any better. Can you tell me anything about his illness?"

Without saying a word, Isaac places a sheet of paper in front of him and takes up a pencil. He closes his eyes and we wait ... and wait ... and wait. For about 15 minutes, he sits perfectly still. I look around the room uneasily, afraid to move in case I bring him out of trance.

No sounds at all disturb the absolute silence, except for my own breathing, and I try to do that as quietly as possible. A long, diagonal sunbeam angles into the room, catching the dust in the air. It's surreal, like time has halted for everyone and everything on the planet except me. Everything's in suspended animation.

What shall I do? I wonder. Maybe he's died in trance. Should I go over and shake him to find out? But if he isn't dead, that will bring him out of trance. Shit, what shall I do?

My dilemma is solved when Isaac shudders and his hand makes several jerky movements over the paper. This is even more weird. His eyes are closed and his hand and arm are going into spasms. After about a minute of this, he stops, shudders again, and opens his eyes.

Isaac hands me the paper. "Here," he says. "There's your answer."

I look at the paper. Three graphs perfectly fill the space. They look machine-drawn, but they can't be because the paper was blank when he began and there's no way he could have switched paper.

"What's this?" I ask.

"That's your father."

"What do you mean, it's my father?"

"These show his lungs, kidneys, and heart," he says, pointing to each of the three graphs in turn. "This one shows that the lungs are erratic which overtaxes the heart. And it looks like he's on some medication for his kidneys, which are in poor shape."

"My God," I shout, "that fits! He's already on eight liters of oxygen a day."

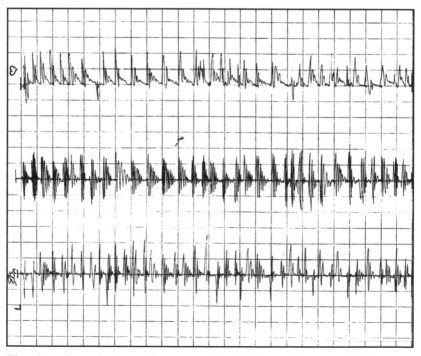

The chart drawn by Isaac showing my father's lungs, heart, and kidneys

"I don't know what the medical term for this is," Isaac continues, "but it's very rare and always fatal."

"Are sure there's no cure?" I ask.

"I don't think your medical profession has this one figured out yet."

"So how long has he got to live?"

"It takes two years to run its course, maybe a few months less."

"Two years! But he's already been sick for a year."

Until now, my father had just had an unexplained, progressive illness from which he didn't seem to be recovering, but now, a theoretical possibility was almost a certainty. And oddly, nothing in me doubts Isaac's diagnosis.

"Just remember," Isaac continues, "he set this whole thing up, no matter how unlikely it seems. He chose the manner of his death. Very exotic and imaginative, don't you think?"

Some reassurance, I think, tears welling up in my eyes. My visit feels like it's over so I offer my thanks and leave. I have a lot to think about.

The following day, I showed the charts to an RN friend. "Here, what do you make of this?" I asked.

She studied the charts for a full minute, her brow deeply furrowed as she tried to make sense of it. She turned the paper sideways and upside down, cocking her head to look from different angles. "I don't get it," she finally said. "It's tremendously detailed. Where did you get this? Which hospital did it? And what equipment did they use?"

"A friend of mine drew it."

"What do you mean, a friend drew it? By hand? That's impossible. This was done by a graph plotter."

"Yes, by hand. And with his eyes closed!"

"Who is he? And where does he practice?" she asked.

"As far as I know, he has no medical training at all."

"No, it's just not possible. No one could have drawn this by hand."

How had Isaac managed to pull off a feat that is impossible, even by today's medical standards? How could he have outdrawn a computer and printer? Did he somehow scan my father internally? Or was he in contact with other ETs who had advanced technology and had simply charted their findings? Thinking about the medical technology portrayed on the TV series, *Star Trek*, the latter didn't sound so preposterous. a million questions rolled around in my mind for the next few days.

Things took a new turn when we got my father's biopsy report from the Mayo Clinic on the East Coast. My father's doctor had been totally stumped by this mysterious illness and had sent a tissue sample to one of the best labs in the country. Their finding was that my father had one of the rarest illnesses ever recorded: pulmonary venal occlusive. In this extremely rare condition, the capillaries of the lungs inexplicably shrink. As the blood flow decreases, oxygen is no longer carried to the body's organs and the whole body just seems to shut down. There have been only 75 recorded cases in this country, each of them an unsolved mystery. With so few cases, no research had been done, no cause had been identified, and neither had a cure. There was no treatment whatsoever.

I set up a private meeting with the doctor. He shook his head. "You know, Robert, I've had one other patient with this condition. Considering that there have been only seventy-five cases, the coincidence of my having two is remarkable. And that first time, I was sure that I'd never see another. This is weird."

"How long did that other patient live after the onset of the illness?"

"Just under two years. I can't lie to you, Robert. This, too, is terminal, and he has less than a year to live. I wish there was something else I could tell you."

I left the doctor's office, deciding to keep quiet about Isaac and his amazing chart. Who would believe me anyway?

The Untold Story of Nikola Tesla

Probably the greatest visionary this planet has known is Nikola Tesla, one of history's great unsung heroes. This enigmatic character has fascinated me all my life, even more so after I read a book, *Return of the Dove.* Some of the material in that book is woven into a biography of Tesla written by my co-author, Tony Stubbs.

Published in 1957, *Return of the Dove* is shrouded in mystery. Soon after its publication, the story goes, all copies were removed from the publisher's premises and bookstores by

[Photo courtesy of the International Tesla Society

parties unknown. Very few copies had been sold by that time and therefore survived the swift censorship. Something in that book disturbed some very powerful people. Amid the paranoia of the Cold War in the late fifties, the talk of free energy devices and the wireless transmission of unlimited amounts of electricity would certainly not have helped the climate of fear the U.S. government was trying to maintain.

Here are a few spellbinding details of one of history's least known but most important figures. Nikola Tesla's inventions totally dwarfed those of his competitor, Thomas Edison, but the latter is still heralded as the "father of electricity" in our school textbooks because, I believe, he was an American, and not a Yugoslavian immigrant. But was he?

According to *Return of the Dove*, Tesla was, in fact, a higher dimensional citizen of Venus. Yet J.W. McGinnis, President of the International Tesla Society since 1988, told me that Tesla's Venusian origins were "highly speculative and, for the most part, embellishments on the part of metaphysical thrill-seekers." Furthermore, he added that "these stories are upsetting to those family members still alive and offensive to the memory of Nikola Tesla."

Although Tesla is undoubtedly unsurpassed as an inventor and wrote hundreds of patents, he stressed that he was human just like the rest of us and that we all could do what he did if only we put our minds to it and stretched our faculties as he did.

Born on July 10, 1856, the son of Rev. Milutin and Djouka Tesla was remarkable from day one. His most notable features were his piercing, deep-set eyes and exceptionally long fingers. Tesla also had psychic sight and was bothered by the "dirty" auras of those around him. This later led to his "eccentricity" of not wanting to shake hands with anyone and of washing his hands afterwards if this could not be avoided.

This psychic vision also gave him an enormous advantage: apparently he could see the higher dimensions that surround us all the time, and he saw phenomena that others did not. On an internal "screen," he saw objects and hypothetical scenarios with such clarity that he would often confuse physical reality with higher reality. When he discussed higher dimension phenomena with his friends, however, their derisive laughter convinced him not to share his visions with them.

School was all-consuming to the young Tesla, and his vision allowed him to visualize the school blackboard in a special way. When set a math problem, he would watch the solution materialize on the board as though it was solving itself, although at a much faster rate than physical chalk could move. Likewise, he would watch physics and mechanics problems "solve" themselves in the higher dimensions, often going beyond what he was being taught. He only had to think of an object and it would materialize in front of him. He would watch a device he had created in his mind, leave it running, and come back to check on it later.

When his physics teacher demonstrated an invention consisting of a bulb that spun wildly when connected to a machine that generated static electricity, Tesla was overcome by a precognition of working with the mysterious force called electricity. On encountering an engraving of Niagara Falls, he saw clearly how the water could drive a huge turbine wheel, and had the odd sensation that one day he would harness the raging waters, a prophecy that would take 30 years to come about.

In his second year at college, during a demonstration of a Gramme machine, a device invented by the young American, Thomas Edison, Tesla remarked at its crude design that caused arcs to flash across the commutator. The patronizing professor explained that as long as electricity flowed in one direction, a commutator was necessary. In a brilliant flash of insight, Tesla saw how the direct current device could be improved by using alternating current instead. With typical indiscretion, he shared his insights with the professor who then turned on him for his blasphemy and insubordination. "Many men better than you," he stormed, "have experimented with alternating current and failed. It is against the laws of Nature."

Stunned by the viciousness of the attack, Tesla retreated but never doubted the validity of his own insights. Visions of motors and generators still swam before his eyes in perplexing patterns. Slowly the pieces were coming together, but it would be a few more years before everything suddenly became clear in one blinding revelation.

In February, 1882, Telsa's true genius emerged. As he walked with a friend in a Budapest park reciting Goethe's *Faust,* Tesla suddenly stopped and stared into what looked like empty space to his friend. Tesla was observing a fully-functioning alternating current device in the higher dimensions.

"See how smoothly it runs. And backwards, too!" Tesla cried in delight to his puzzled friend. From then on, Tesla would "return" to the device to check for wear and tear. Many times in his life, he would build machines on this inner dimension, returning to check for wear and get measurements. He described this process of working out all the details, including minute measurements in his mind, as "incubation."

To complement the image, a vast body of information on the alternating current motor flooded into him. He immediately began drawing diagrams in the mud with a stick, excitedly explaining them to the stunned friend. Years later, he would present these same diagrams to the American Institute of Electrical Engineers, but for now he held the images in his photographic memory, the devices complete in every detail. There, Tesla would set them running and check on them periodically for wear.

The fact that he wrote little or nothing down would later rob the rest of us of much of his legacy. On his death, the F.B.I. seized his papers and handed them over to the Alien Property Office even though he was a naturalized American citizen. Requests for release of these papers under the Freedom of Information Act is met with the usual official "denials."

The years passed and Tesla continued to invent, receiving a small income from his patents. The passion of his life was still the universal principles behind the rotating magnetic field. He often reflected on the role magnetism and electricity could have played in ancient civilizations, such as early navigation. An uncomprehending public preferred the sensationalism of his predictions of communicating with Mars.

He refuted any serious interest in the occult, but by implication his name was often drawn into the hoaxes, flying saucer rumors, and con-tricks of the day. He believed that mysticism and the occult distracted man from getting in touch with the more fundamental truths of the universe, a great paradox for one of the greatest mystics of all time. He believed that there was no problem that man could not solve given enough time, and in just one lifetime, his inventions foreshadowed the computer, the laser, and the wireless distribution of electicity.

Ironically, Tesla was blessed with a photographic memory, supernormal sight and hearing, and the ability to see clearly into the higher dimensions. Publicly, he denied that his talents were anything more than the workings of what he called "the human meat machine." He had many psychic experiences in his life, but took every opportunity to staunchly deny the existence of the psychic realms. What we call "supernatural," he called natural.

Tesla's eccentricity was legend. For example, he was avidly superstitious about the number three in all aspects of his life, favoring any number divisible by three. He was obsessed with personal hygiene and would not contemplate sitting down to a meal without at least 12 clean napkins at the table. He maintained a wide distance with women, seeing them as a distraction to any serious inventor, yet he enjoyed the beauty of elite New York society women.

His premonition of harnessing the power of Niagara Falls was fulfilled when he was selected to design the giant turbines near Buffalo, NY, that today power much of the Eastern seaboard.

In his later years, the sight of this old man wandering the streets of New York feeding the pigeons on street corners was a common event. He was especially attached to one particular white dove, and would pay a delivery boy to feed the pigeons for him if he was too ill to walk the streets himself. The dove visited him nightly by flying to his hotel window.

According to *Return of the Dove*, in 1940, Tesla would confide to a John O'Neill who he'd taken on as an apprentice that the white dove was his Twin Flame, who had come to be with him. He'd retell the beautiful love story, how the dove had once come to him to announce that it was her last visit, that she was about to leave her physical body. His grief at the death of the white dove suggests a bond far deeper than a simple love of birds. What he really felt died with him, except for his telling O'Neill, "I loved her as a man loves a woman."

A visionary dedicated to the service of mankind, Tesla refused to be part of the Manhattan Experiment that developed the atomic bomb, preferring his so-called "Death Ray" that could deliver 50,000 volts to a pinpoint in space up to 400 miles away. This would destroy enemy aircraft in flight without taking a huge toll in innocent lives, but the U.S. military were not interested, possibly because the Administration wanted a weapon that would "end the war once and for all."

Tesla's name also crops up in connection with the Philadelphia Experiment that attempted to render naval vessels invisible to radar by containing them in an "electromagnetic bottle." He worked on the project in the early 1940s but left in protest over the lack of safety for the crew. Tesla died in January, 1943, but was proved right when, on August 12, 1943, the USS Eldridge disappeared from the Philadelphia Naval Yard for four hours. It was seen at the Naval Yard at Norfolk, over 400 miles away. When it returned to Philadelphia, some of the crew rematerialized in the ship's bulkheads, dying in agony. Those who survived returned insane and were promptly discharged from the Navy.

Tesla's most important discovery was probably the transmission of electrical power without wires. Using the Earth as his conductor, he was able to transmit electricity 20 miles away from the magnifying transmitter. His plans for a planetary "free energy" grid were thwarted by the investor tycoom, J. P Morgan, for the simple reason that Morgan saw no way to make any money from it. Only today is science beginning to catch up with Tesla despite the resistance of countless opposing vested interests. Nikola Tesla undoubtedly possessed a large part of the Divine Blueprint, but a part he unfortunately didn't get to share with the rest of us.

Today, the International Tesla Society is pledged to provide a platform for Tesla technology and for emerging "new" technologies. Membership is open to anyone with an inquiring mind (see Resources for more information).

Visions

Throughout history, people have had visions that changed their lives. I, too, have been blessed with more than my fair share of life-changing visions, two of which follow.

Just before going to press with this book in July 1998, I had a private session with Melinda Connor, a local clairvoyant and a devout Buddhist. Previous sessions with Melinda had left me astonished when she had arranged for me to speak with my parents who'd died about three years earlier.

In the session, I asked to meet my guides in order to form a deeper, conscious relationship with them. Of course, they were already in the room with us, and Melinda saw them very clearly. Looking across the room, she asked them, "Well, is he ready to meet you?"

After a short pause, they replied telepathically, and she said, "Oh, good. They say that they'll be at your place tonight. They're going to show you what the astral plane looks like."

The rest of the day passed slowly as I anticipated that night's trip to the astral plane. Eventually I fell into one of the soundest sleeps I've ever had.

I awake to the sounds of tremendous activity around me. Several people seem to be talking over a background noise of a loud hissing and the hum of a vibration. I realize that I'm sitting up in bed even though my body is still prone. Several semi-transparent men and women stand before me, saying, "Well, here we are. You wanted to see us."

A tiny part of my mind tries to sort this out, but most of me is willing to go with the flow. One of the guides steps forward and asks, "Would you like to look around?"

I signal yes, and two of the guides reach out to me and ease me fully out of my sleeping body until I am standing. A thought flickers through my mind: So this is the astral plane. I am a little disoriented since I can hear everyone else's thoughts in my head and I feel connected with everything around me. As we move away from my bedroom, the sensation feels like swimming through lots of disembodied people, thoughtforms, energy patterns, and guides.

I note that I can move just by willing it so, and float through the rest of my house. The furniture looks different somehow; manmade objects such as plastic have only a faint aura but natural materials such as wood have bright auras, probably because they were alive at one time.

My body feels as though it has electricity running through it and the constant buzz is uncomfortable. (Melinda later told me that this was because I was insufficiently grounded.)

What strikes me most about the astral plane is how busy it is, with people and energy in constant motion. Every event on the third dimension is also attended by beings in the fourth dimension. Nothing that happens in the third dimension is isolated, but is shared by countless beings in the fourth.

The knowing enters my mind that entities from all over creation come here to study the mental and emotional aspects of human experience, and how we exercise free will. Our every choice is observed, monitored, and analyzed to find out what factors go into our decisions. The observers are fascinated by how we make our decisions—out of love or fear.

I also see how those in the fourth dimension influence us with thoughtforms, and how not all our thoughts are, in fact, ours but are shared with our guides and others. So much for privacy, I think.

I look round and tap into astral thoughtforms for an unknown length of time until my guides lead me back to my body. Then things begin to get dim, as a dream recedes when you wake up. I lie down over my body and slip into its sleeping form just as my guides finally fade from view.

I slowly woke up, trying to focus on the third dimension. What just happened? I asked myself, feeling disoriented and not really sure where I was. Then it hit me. Melinda was right. They came ... my guides really came and we really did go to the astral plane!

In the fall of 1984, I was in a light meditation, when suddenly I was transported to a different time and place:

I'm walking through a crowded marketplace looking for someone but I don't know who. It's late afternoon on a warm, sunny day. The sounds and smells of the street surround me as market stall-holders call out to passersby. I hear the clink of coin as goods and money change hands.

In my search, I look over my left shoulder and see a man dressed in a simple coarse, white robe, addressing a group of about twelve people gathered around him. They listen intently to his words as he talks of love and God. A couple of children who would rather be off playing fidget and pull each other's hair.

The speaker is taller than most and I see the sunlight glinting in his shoulder-length, chestnut hair. A surge of love wells up in me as my mind echoes with an ancient memory. I stare, riveted, and then it hits me: it's ... it's Jesus! Oh, how I love this man, my teacher, my beloved, my savior.

Tears well up in my eyes. I remember Jesus. I realize that I'm one with him and have always been one with him, his essence permeating my spirit throughout all my lifetimes. I am blessed to encounter him again.

Without warning, the scene fades, a rushing sensation overtakes me, and I am slammed into current time, waking up in my own bed.

All of my life, I have been fascinated with the life of Jesus, beginning with the New Testament accounts and later with more esoteric reading, such as the lost books that never made it into, or were taken out of, the Bible. In my search for the truth about Jesus, I have felt his spirit move through me and guide me. I am in awe of how this one man has remained at the center of a major religion for two millennia. My personal feeling is that he has truly earned his place as world teacher and I feel enormous gratitude for his influence in my life.

Chapter 7

Devon's Blue Angels:
All That Glitters Is Not Gold

WITH SO MUCH EXCITING material out there pulling on your time, discernment becomes paramount. Just because something looks like the magical silver bullet for enlightenment doesn't mean that it is; equally, it doesn't mean that it is not.

"Too good to be true" is often countered by "Too good not to be true." There's an old saying, "The dictionary is the only place where success comes before work." I always leave room for spirit to work miracles in my life, but sometimes, you've just got to raise a sweat or a blister in the cause of service.

In this chapter, we take a look at a few salutary examples that have impacted me in my life and see what we can glean from them. The first involves the tragic story of Devon (not her real name) in the summer of 1992.

Devon's Blue Angels

I wake up in the small hours of the morning to see an electric-blue figure standing next to the bed on Devon's side. (With five people in one motel room, we've had to double up on the sleeping arrangements. I've never been one to refuse sharing a bed with a beautiful woman, even though we are only "good friends.")

The five-foot blue figure looks like an angel, with long wavy hair cascading down over her shoulders and framing one of the most beautiful faces I have ever seen. (Why do you never see an ugly angel? I've often wondered.) She looks down at Devon with a mixture of love, compassion, and concern. I watch in awe for about five seconds and then the angel looks up at me. An electric current of the purest love hits me. The next thing I remember is waking up to sunlight streaming into the room.

I run outside and announce, "There was an angel in our room last night. Did you see her? Did you see her?" The general reaction, however, is focused on the fact that I sleep nude and had forgotten to put anything on before storming the great outdoors. A naked, raving man is just what everyone wants to see before breakfast.

Devon, 32 and very attractive, was a good friend who was fascinated, even obsessed, with anything to do with the paranormal. From angels to Zeta (the homeworld of the gray ETs), Devon was totally absorbed, to the point where "normal" life was second or even third on her list of priorities.

I'd known her for about six months and although we were not romantically involved, we'd become very close in that time. Along with another good friend, Bev Geiger, we'd gone to Mt. Shasta in Northern California to attend an event called Ascension Celebration.

On the five-hour drive from the San Francisco Bay Area where we all lived, Bev cautioned Devon about her obsession with leaving her body during meditation to, as she put it, "walk with the masters on the inner planes." The masters are very powerful non-physical entities who are pledged to work with our planet from the higher dimensions. Devon would enter into lengthy meditations and her consciousness would leave her body for long periods, often for several hours.

Advanced meditators routinely leave their body but they have the skill and experience to "keep one foot on the ground" while off traveling. Bev and I were worried that Devon's spiritual ambitions exceeded her abilities.

It was the day after the angelic appearance and the final day of the conference. I was leaving that afternoon but Devon planned to stay the rest of the day and return with someone else. As we hugged farewell, I had a sudden twinge of premonition and asked her to be careful.

Devon was due at my house around noon the following day. All morning I had the oddest feeling that she was in the room with me. I'd look over my shoulder, expecting to hear her soft voice say, "Hi, Robert." Noon came and went and by late afternoon, I was beginning to get concerned. Why hadn't she at least called to tell me she'd be late?

I'd planned to have dinner with Art Martin. When we returned from dinner, I took the messages off the machine and found one from Bev. She recounted a few details about events since I'd left the previous day and ended with: "Oh, by the way, Devon died last night."

Bev wasn't big on the drama surrounding death, regarding it as simply a flicker while your focus of attention shifts from your physical body to the astral plane and beyond. Hence her low-key dispatch of the information.

I replayed the message and sure enough heard, "Devon died last night." My first reaction was anger. Then came the grief. How could that beautiful, vivacious, young woman be dead? Devon, who had so much to live for.

I was so angry I pounded the refrigerator door over and over, enough to cause Art to rush into the kitchen. "What's happened?" he asked, alarmed to find me punching out the fridge.

"Devon died last night," I managed to get out.

Art looked at me. "Okay, Robert, when you've calmed down, let's do a session and find out what happened.

A few minutes later, we were in my office. Art cleared his mind of all thought, took a few deep breaths, and went into trance.

"She's right here in this room," he begins, "standing next to you."

"What's she saying," I ask, looking around but unable to see her.

"She knows I can see her and communicate with her. She's asking, 'Is this a dream? Why can't I wake up? I just want to get back into my body and I can't.' "

Art looks to a point about two feet from me, to where Devon is apparently standing, and says, "Devon, listen to me very carefully. This is not a dream. You are no longer connected to your body. Tell me what happened."

Devon's guides make themselves visible to Art. "Devon's guides are telling me that they supported her for a long time during her prolonged meditations. They would care for her abandoned physical body for hours, ensuring that the silver cord stayed intact. When a soul has an out-of-body experience, a silver cord keeps it connected to the physical body. At death, this cord is severed, allowing the soul to leave permanently. But Devon would stay out so long and so frequently that the cord could no longer be sustained and eventually her guides had to stand by and watch the inevitable happen. And worse, instead of leaving her body through the crown like most people, Devon developed the trick of leaving through the solar plexus center, not a wise thing to do apparently.

Art turns his attention back to Devon, who is understandably freaking out by this point. She tells Art that she'd pounded on her body all night, trying to get back in but couldn't. She'd become alarmed that her body was no longer breathing, that her heart was no longer beating, and that her body was getting cold. She'd watched as a friend came into the room, shook her body, and told her it was time to get up. As the friend became alarmed at finding the dead body, Devon screamed in her face, "I'M HERE! RIGHT HERE, AND I CAN'T GET BACK IN MY BODY. PLEASE HELP ME!"

Devon followed the friend out to the kitchen as she made the phone call, all the while shouting, "I'M HERE! WHY WON'T YOU HELP ME?" She watched as her body was loaded into the coroner's van, staying with it all the way to the morgue and the unceremonial placement in a refrigerated "filing cabinet drawer."

Totally freaked at this point, Devon thought, *Robert! He'll help me. He'll know what to do.* And whoosh—she was in my living room. All day, Devon had been trying to get my attention. That was why I'd felt her presence so strongly.

Art tells Devon that she's really dead and to seek out her guides, who would help her. Hearing this, Devon breaks down and tells Art, "I've been really dumb. Why was I so stupid? Why wasn't I more careful? Why was I so headstrong? I guess I've paid the price for it all now."

So Devon's obsession with the inner realms finally cost her her place in the outer realm, a heavy price indeed. In hindsight, the angel may have appeared the night before Devon died to either warn her or prepare her for what would happen. Time is linear only here on the physical plane; in all other dimensions, you can move easily into the past and future. It would be only Devon's ego that would be surprised at her death. Of course, her soul knew, and probably planned this event long before incarnating as Devon. Before incarnating, the soul has the lifetime pretty well planned out, including the means and time of death, which casts murder in a different light. The souls of the murderer and victim have had the whole thing planned out since before they both incarnated.

Why Devon did this, I'll probably never know for certain. Devon-the-ego was stubborn and self-willed, refusing to believe in her own limitations. Maybe Devon-the-soul had crafted that ego for a specific purpose, maybe that particular death experience itself. Death is no big deal to the soul, of course, which has planned and executed countless deaths during its cycle of Earth lives. The ingenuity of the soul in finding new ways to die always impresses me.

Devon was a "topper" in that if you told a story, she would top yours with a bigger, better, faster whatever it was. She died as she lived— one step beyond everyone else. She was a perfect example of the saying, "Don't fly faster than your guardian angels." Like Icarus, she had flown too close to the sun and melted her wings.

Five days later, I delivered the eulogy at her memorial service, and told those attending, "This beautiful, spirited young woman was a spiritual pioneer and like many explorers, gave her life to the cause. Unfortunately, her courage and persistence outweighed her discernment. But Devon did not die in vain. She has left us with a valuable gift, a clear warning that we should always exercise discernment in our spiritual work. I will always remember Devon as a brave, loving person, unique in her dedication to her spiritual mission and as someone who died to teach us all a valuable lesson."

Knowing that the departing soul invariably attends its own memorial service, I looked up into the lofty reaches of the church and said, "Devon, I love you and I thank you for the time you spent with us and the great gift you gave us. Farewell, and God speed."

People on this planet are hungry for a celestial event that augers great change. A thousand years ago, as the old millennium gave way to the new, mass suicides heralded either the dawn of a new era or the end of life as they knew it, or both. It's happening again. The odd thing is that the way our decimal numbering system carves time up is purely arbitrary. We could have chosen a system of twelve to count by, or sixty as did the ancient mariners long ago. (That's why there are 360 degrees in a circle.) But no, we count in multiples of ten. How can we expect a celestial event to honor our arbitrary numbering system? We can't, so any hysteria based on our calendar and a decimal numbering system is way off base.

I urge discernment at anything special having to do specifically with the change in the first digit of our system of counting years. If ETs, angels, ascended masters and so on are going to drop by, they certainly won't be looking at the calendar.

Even the New Testament urges patience in dealing with celestial events and cautions us to use prudence and discernment in choosing the factions with which we align ourselves.

All That Glitters Is Not Gold

"Robert, how would you spend a million dollars?

"Sorry, Bev, I'm in no mood for jokes," I grumped. What kind of a dumb question was that?

"No, seriously, I mean it. If someone gave you a million dollars and said it's yours to spend however you wish, what would you do?"

I was having coffee with my friend Bev. We'd just ordered and she fixed me with those piercing blue eyes of hers. She wasn't about to let me off the hook. The way she held her mouth told me she wanted an answer.

"Let me think about it for a moment," I said as the waitress set our coffee down. "Well, I guess I'd use it to help people in some way. Maybe open a retreat center of some kind for healing. What's it all about? Who's gonna give me the million dollars?"

"I want you to come to a meeting tonight to meet a group of people who are working on an unbelievable project."

"What does that have to do with a million dollars?"

"You'll see," she said mischievously. "I'll pick you up at seven."

When Bev and I arrived at the meeting, the air was charged with excitement, like static clinging to your clothes. The house was packed. Groups huddled everywhere in heated discussion. I caught snatches of conversation like, "… when the money arrives…," "I'm getting two million," and "… opening a healing center on the Oregon coast."

I found a table stacked with documents, legal papers, stock certificates, fliers about spiritual events, and so on. With my curiosity off the scale, I asked a woman at the table, "What's going on?"

"There's going to be an arbitrage," she said, as though that explained everything.

"What's an arbitrage? I asked.

"Basically, it means the buying and selling of money, although it's also a giving away of money."

Okay, I thought, that's where Bev's million dollar mystery question comes in. My reverie was broken by someone asking us to assemble in the main room.

"Ladies and gentlemen, tonight I want to introduce to you an extraordinary opportunity. There are areas of the planet that are holding unbelievable amounts of hidden wealth, wealth that is beyond your wildest imagination—gold bars, precious stones, rare coins, works of art, and mountains of currency.

"We have been told by the Spiritual Hierarchy that there is going to be a disbursement of unparalleled magnitude to those lightworkers seeking to help this planet. There has been a master plan since the mid-forties to release enormous sums of money to the metaphysical and spiritual community at the close the twentieth century.

"The purpose of this is to allow us to go out and spread the word to the world about the return of the Spiritual Hierarchy. As you all know, money is just another form of energy, and this is how the Hierarchy proposes to support you in your work."

My reaction was pure amazement. I was stunned at the magnitude of the project, and in awe of the Hierarchy that had masterminded this brilliant scheme. What incredible foresight to be providing resources just as we're all ready to march boldly into the new millennium.

"The money is being held in trust by a dedicated group of people who are in constant touch with the Hierarchy. The grand plan has been unveiled to them but, of course, they can't reveal too much of it until the Hierarchy gives them permission. But the plan is already underway to release the funds. Secrecy is obviously very important when you're dealing with such huge amounts of money. It must be carefully guarded and moved around the world using anonymous accounts in offshore banks so that none of the governments have any idea what's happening. It's being funneled through countries like Liechtenstein where the controls are less rigid.

"When you receive your money, the trustees want you to secure it carefully and keep quiet about it. You will be asked to sign a non-disclosure agreement because if word got out, it would upset the world's money markets. They'll set up offshore trusts for you, so that although the money's yours, it won't be held in this country.

"Now let me tell you how this works. There will be a number of windows opening and closing. If you get in during one of these windows, your money will be disbursed within thirty days. In the window that's currently open, for every hundred dollars you put in, you'll receive fifty thousand back. In future windows, the return will be a hundred thousand or even two hundred thousand dollars."

I took in this brilliantly planned, well-presented program, as did everyone else. People shared their amazement and excitement with those sitting on either side of them. The room was abuzz with agreement about what a wonderful opportunity this was. We were all impressed by the professional charts and graphs showing the projected rollout of this secret superfund of trillions of dollars hidden around the world, how billions were moved every day from one offshore account to another to cover the tracks. I couldn't have been more excited if I'd just come face to face with the Ark of the Covenant.

It all made sense to us. The tiny number of lightworkers just weren't making any headway with taking our message into the mainstream population. Meanwhile, we saw the planet plunging into chaos. It was 1992 and the Gulf War madness was still a fresh memory. For every hot spot doused, two more seemed to spring up. We lightworkers needed support if we were going to make any progress against the ignorance and darkness threatening to grip the world.

For fifty years, the Spiritual Hierarchy had been squirreling money away, ready for a final thrust at the turn of the millennium. And now they had spoken. It was time. Finally our prayers had been answered. I wanted into this program in the worst way.

I signed up for two hundred dollars that night. All the way home, Bev and I toyed excitedly with what we would do with our first hundred thousand dollar windfall.

Two weeks later, I heard through the grapevine that another window had opened up, this time with a hundred thousand dollar return. Four frantic phone calls later, I found how I could sign up. I called my friends; they called me. The '49 gold rush had nothing on this as we burned up the phone system with our hysteria and stood in long bank lines to get our cashiers' checks. This time, I went in for a further three hundred dollars. I'd be another three hundred thousand dollars richer in just a few weeks.

A few weeks later, yet another window opened up, promising an unbelievable *two hundred thousand dollars* for every hundred we put in. By now, life was pandemonium as all my friends called each other every few minutes to keep up with the latest gossip. I raced to the bank for a third time, got my cashiers' check, and dashed to the Federal Express office. This latest investment would push me way over the top. I kept thinking of the thousands of people we would be able to help and all the lives we would touch and heal.

All my close circle of friends could talk about was what they were going to do with their money. But the days were going by. We were already many weeks past the date of the first window's payoff and nothing had happened. Every time I called the contact person, I was told,

"It's going to happen real soon. There's just been a hold up with one of the offshore banks but that's been cleared up, and the money will be disbursed in a few days." With such plausible reasons, we hung on, believing in the integrity of the plan and its trustees. After all, this *was* sponsored by the Spiritual Hierarchy itself.

All through the summer of 1992, the hysteria grew to epidemic proportions. It seemed like everyone who could channel was pulling in some member or other of the Spiritual Hierarchy who had something to say about the arbitrage. In our feeding frenzy, we took even the most innocent message to mean that the Hierarchy was behind the program.

Every day we waited anxiously for the Airborne courier to arrive. We made sure that there was always someone home, and if that person had to use the bathroom, he'd leave a note on the front door asking the caller to knock loudly. We didn't want even the remotest chance that we'd miss the arrival of our first check.

"It will be tomorrow, without question," headquarters promised. "STAY HOME." Art and I danced around the living room, patting each other on the back, giving each other high fives and shouting, "How does it feel to be a millionaire?" We could hardly contain our excitement as the scheduled time for the Airborne courier approached. We both agreed that we needed a break before we started to set up our retreat center and argued about whether to go to Hawaii or take a Caribbean cruise.

Art and I encountered all kinds of people during those heady days. Some managed to stay centered and put in only a hundred dollars, mainly out of curiosity. Others were consumed by greed and sheer, primitive lust.

With each new promise of "It'll be tomorrow," we began to understand the wisdom of the old saying, Tomorrow Never Comes. The days rolled by and the Airborne courier didn't come. I lived a mixture of the most incredible highs at the prospect of receiving over two million dollars and the dread that something might go wrong. Initially, my confidence allowed me to wash away the doubts of everyone who called wanting to know what was happening, but as the days of waiting turned into weeks, and then months, even my confidence started to wane.

Summer turned to fall and then winter. 1992 rolled into 1993. Still no word. Every inquiry was deflected by some excuse or another. By now, a heavy dose of realism had set in, but there was nothing we could do. Always, some bank or another, or a firm of accountants, were blamed for holding things up.

In July, 1993, our hopes took a beating when the bonanza fizzled out in a Georgia bankruptcy court. We were urged not to worry because the funds had been secretly moved to other offshore accounts so that the court couldn't get possession. Buoyed by this news, the enrollments continued to come in and, as late as 1994, people were still shooting for their piece of the pie.

Over the next two years, the scheme just ran out of steam. No one came clean and said, "Sorry, folks, you were ripped off." Everyone was totally disillusioned. Phone calls and letters disappeared into a black void, never to be returned. All our hopes and dreams for a golden future lay in tatters in the gutter.

As a postscript, in 1997, I received a letter from the State of Virginia District Attorney advising me that the principals of the scheme were now serving time for felony fraud and asking me if I wanted to join in a civil suit against the organization and its founders. But I decided to just walk away and chalk it up to experience.

It has since become apparent that the founders saw the metaphysical community as ripe for the plucking. A blend of naiveté and idealism left us wanting this to be true so much that we were blinded to the obvious risks involved. When we started to channel messages that the Hierarchy was behind the program, the founders picked up on this and amplified it by saying, "We've been getting the same information."

The metaphysical community really sold the program to itself, which must have given the founders a great deal of amusement. A tight-knit network and gold fever guaranteed that the word would spread like an out-of-control forest fire, consuming all doubt. In fact, doubters were ridiculed for their lack of faith in the word of the Hierarchy. What a wonderful example of the *Emperor's New Clothes!*

Did I regret getting involved in this whole thing? Not a bit, for while we were all caught up in the drama and excitement, I saw myself and many others grow tremendously in self-knowledge, understanding, and discernment. We each had our own reasons for getting involved and I saw many mainstream people initially attracted only by the glitter adopting a spiritual way of life as a result of encountering so many lightworkers. But some of those attracted only by greed were faced with another brutal lesson that hopefully taught them something.

Those of us with a spiritual motivation were left confused by the involvement of the Spiritual Hierarchy and were led to the realization that the only source of what is true for each of us is our own inner knowing, our own piece of the Divine Blueprint.

Ah, but what a dream it had been while it lasted.

****

Let me close this chapter on discernment with an observation. One disturbing thing I've noticed in the New Age movement is that many people are looking for shortcuts to both material and spiritual advancement. In addition to the Arbitrage scheme, we've also seen other networks, basically pyramid schemes, sold as a "matrix." With an enrollment fee of $100, you recruit more people beneath you and receive a payout. Like all these schemes, a few people at the top get paid off, but many, many more are left holding worthless enrollment certificates.

It seems like one of these schemes emerges every four or five years, when people have forgotten how painful the last one was. Of course, a scheme may have a new twist to distinguish it from others, but they're basically all the same.

Another trait I see in the New Age movement is when spiritual people think it's cool or cute to dodge the obligations of living in society. In the belief that not being part of the system is to beat the system, they eschew every contact with officialdom they can.

Yes, the system is huge and, yes, it is corrupt in places. Yes, it is outright dumb in many regards but it's here and *it's not going away*. It will change, and hopefully media watch dogs will expose the most flagrant excesses of greed, corruption, and stupidity. But for now, it's all we've got, so let's work with it rather than against it, for the benefit of all.

I'm often amazed at the lengths people go to resist the system to avoid the control it would have over their lives. These people don't realize that by taking elaborate countermeasures against it, they are actually allowing it to control them. *Focusing on resisting the system is still focusing on the system.*

One of the hallmarks of a spiritual person is that of taking responsibility for your life. To me, this means working responsibly *within* the system and not ducking out of it like a child cutting school. Playing with feathers and crystals while ignoring our responsibilities does not sound spiritual to me.

This is probably best summed up by the words of Jesus when he said, "Render unto Caesar that which is Caesar's, and render unto God that which is God's." By denying Caesar his tribute, we demonstrate a "me first" attitude rather than "we together."

Chapter 8

Death, Dreams, and Divine Intervention

The Bad News Is My Parents Died; the Good News Is They're Alive Again

Good-bye to My Mother

IN MAY, 1994, MY mother was diagnosed with ovarian cancer. The prognosis was bad: two months to live. At the same time, my father was in and out of the hospital with numerous complications. They were both dying at the same time and caring for them both and learning how to manage their lives was an all-consuming task.

By June, my mother was on chemo-therapy and drugs. By July, she was in a hospice. Meanwhile, my father, back at home, needed almost full-time care. He was unable to walk even across the room.

On July 28, I cradled my mother in my arms and thanked her for all she had done for me. "I'm going to devote my life to world service in honor of what you've taught me. I'm letting you go now, Mom, because I know it can't be easy in that body. You've done a wonderful job in this lifetime; now it's time to let go. But I want us to try and stay in touch. You're not getting away from me that easily."

Driving home, I reflected on my mother and her life. Seeing that frail woman in her hospice bed, it was hard to imagine the vivacious, glamorous society queen. Always exquisitely coiffured, manicured, and adorned, she made a gracious hostess. But her real forte was money—making it and playing with it. She had another side, however, that few people saw: the poet and metaphysician. She and Shirley MacLaine had a lot in common, I thought—the public and private selves. Shirley was her role model, her books my mother's inspiration. It became a family tradition that every Christmas, I would buy Shirley's latest book for my mother.

I thought about how I personally also owed Shirley a huge debt of gratitude. Her first book, *Out On a Limb*, inspired me from the day I read it. It was instrumental in giving me the impetus I needed to go public with my own story.

My reverie was interrupted by my mother. "Robert, Robert." I looked round, half expecting to see her in the rear seat. When I got home, my father called to tell me that my mother had died. The time he gave was exactly the moment I heard her voice. No matter how much I expect things like this to happen, a part of me is always surprised when they do.

It's ironic that she had been my main supporter when I went public, yet she had never heard me speak. What a shame that she would not be around to share in my growing success.

My mother's memorial service was a beautiful affair, held in a rustic, period building on the outskirts of Sacramento. After the cremation, my sister and I went up to Lake Tahoe to disperse the ashes. Nevada law forbids airborne distribution, so a family friend, the manager of Harrah's Casino in Stateline, offered us the use of a yacht. In a beautiful little ceremony, my sister and I left my mother's remains in that place on the planet she most loved.

Good-bye to My Father

In the fall of 1994, my father's days were fast coming to a close. The doctor estimated that he might have two or three months left. I decided to spend the short time we had left together in his company and we discussed everything from the nature of time-space to the mysteries of death.

In his last few days, I approached him with an idea. It was radically different and certainly a departure from anything I'd attempted in previous experiments. "Dad, if as we agree, death really is an illusion and the essence of who you are really does continue, how about trying an experiment? Let's put it to the test. Let's try to continue our relationship, even though you may not be physically present in a body."

The experiment I proposed to my father was based on the premise that, at death, we continue our existence without missing a beat. All we need do is set our intent to continue our relationship and open our belief systems to allow it to happen. We talked more about what that would mean and he agreed to give it a shot. So, together, we set our intent and sealed it with a handshake.

When my sister heard of this, her reaction was, "Robert, you're always experimenting. First, it's extraterrestrials and now it's raising the dead!"

"Dennie," I explained, "many people believe that death is 'the final frontier' that marks the end of existence, that memories are lost, that identity ceases, and that the living can't communicate with those who are no longer attached to a physical body. But the truth, as I see it, is totally the opposite. Bearing in mind how limited we are stuck in physical bodies, you could say that 'real life' begins only when you *do* die. Forget about life after death; is there life after *birth*?"

Our experiment began with me facilitating a life review for him, much like we believed he would undergo after leaving his body for the last time. We went over all the major decisions in his life and he reflected on what they had meant and what the outcome could have been if he had decided differently. For example, what if he had married someone other than my mother? What if he had chosen a life as a politician or military officer? But the most significant outcome from this review were his answers to the question, "If you had your life to live over again, what would you do differently?"

His biggest regret, it turned out, was getting sucked into earthly dramas at the expense of his spiritual values. He especially questioned his obsession with making money: "Money was too important to me. Striving for *quantity* caused me to neglect the *quality* of life. I wish that I'd focused more on who I *really* was and my relationship with the planet and nature. I now see these things as my *real home*. I see now that I was just following the values I had inherited from my parents—that amassing wealth was the number one indicator of a successful life. I wish now that I'd spent more time exploring spiritual values and truths, like who I really am and what the world is really about. I wish that I'd read more of the great metaphysical books and attended more lectures and workshops by the great spiritual pioneers. And I wish that I'd been able to clear up old grudges when they came up. Listen, son, make sure that you quickly forgive anyone who harms you, and that if you harm anyone, you apologize and get their forgiveness."

My father's review left me with two salutary lessons. First, don't put off your life review until after death—it really is too late then. Try to make it an ongoing process. Second, take every opportunity to immerse yourself in your own spiritual evolution. Read books, attend workshops that interest you, talk to people of like mind, see your relationships as "works-in-progress" and keep enhancing them, for as the old saying goes, "you're a long time dead."

But the most important issue that troubled my father was that of self-love. The first thing you realize on the other side is just who you really are, how awesome a being you really are. If you haven't lived a life full of self-love, you really kick yourself when you realize what an opportunity for joy you missed.

On the morning of January 14, 1995, I was looking out of the sliding glass patio door of my father's home just outside Sacramento at the golf course of the exclusive gated community. Sheets of rain came down so hard that it was like being in a carwash; small lakes had formed around the course. No one will be playing golf today, I thought. The only golf balls around were the hail mixed with the rain. They crashed onto the patio and exploded, turning into freezing mush.

In the room behind me, my father reached down to pick up the newspaper he'd dropped. In that movement, something snapped in his chest. He gasped as his lungs collapsed and finally gave up their battle. From that moment, every breath became a supreme act of willpower.

"Son, can you grab that file of papers out of my office? It's on the desk," he asked, his voice rasping between breaths. As I did so, he cranked up the oxygen supply another notch. Those two sentences had cost him dearly.

The three-inch-thick file contained summaries of my father's complex business dealings and real estate holdings. And what a tangle: Nevada apartment complexes, commercial properties in California, and countless other matters. Each one had its own twists and turns, partners, and legal and financial angles. My father coached me late into the night on all I would need to know to manage his estate. For more than twelve hours, he would utter a short staccato phrase, followed by several deep breaths of oxygen, and then another phrase. In my agitated state, it's a wonder I remembered anything.

"Why have you left all of this until the last minute, Dad?" I asked.

"Because until today, I thought that all those doctors might be wrong and I'd get better. Now I know I won't."

That admission capped the depression created by the appalling weather. I was in no mood for all this legal and financial detail but it had to be done. He tried to lighten my mood by joking, "I never thought I'd die. Hell, I've never done it before."

Bravely facing death with a wisecrack—how I loved him at that moment.

After midnight, we called it a day and caught a few hours sleep. I was pulled out of it by my father's breathless, raspy voice. "Rob, Rob."

The clock showed 5:15. It was still dark outside. To look down at the tortured body of this once giant among men broke my heart, doubly so when he meekly agreed that I should call for an ambulance. He knew the end was near.

Minutes later, the paramedics had him strapped on a gurney and in the ambulance. Those angels with the sirens and flashing lights were out of there before I knew what was happening. I threw on some clothes and dashed out to the Jag, my father's favorite toy. His biggest regret of late was that he'd been unable to play with that particular toy.

With the pedal floored, even the Jag couldn't catch that ambulance as it screamed to University of California Medical Center at Davis. I arrived to find him already in the emergency room. I paced the waiting room as countless other anxious relatives had done. In the background, an obnoxious evangelist was preaching from the TV, "... and everyone who has not accepted Jesus Christ into his or her life will burn in hell forever."

"Not *my* father, you asshole!" I replied angrily and, with a sharp jab to the power switch, I consigned the preacher to the void. There's no way my father will burn anywhere, I thought. I've never known a man benefit so many charities and good causes. He was especially generous to employees and their families, valuing integrity above all other human qualities.

I continued to pace for what seemed like hours, until an ashen-faced doctor in scrubs appeared. "It doesn't look good," he said, shaking his head and mirroring my thought. "It's almost over."

As I took this news in, my heart sank into my shoes.

"He expressly told me that he doesn't want life support to extend his life and that you alone, Robert, are to make that call when the time comes."

Oh God, the turmoil. It was to be my decision that would finally kill him. All my studies into life after death were on the line. I would be freeing him from that tortured body to enjoy the glories of the higher dimensions, but how would I feel when the time came? Could I pull that plug and end his life?

"So what are his chances on life support?" I asked, shaken.

"Almost none, I'm afraid. "And it would be no kind of a life, anyway. But he said he didn't want that, under any circumstances."

"And what are his chances off life support?"

"None." The doctor shook his head. "No chance at all. It's only the machines that are keeping him alive at this point. Without them, he'll die. What do you want to do?"

"Can you give me two minutes?"

Two long minutes of more pacing as I fought with the conflict in me. I grappled with my feelings at losing my father but in the end, of course, his wishes to be spared a long drawn out death were paramount. Part of me wished that the other members of my family were here to share the burden, but at this time of the morning, I was on my own.

I took a deep breath and went into Intensive Care. My father was barely visible under the tangle of tubes keeping him alive, the wires monitoring his final battle. "Okay, doctor, I'm ready. Let's do it," I said quickly, before I change my mind. "And I want to be there."

My father was not conscious as I cradled his head in my arms and the medical staff freed him from his artificial life. I asked that his guides be present to meet him once he left his body. The audible heart monitor was already slow. Soon it began to slow until it was just a continuous tone. After a two-year struggle with that mysterious disease, he was free.

The sound of the monitor hung in the air, a postscript to my father's last moments. Thankfully, a nurse turned the awful sound off, and I was alone with my father's body.

I knew that the newly-released consciousness often lingered for a while so in case he was initially confused, I said, "Dad, look for someone familiar. Is there anyone you know there to meet you?"

I stayed with him for some time until the nurse and doctor finally led me out of the room. As tears streamed down my face, I took one more look at him and said, "Bon voyage. I love you, Dad. We'll be in touch. Remember our agreement."

With that, I turned and left. A cold January wind scurried the low, gray clouds overhead but to the east, the sun broke through and a long sunbeam angled down, reminding me of that afternoon in Isaac's apartment.

Within 48 hours, I was bombarded with questions about my father's estate: what to sell, what to renegotiate, what to leave alone. Lightning-fast decisions became my life; I had no time to grieve my father. On top of everything, in the midst of all this wheeling and dealing, I had funeral arrangements to make.

The family gathered at his house and once, as I entered the room, the hushed conversation halted. A moment of silence hung in the air as my sister looked at me and said, "Well, Robert, you're the godfather now."

I laughed and that broke the tension we were all under. Soon everyone was laughing, crying, or both.

The memorial service was held at the golf club clubhouse; the 19th hole had always been my father's favorite. I began my eulogy with, "Every man is born to die, but how many men truly live? My father was such a man, a man who lived life to its fullest. Few men have exemplified greatness and leadership as he did. Don walked like America. He had the swagger of John Wayne and the polish of Frank Sinatra. He had style and showed us the rewards of hard work, dedication to your goals, and taking responsibility for your life."

As I said that, Paula, my psychic friend, gasped, I continued speaking but was very curious about what she had seen. My father, she later told me, had been standing next to his casket, beaming with pride at my words and exuding incredible love in my direction. To her psychic sight, he was just as real and solid as anyone else in the room. Now I know why we say, "Don't speak ill of the dead." Chances are, they're standing right next to you. My father's antics were not over yet, though.

The minister conducting the funeral service had brought a colleague along who chose to use this occasion to score some religious brownie points. He got up to tell us, "Don was a deeply religious man whose constant words were, "Praise the Lord.""

In fact, my father had been a deeply spiritual man, but religious? No. Paula later told me that my father had held his nose and waved his hand as if to say "You're full of bologna." What Paula didn't know was that this was a very common gesture my father used at anyone with whom he disagreed. Score one for the after-life!

Remembering our agreement to conduct research, I began to look for signs of communication. It had been a hectic week for me because, even though he had worked hard to straighten out his business affairs, many of them were so convoluted that several tangles had to be unraveled. This left me physically exhausted and mentally depleted on top of the emotional distress of losing a father and a good friend. In retrospect, even if he *had* been trying to contact me during that week, I was probably not in a receptive state.

The day of the funeral, however, just as I was on that threshold between sleep and wakefulness, I heard two words in his voice so clearly that I thought he was by my bedside: "Hi, Rob."

Still groggy, I opened my eyes and looked around the room. Then it dawned on me: he had slipped his greeting to me before my overworked mind could get involved in the day's activities. Nice job, I thought. I relaxed and enjoyed the energy of "it's all going to be okay" that he somehow wrapped me in.

With that masterstroke of my father's, seven days of tiredness, grief, worry, and doubt evaporated. Yes, he's still around, I thought. Yes! I bounced out of bed, full of hope, optimism, and joy bordering on ecstasy. I threw on a robe and ran into the kitchen where everyone else was fixing breakfast. "Listen up, everybody. I have an announcement. Dad's alive! He just spoke to me and everything's going to be just fine!"

Twelve blank faces stared at me as though I was a raving madman. They had no idea that I and my parents had a "spooky" side. I could imagine what was going through their minds: "Poor Robert's finally cracked under the pressure. Grief and anxiety over Don's business affairs have pushed him over the edge. We bury the father and commit the son to an institution all on the same day. What a mess."

My sister Dennie said, "Robert, you're tired."

"I'm not tired!" I snapped back. "I'm telling you, Dad's alive."

"Then what in the holy hell is going on here?" she asked.

"What do you mean about everything's going to be fine?" someone else asked timidly, not wanting to provoke the madman too much.

"Well," I said, "it wasn't so much what he said but the knowing that he immersed me in. As though he washed out all my doubts and fears and replaced them with confidence and security. I don't know how he did it, but he just spoke to me. These seven days have been hard, the not knowing. But now I know, it's true. It's really true!"

I stopped there, thinking that my wild babbling might prompt someone to call 911. I decided to bask alone in the warmth of my father's love, to enjoy it without anyone trying to talk me out of it. And enjoy it I did.

The weather for the funeral was appalling—dense fog, light rain, and low clouds hanging on the surrounding hills. Paula told me later that during my eulogy, my parents stood together, watching the proceedings and that at one point, my father came over to me and put a captain's hat on me. I guess that meant that I was now, indeed, the head of the family.

Dreams and Divine Intervention

About three months passed before the next contact, despite my daily ritual of reaffirming our contract and restating my intent for our relationship to continue. It began with my waking up and knowing that I had been dreaming about my father and my mother. I wasn't able to bring to conscious awareness the substance of our meetings, but I always awoke with the deep feeling of being loved. I would go about my day held in that warm glow.

One morning a few weeks later, I awoke with a clear memory. I had met my father and had been aware that, although I was present with him, my physical body was asleep elsewhere. This was my first lucid dream with him.

I hug him and with tears streaming down my face, I say, "I love you, Dad." He looks at me with tremendous love in his eyes and I feel his love wash over me and through me. Without moving his lips, he says something about being emotional. Suddenly, a spinning sensation overtakes me, everything goes black, and I hear a thump. I am back in my own bed, startled by the sudden change of location.

It then occurred to me what his warning about emotion meant. He was warning me that being overly emotional would break my connection to the dream dimension, and was telling me not to get so excited. Breaking the connection is, of course, a valuable safety valve when the content of a bad nightmare gets too intense and you wake up sweating and your heart racing. Any emotional intensity will cause you to slam back into your sleeping body, regardless of whether those emotions are enjoyable or terrifying.

I was almost beginning to lead two lives: an outer life resolving a very troublesome legal situation I inherited from my father, and an inner life with him at night. This led me to refute the deeper reality of death. In fact, I was "dying" myself every night when I met with my father, except it was a "temporary death" because I came back to my physical body afterwards.

I now had trained myself to avoid excitement during our meetings and would greet him with a calm, "Hi, Dad." Equally calmly, he would reply, "Hello, son." At one meeting, I noticed that he was looking younger and slimmer, with fewer lines in his face. He was wearing his favorite polo shirt, slacks, and shoes. Telepathically, he asked if I had any questions.

"Where are we?" I asked.

"We're right here, son. Because here is the only place we can be."

Of course, I thought. Here *is* the only place you can be. That profound insight had great inner meaning for me, although much of the meaning would unfortunately be lost to my waking consciousness. Don't you hate it when that happens?

"So, how are you, Dad?" I asked.

"Fine, son, just fine." He smiled and began answering my next question about what he did all day even before I'd begun to form it in my own mind.

"I'm going to school right now, playing catch-up on what I missed during my Earth life. And the subject is … me. I'm learning about what I'd hoped to accomplish on Earth versus what I did accomplish. I'm replaying every decision I made to explore what would have happened if I'd decided differently, and which would have been the best decision for everyone involved. I'm re-enacting every experience I ever had to see how it served me, everyone else, and even the creator.

"The bottom line is that, apart from the regrets we talked about, I lived a good life, an honorable life. I'm even drawing up some tentative plans for another lifetime and deciding what I would want to learn and accomplish."

My meetings with my mother revealed that she, too, was conducting her own life review—her life plan, her actual accomplishments, what had served her, and what hadn't served. Her findings were very different, of course, because her personality's attachment to material wealth was different. Her regret centered on pre-life goals that weren't achieved. She seemed to feel more sorrow about unachieved goals, whereas my father could blow that off more easily. I wondered if this was due to our having already conducted a life review while he was still alive. Mother expected more of herself, was harder on herself in her review than my father was.

It occurred to me that after death, it's important not to get too hung up on what had been done or left undone and simply plan to tackle it in another life, which adds a new literal meaning to the saying "life goes on." It's important to accept what is and move on.

Was any of this real or was I making it all up? I needed some outside input so I called on Paula. I asked her to conduct a session in which I would try to speak to my father.

As soon as the session began, Paula reported that my father's presence was extremely strong. This didn't surprise me because many entities stick around for some time after death to observe their loved ones and maybe help out where they can. I imagine that knowing how people feel about you after your death is useful input in a soul's review of a lifetime.

"Your father wants to convey some important information to you. He has many things to say to you. First, he congratulates you on helping him through the transition. He also wants you to know that he is impressed with how you handled all the tough decisions with the estate. He knew that it would call on all your leadership abilities, and he is very pleased with what you have done. He also has a warning for you."

Suddenly alert, I urge her to proceed.

"He says it's to do with the apartment complex in Nevada. (This was the tricky legal problem I'd inherited. He had made a real estate investment two months before he died and had formed a partnership with two other people.)

"So, what's going on with the investment?"

"One of the partners is dangerous. It appears that two liens have been placed on the property, that there is a legal problem with the roof, and there's some kind of 'fudging' going on."

I know exactly what he means by 'fudging' because it was a term my father often used and he's the only person I've ever heard use it. This confirms that it really was my father on the line.

"Listen very carefully," Paula continues. "This is a very serious situation. You have to get out of the investment as soon as possible. You'll need to take a strong stand to pull this off, but it's vital that you act, and act very quickly."

After the session, I began to think furiously about what I should do. I couldn't accuse the partner of some very serious crimes without proof, but I was not involved in the day-to-day management. How could I obtain the proof I needed without raising his suspicions?

I was faced with hiring a team of lawyers and accountants to begin sorting this mess out. In the back of my mind, I knew that I had the best advisor of all—my father—and he was motivated because it was his lack of judgment that had gotten me into this situation in the first place. Unfortunately, I had to keep this from my family. Their mid-Western beliefs would not have allowed them to accept the source of this information.

However, I didn't have that luxury with the third partner—a born-again, Christian evangelist minister. How could I explain to this ultra-conservative minister that I had received this information from Don after his death via a psychic? "Talking to the dead is no big deal. I do it all the time." I'm sure he would have commanded an exorcism on the spot.

My dilemma was resolved during my next visit to the complex. The secretary approached me in tears and told me that the complex had a bad roof and someone was suing us. She also told me that two creditors had not been paid and had filed liens against the property. And worse, money was being siphoned out of the bank accounts at an alarming rate.

I was staggered. This was almost verbatim what my father had warned me about through Paula a few months earlier. And, of course, Paula had no knowledge whatsoever of my real estate dealings so she was incapable of fabricating this information. Never before have I had such positive, unequivocal evidence of existence after death as this. I wandered around in a daze while I assimilated both the bad news about the apartment complex and the overwhelming proof of life after death.

With a powerful team of attorneys and accountants, I managed to force the partners to buy me out. It would take over two years of tense meetings, down-to-the-wire bluffing, sleepless nights, and nerves of steel. But always I felt my father watching from the wings, rooting for me. And I won. Thanks, Dad.

My Darling Beverly

"You're new here, aren't you?" a friendly face in the crowd asked. It was my first Selma group meeting and I was feeling a little lost.

"Me? Yes. How did you know?" I asked this bright, vivacious woman.

"Oh, it's easy to spot a newcomer. Here, let me show you around. My name's Bev, by the way."

That was my first meeting with someone who would, over the years, become my best friend. Bev Geiger was a delight. In her mid-forties, she had salt-and-pepper hair, mischievous eyes like Shirley MacLaine, and an effervescent sense of humor. I was immediately attracted to the unconditional love that exuded from her. A very spiritual woman, she had avoided being locked into any one set of beliefs, and was always on the prowl for new ideas and ways of looking at things.

I was 23 and Bev would listen to me and my troubles carefully. Her advice was always filled with love and humor, free of any hidden agenda. I adored her child-like wonderment at the world around her, and way she could see right through the bullshit that often passed for "new age."

We lost touch for several years, but renewed our friendship in 1992. In our search for the truth, Bev and I had more fun than was legal. We attended lectures and workshops on every wild and crazy subject and talked about them until dawn.

For four glorious years, Bev and I played like two kids who'd just found a secret fort or cave in the hills until early in 1996, when Bev mentioned that she was getting easily tired, and slowed the frequency of our outings. I was out on the talk circuit more and more, and I didn't see her until July, when I got the shock of my life. Gaunt, emaciated, and jaundiced, she was a frail shell of a human being, far from the firecracker I'd last seen.

I went to the doctor with her to get the verdict on her condition. It was cancer, the single most terrifying word in our language.

"I'm going to be done here pretty soon," she said quietly, coming out of her doctor's office.

I knelt beside her wheelchair in the waiting room and hugged her, tears streaming down my face. My sweet, beautiful friend who I thought would never die had been served with the ultimate eviction notice: "unfit for occupation."

It's ironic how we all know that death is inevitable, like taxes, but when it points its finger at you or someone you love, it's always a surprise. I'd lost Devon and my parents and now I was about to lose Bev. Life, the most precious of things, is so fleeting and fragile. Enjoy every moment while you can.

She stayed at my house for a few days. During one of our conversations, often cut short by her exhaustion, I told her that I fully expected to continue our relationship after her death, that she wasn't getting away that easily. I joked that I'd be furious if she left the immediate vicinity of Earth without a word so we agreed a secret code by which I'd know it was her.

Bev knew fully that life and death are simply two states of being; she had no qualms about her upcoming change in state. She went into death with magnificent composure despite the physical side-effects of the treatment. I got the phone call on Wednesday, August 21, and although I'd been expecting it, the shock still hit me like a blow in the abdomen. Apparently, she died with a broad smile on her face, as if she was off on the grandest adventure of all.

I didn't have long to wait for Bev to make good her promise to keep in touch.

About 5 a.m. one morning, I wake up in the middle of fascinating conversation—with Bev. We're chatting like the old days about anything and everything. As I continue to wake up, the truth dawns on me. "But wait, you died," I protest.

"Yep, that's right," she smiles back. "I made it."

I open my eyes and there she is, stretched out on my bed, head propped up on one hand, looking at me with a broad smile on her face. Then slowly she disappears, just like the Cheshire cat! I couldn't believe it; Bev, a full-body apparition!

Waves of emotion swept over me and tears of joy flowed down my face as I marveled at the miracle of life, and life after life. What a wonderful example of the continuity of the human soul.

In the midst of my surprise, the thought flashes through my mind: *Don't be surprised. You should listen to your own lectures, Robert.* And then suddenly I burst into tears at my next thought: *It's August 23. My birthday!* Oh, what a beautiful gift, Bev. Thank you so much.

A few weeks later, I asked Paula to get in touch with Bev. She promptly showed up and proceeded to regale me with her impressions of life after death. I began by asking whether time is the illusion we figured it to be.

Bev answers, "Time is so different on this side that I can't even begin to explain how."

Then I ask, "Is the Earth really watched over by a Spiritual Hierarchy just like we figured?"

"Yes. It's a very well-organized structure of observation, management, and recording. I haven't had time to get involved but trust me, I will."

"Tell me about the Photon Belt."

"Wait ... they're showing me something. It's a very complex consciousness, of the essence of the Creator itself. It's so complex that hundreds of different life forms throughout the galaxy are studying it. I'm sorry but there's no way I can describe in English what I'm seeing."

At this point, my analytical side kicks in. "Bev, how do I know it's really you?"

I gasp at what she says next. Only she and I know that secret code and that's exactly what I hear: "Old friend."

There's no way Paula could have known that phrase, and it's not something she ever calls me. Therefore, it really was my dead friend Bev, alive and well in the higher dimensions, getting into as much mischief, I hope, as she did on the physical plane.

Dannion Brinkley

No chapter on death would be complete without mentioning Dannion Brinkley, who documented his amazing story in *Saved by the Light* (see Reading List). The night of September 17, 1975, when Dannion was 25, a thunderstorm rolled through South Carolina. Just as he was trying to wind up a phone call to ward off something he had feared all his life, it happened—a flash of lightning and millions of volts crashed through him, blowing him clear across the room, leaving his boots welded to the floor. From above, Dannion watched as his wife performed CPR on him and his body was carried off in an ambulance.

As the tunnel opened, Dannion was pulled into it, and he was met by a "Being of Light." The Being radiated overwhelming love, which was just as well, since Dannion's life review was grueling. His boyhood label of "troublemaker" had been well earned, and his military service had resulted in many deaths and great misery for countless people. Well, he got to count every single one and experience their pain and suffering. The "ripple effect" was particularly hard because he had once been involved in arms distribution. He got to experience the awful harvest of death reaped from each and every gun.

The Being of Light left him with his anguish for a while and then helped him work through the guilt. Then the Being told him that humans are capable of great good that is usually expressed in small, spontaneous, one-on-one acts rather than through great deeds. His delight at this awesome insight was dashed by the realization that he was dead and couldn't apply it.

Dannion was transported to a crystal city, ushered into an auditorium, and became the focal point for telepathic information by several more Beings of Light who revealed 13 remarkable sets of visions of the future of humanity. Of the 117 visions, 95 had come to pass by 1993 when his book was written. We only have to watch the evening news to share in those visions: the fall of communism, Desert Storm, Chernobyl, Iraq's chemical weapons—Dannion saw it all. However as of Spring, 1998, the worst outcomes are yet to come.

The grisly show ended with Dannion being told that none of this was cast in stone and could be averted. His mission was to report this information back to us and to build a series of "stress reduction" centers for the benefit of mankind. For the latter, he was shown the equipment needed, and the blueprints for creating it.

Dannion returned to his body and the excruciating pain had him wishing that he *had* died. Every nerve in his body had been fried and screamed in agony. Over the next several months, his only relief from the unbearable pain were visits back to the crystal city for more coaching on the healing centers. He talked incessantly about his passion—the centers—to the point of driving people to boredom until finally, he met Dr. Raymond Moody and was able to begin making sense of what happened.

In *At Peace in the Light*, the sequel, Dannion describes the three worlds he lived in while recovering from the lightning strike: (1) the everyday world in which he could barely function, (2) the spirit world where he would meet with the Elders for continued instruction, and (3) the life of whomever he was with. It was this last world that caused him the most trouble because people got angry or defensive when Dannion revealed that he knew their thoughts and emotions. Today, he enjoys playing in these three worlds, but in 1975, he really thought he had gone insane. What he didn't realize at the time was that he was one of the sanest people on the planet.

Dannion also describes how he had the ability to accurately predict the future. This drew him into the world of gambling for the income, but deep down, he knew he was misusing a remarkable gift from spirit.

After stumbling in the dark, searching for his mission, Dannion was finally pointed in the right direction by a wise old man who told him that if people heard about Dannion's NDE, it would dispel the fear of death. He discovered he had a wonderful ability to counsel people on their deathbed and lead them through a life review so that they died in peace.

In countless hours at hospices, Dannion had some truly heartwarming experiences as he walked the dying through death. I was touched by every one of them because they brought back the role I played in my father's death. Dispelling the fear of death, as Dannion does, makes the best case I know for not artificially prolonging life. Keeping someone alive is often done simply because the relatives don't want to lose the person. I'm convinced that if people have no fear of death, they should be allowed to go through their transformation at its natural pace, ideally surrounded by loving relatives wishing them *bon voyage*.

Every patient encounter is a healing experience for Dannion, and often, at the moment of death, as the ego finally crumbles, the pure light of the soul shines through. That, Dannion says, is his payoff.

Through thousands of hours spent in hospices at the bedsides of the dying, Dannion has touched so many lives and helped them face the ultimate mystery without fear. His compassion for his fellow man touches us all. His noble service comes at a time when we are most vulnerable, and Dannion gently helps us cross the threshold of the unknown. And I am amazed at how spirit changed his life so that he could fulfill his piece of the Divine Blueprint.

Dannion's experiences led him to form Compassion-In-Action (C-I-A), a non-profit organization working to train a network of counselors to assist those in hospices through their death process. Dannion's credo is, "No one need die alone." (For information on how to contact C-I-A, see Resources.)

Chapter 9

Echoes of Ancient Egypt

Death On the Nile

THOUGHT I WAS going to die. The sweat poured off me, soaking the blankets I was wrapped in. A temperature of 101 wracked my shivering body as my friend Ruth Lowery wrapped me in dry blankets to break my fever. In the midst of the worst physical pain I thought a body could endure, a part of me wondered how I could go back and tell my friends that I had traveled nine thousand miles but fell five hundred yards short of the Great Pyramid of Giza. The grand finale of our Egypt trip was to have been the visit to the King's Chamber in the pyramid at Giza on the Spring Equinox.

For twenty years, I had been searching for answers to life's "big" questions: who we are, where we came from, what we're doing here, and where we're going. How were we created? Who is God and who are these ETs that keep cropping up in my life? What better place to look for answers than Egypt?

I had prepared for the trip for weeks, pouring over maps and guide-books, and brushing up on my Egyptian history. I'd spent hours planning how I would spend my time in this mysterious land of ancient pharaohs. I remember talking to a friend on the phone before I left. She said, "Robert, you sound nervous. You don't sound happy about this trip."

She was right. For no apparent reason, I was apprehensive. I bit my nails and stared out the window for hours. What would we find? What would the Arabs be like? Despite my preparations, nothing could have prepared me for what I was about to experience. Little did I know that when I left on my expedition to Egypt in search of the truth about extra-terrestrials, I was headed for an initiation where I would die at the Giza plateau and go to the other side.

The day of departure finally came. A loud banging at my front door, along with, "Robert, let's go, man!" announced the arrival of Kenny, a good friend who'd come to drive me to the airport. I quickly pulled the last of my things together, secured my grip, and then closed my eyes and said a prayer: "Father, please keep me safe. As you know, I'm going into the desert to search for answers about You and Your wonderful reality. Guide me, Father. Watch over all of us and hold each of us in your heart."

On the plane, I dozed in and out of dreams. We were somewhere over the Colorado Rockies when, over dinner, the woman next to me asked, "Are you going to New York on pleasure or business?"

"Neither," I replied, "I'm on my way to Egypt."

"Why would anyone go to Egypt?" she asked, a worried look on her face. "It's dangerous."

"Thank you, I already know that. I'm doing research on extraterrestrials."

She was a little startled and then she frowned. "Extraterrestrials? You mean people from outer space?"

"Exactly. ETs have been visiting the Earth for thousands of years and I'm on an expedition with fifty other people who feel that Egypt holds the answers. Nowhere on Earth has the influence of otherworldly visitors been more apparent than in Egypt."

"Oh," she replied, adding, "I once saw a picture of a pyramid with UFOs around it."

"That's why we're going. To find out." I was amused that the average person who knows nothing about UFOs usually associates them with the pyramids.

Dinner trays collected, the passengers relaxed to watch the movie. I closed my eyes and reflected on the trip and that in a few hours I'd be in New York, meeting with fifty mystical, magical people who wanted to walk the halls of the ancient pharaohs' temples and mystery schools. What will we find? What kind of race would build a monument to those who came from the stars? I couldn't help but feel that I would find my answers there. The Sirians? The Orions? The Hathors? I felt connected to the Hathors. I saw the land and people so clearly in my mind, but for some reason, I couldn't shake my apprehension. I'd learned from experience that this feeling meant that something was going to happen, something that might not be too pleasant.

We arrived in New York and assembled in the airport like a bunch of giggling school kids thrilled at the prospect of the experience of a lifetime. We also met the owner of the tour company. For many years, his company had been opening up the ancient mysteries of Egypt to tourists. A very sharp dresser, charming and witty, he was a tremendous source of information about Egypt, ancient and modern. But my premonition stayed with me, niggling at my subconscious.

Poking each other in the ribs, laughing and fooling around, we got on the plane. The mood changed abruptly. What we hadn't realized until then was that Egypt begins once you board an Egyptian airplane: rude cabin staff, filthy seats and aisles, horrible bathrooms, and sinks that didn't work became the norm for the next twelve hours. I just hoped that the engines had faired better in their last maintenance.

I walked through the cabin, saying to everyone, "Welcome to Egypt. It's fast, it's fun, it's Egypt." My morale-boosting got me liberally showered with peanuts.

After a long, exhausting flight, we arrived at Cairo International Airport on a blazing hot Sunday afternoon. The air conditioning must have last worked around the time of Moses for the heat in the terminal was withering. Uniformed military types stood at each corner and swarms of small, scruffy-looking boys plagued us like gnats, their hands out for whatever they could get. The air was blue with acrid cigarette smoke. What a blessing that the bus to the hotel was air-conditioned.

After a brief period to wash up, we were to attend the trip orientation and meet the organizers, Mary Elizabeth Hoffman and Joe Jochmans. Delightful people, perfect to lead us on our quest of growth and spiritual transformation. We also met our guide who had Masters degrees in Egyptology and Hieroglyphics.

During this meeting, Joe gave us two warnings. First, watch what we ate, because we stood a chance of getting some form of food poisoning. The locals were used to the organisms in the food and water, but we weren't and could get sick. Second, be careful with the energy of the sites we were to visit. Having been the focus of thousands of years of very powerful energy, the temples had very thin or nonexistent veils. If anyone was particularly sensitive to energy, he recommended that they use shields against the overwhelming energy. And if you'd had a previous incarnation associated with a site, it was almost certain that you would experience an energetic overlay from that lifetime. What happened then would depend on whatever happened in that lifetime.

At least one of our party was to forget that admonishment and undergo a truly transformational experience as she embodied the actual energy of the goddess Hathor. But I was in no mood for doom-laden warnings; I just wanted to party!

After the meeting, I went to the bar with my new roommate, Colin Reynolds, a huge bear of a man. At six-foot-seven and almost three hundred pounds, I thought he'd be a good man to have around if we got into any trouble. But appearances can be deceptive; Colin was one of the gentlest souls I'd ever met.

On Monday morning, we flew to Aswan to embark on what was promised to be a luxury cruise liner. Reminding me of a river boat from the deep South, she was to be our home for the next several days.

I wondered how I would fare, sharing a tiny cabin with a guy the size of a grizzly bear but I didn't have time to dwell on it. With just enough time just to drop our things in our cabins, we were off in a felucca, a small flat-bottomed river boat that held about fifty people, with only an awning for protection from the merciless sun. Our destination was the Temple of Isis at Philea. Isis, Osiris, and their son Horus were ancient Egypt's "first family."

Isis was the ultimate goddess/mother. Her personal symbol was that of the throne, indicating she was the archetypal goddess. Married to her brother, Osiris, she sought him out after he had been slain and dismembered by his wicked brother, Set. Isis resurrected Osiris and conceived their son, Horus, who became the Sky God. In a famous battle, Horus sought revenge against Set, losing an eye in the process. However, Thoth intervened to negotiate a reconciliation in which Set ruled Upper Egypt and Horus got Lower Egypt. Since that famous battle the Eye of Horus has always been seen as symbolic of divine protection against evil.

The sheer magnificence of the temple's structure is impossible to describe: two-hundred-foot walls with one-hundred-foot figures carved into them, surrounded by carved hieroglyphics still as fresh-looking as the day they were carved, despite the scouring winds that blow through the temple daily. Courtyards as large as football fields conjured up images of what it would have looked like five thousand years ago when priests and priestesses would walk in groups either silently or in deep discussion.

What really struck me was that, unlike Western statues that may bear a name or inscription, these buildings were literally covered from end to end and floor to ceiling with hieroglyphics. No piece of stone was left uncarved or unpainted. Each wall tells an amazing spiritual story that is still as valid today as when it was over seven thousand years

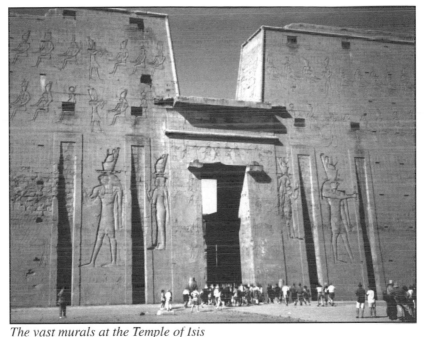

The vast murals at the Temple of Isis

ago. Imagine the walls of the White House totally covered in thousands of phrases and sentences in purple, green, blue and red ink, each extolling the virtues of the office of the presidency or explaining the highest ideals of the republic. Egyptian buildings aren't just places to keep the weather out; they are information sources in their own right. How colorful those cities must have been in their heyday.

We entered the temple, and, as in all later rituals, we were invited to place an object significant to us on the altar of the temple. This would charge the object with the energy of the site plus the energy of whatever spiritual work we did. It would then serve as a focal point for integrating our achievements long after we returned home. I strongly recommend this practice and suggest taking a crystal with you whenever you visit any high-energy place or sacred site.

Mary then led a ritual to celebrate the family of Isis and express our gratitude to her and the other founding entities of the Spiritual Hierarchy for their achievements in times long ago:

"Isis, we call upon your wisdom now as we give birth to a newer, higher aspect of who we are. Help us to step into our wisdom in a way that will benefit ourselves, our families, and all of humanity.

"We ask that you assist us in creating this bridge from where we are now to where we wish to be, and for you to be our guide on this path as we journey across bridge after bridge, ever-expanding until we become our God-selves."

Joe Jochmans explained that a common inscription on the temple walls was a sobering reminder to the aspiring initiates: NO ONE HAS UNCOVERED THE LAST VEIL.

"This means," he said that as long as we're limited by our five senses, the Mystery will elude us. In fact, there is no final veil, because no matter how deeply we plumb the depths of the Mystery, we will always have farther to go. Enlightenment is an everlasting search into the Great Mystery."

For the first time, I sensed the immeasurable passage of time that only an ancient place like Egypt can bring. Even the air in the temple smelled old but what really struck me was the heaviness and density of the energy. For thousands of years, people came to this place to worship Isis and in doing so, evoked the energy of the goddess herself. The presence of vast, ancient beings was almost overwhelming and out of respect, if we wanted to speak, we either waited or whispered. Whenever we entered a temple, I couldn't shake the feeling that something enormous and ancient was watching us. We'd been told that while we might find the energy intimidating, the high priests and priestesses were trained to work with it at levels far higher than we were experiencing.

Next came the Temple of Khnum on Elephantine Island. Khnum was celebrated as the father of the gods because he would create them by fashioning clay figures and implanting them in the body of his mother. As creator of the gods, he also embodied them and all their powers.

Here we celebrated our ability to create our own potential in conjunction with our own spirit, which is our only real and true identity. We were reminded that, at every moment, we are in full choice as to who we want to be. That is the most amazing thing about us as a "free will" species. I silently vowed never to forget the personal power to express who and what I want to express in the moment.

Sailing overnight brought us to Kom Ombo (dedicated to Sobek, or Suchos, the crocodile-headed god) on Tuesday morning, where we performed an early morning ritual of letting go of our past and the choices we have made. Letting go of our old identity leaves us open to embrace whatever new possibilities our spirit suggests in the moment.

Mural at the Temple of Sobek, the crocodile-headed god

It is also important to examine our emotions and belief systems for old limitations that no longer serve us. It is vital to periodically "clean house" and discard the old to make way for the new. I have found that the best way to do that is simply to expose yourself to a wide cross-section of new thoughts and beliefs, dipping more deeply into any material that inspires you. Never stop searching for new and larger truths within your piece of the Divine Blueprint, and *never* think that you've got it all figured out.

This is redefining ourselves, but before we can do that, we must throw away all previous definitions of who we are, or who other people tell us we are. This is known as being released from the jaws of Sobek.

I vowed never again to allow anyone to impose on me a limiting picture of who they wanted me to be.

Mural showing a stethoscope

Following in millennia-old footsteps of deities and priests was heady stuff. It brought up an empowering and ancient essence of myself.

One of the murals that personally intrigued me the most was at Kom Ombo—of a man holding a stethoscope. This showed quite an understanding of the workings of the human body.

Before we left, I stopped in at a temple dedicated to Hathor. I knelt before her statue and put my forehead against it. "Hathor, what do you want me to know?"

As clearly as if someone next to me was speaking, I heard, "Remember that the one with the most integrity wins."

We continued down the Nile. Sitting in the warm sun by the Emerald's pool, munching hors d'oeuvres and watching the changing scenery slide by was something I'll never forget. A sudden sense of timelessness overwhelmed me. Farmers were tending their fields, herding animals, and digging irrigation ditches as though the last five thousand years hadn't happened. Fishermen threw nets out from small boats just as they did during the time of the pharaohs. The feeling was oddly weird and exhilarating at the same time.

At Edfu, we visited the Temple of Horus and Hathor, built to celebrate their union. Hathor (also worshipped by the Greeks as Aphrodite) was the daughter of Ra, the Sun God. She married Horus and was revered as the goddess of love, joy, dance, and celebration—a regular party animal. For the longest time, they were Egypt's "first couple."

As soon as my friend Lorin, one of the group leaders, entered the temple, she said to me, "I've been here before."

Then, looking at Colin and me, she added, "In fact, we've all been here before."

During our ritual, many couples reaffirmed their own union and renewed their vows to each other. This was a beautiful ceremony to observe and many couples found that their love for each other rose to new levels. We also celebrated our partnership with

At the Temple to Hathor   our own higher self, vowing deeper levels of love for our true nature as we approach the new millennium. Again I was impressed and overwhelmed by the awesome majesty of the energy.

We all felt Hathor's energy, but no one more than Lorin. After the ritual, I found her curled in a fetal position, immersed in an incredible energy of love. I helped her up and, on impulse, grabbed her camera and took a couple of shots. When the prints came back, Lorin was amazed at what she saw on the photograph. Three white globes of energy circled her head and a huge spiral of energy ran vertically through the frame. Lorin said later that the globes were her spirit guides and the spiral was Hathor. Moments later, Hathor's energy entered Lorin's body fully. She said later that she had felt very tall. At one point, she spread her arms wide and said, "These are my people."

Apparently, Lorin had been overtaken by the energy of the ancient goddess Hathor and experienced a deep communication and union with this incredible goddess. It was a remarkable thing to witness and tremendous for our understanding of the awesome power held in these sacred sites.

Lorin experienced a sense of great joy and love but someone else might have experienced a great pastlife trauma. Think about it. If you've had, say, a hundred other life-

Lorin in the Temple of Hathor

times, you've also had a hundred deaths, presumably not all of them pleasant. The soul retains *every* memory, and these memories are the sources of irrational phobias like fear of water, fire, heights, cold, or starvation. A sudden memory recall across lifetimes can be unsettling but also revealing.

More carvings at the Temple of Isis

Back on board the good ship *Emerald*, I enjoyed a cold beer in the bar. In addition to all the different conversations going on, I distinctly heard another set of conversations, but they were in my head. Too weird. After only three days in Egypt, I was suffering from jetlag and culture shock, and was sleeping poorly. Not only were we in a strange, foreign country where all the rules were different, we were being haunted by ancient spooks everywhere we went.

After a short nap, we got ready for that night's costume party: "Come As You Were: Been That, Done There." What a sight we were, drumming, chanting, and dancing. We put on a play in which I was cast as Set, Egypt's arch-villain. We reenacted the dismemberment of Osiris, substituting a cucumber for his godly manhood, or was it manly godhood?

The next morning found us at Luxor and the famous Valley of the Kings. The scale of the valley and its temples left us breathless and once again I was in awe of this 5,000-year-old civilization that constructed buildings still unrivaled today.

Akhenaton, showing clearly the elongation of his head. ET or what?

The temple walls of Luxor tell the fascinating story of the 18th dynasty (1580–1350 BC) pharaoh Amenhotep, who survived a battle between the gods Amun and Aten. Aten won and Amenhotep, no fool, promptly decreed that only Aten could be worshipped. He even changed his name to Akhenaton in honor of this new sole god. All the other gods were furious when their names were obliterated from every temple wall in the land. Ancient Egypt's only period of monotheism came to a halt with Akhenaton's death, when the other gods could once again assert themselves during the 19th dynasty under Ramses III.

The mythology of Egypt takes on a whole different meaning with the theory of some researchers that these gods were not gods at all but actually ETs. Extraterrestrial families and factions were, it is said, in constant conflict over the control of the affairs of humans, who they saw as "worker class" beings. The primitive human population had no other way of explaining the ETs' power, influence, and technology except to view them as gods. And, of course, the ETs did nothing to disabuse them of the idea.

Tricia McCannon has extensively studied the ET-human connection in many cultures and I heartily recommend her books and tapes, *UFOs and Ancient Civilizations* among them (see Resource section). Also, in *You Are Becoming a Galactic Human*, Virginia Essene and Sheldan Nidle relay the information from the Council of Sirius that three factions warred during the period 15,000 to 10,000 BC over who controlled the civilizations in Egypt, China, and India. The factions were led by ETs named Osiris, Set, and Horus!

The highlight was the Temple of Nefertiti, the wife of Akhenaton. It was here, in the Temple of Nefertiti, that I hoped to get some insight into the oft-mentioned ancient influence of explorers from the star systems of Sirius and Orion, something that has always fascinated me. Many ancient manuscripts and carvings portray half-man/half-animal beings, or beings with large eyes and elongated heads, clear hallmarks of ET/human interbreeding.

The Temple of Nefertiti is unusual in that the entire temple—about a quarter the size of a football field—is underground, entered by a small opening in a cliff wall. The walls inside are covered by magnificent hieroglyphics, perfectly preserved from the elements. The most revealing carving, however, portrays Akhenaton with the telltale elongated head offering an ankh to the jackal-headed Anubis. (Anubis, incidentally, helped Isis bury the body of Osiris and became revered as the Lord of the Mummy Wrapping ritual, and the God of the Dead).

And just what was the ET-Egypt connection? How could a primitive desert culture suddenly blossom with buildings that can't even be duplicated today? And what about their advanced math and astronomy that would take humanity another 5,000 years to rediscover? There *had* to be a connection.

We were also introduced to the Hathors in the Valley of the Kings. The Hathors are another ET connection. Apparently an inter dimensional, ascended civilization came to Earth long ago from the same parallel universe as the whales and dolphins. It is said that they came here at the request of Sanat Kumara, the being "in charge" of this planet who was concerned that an impending natural disaster would wipe out all life on Earth. Sanat Kumara knew that the Hathors had averted a similar situation on their own world and their high level of compassion would impel them to help here.

The Hathors are renowned for their incredible God-realized unconditional love and have held this in the higher dimensions as a sort of role model for our continued evolution. They work with us but always allow us our free will. They are intertwined with us genetically and will help any soul who calls out to them for assistance in transmuting fear-based emotion, and in returning to Christ consciousness long before the birth of Jesus on this planet. They encourage us all to remember the beauty and divinity that is our heritage.

We returned to the ship for dinner. Meat again ... ironic for a mostly vegetarian group. After dinner, we rushed off to a ritual celebrating our connection with the Earth.

The entrance to the Temple of Amon at Luxor is guarded by two huge stone statues of lions, imposing and intimidating to the initiates of long ago. They still are. I crept warily past them into the enormous amphitheater surrounded by 200-foot statues of Horus lit by flaming torches. We gathered in a circle around Colin who been "volunteered" to read a prepared address.

In a deep, booming voice, Colin said, "Hear the words of Osiris. We have gathered in recognition of your service as lightbearers."

As he continued, Colin's voice began to boom even more with an edge that concerned me and the energy around us got very heavy. I had the feeling that Colin was no longer reading. He dropped the paper,

The dinner before Luxor, featuring Joe Jochmans (right), Mary Elizabeth Hoffman, Colin (center), Kathleen Dean, and the author (left).

looked up at the sky, and raised his hands to the heavens: "I, Osiris, am here to speak with you."

Holy shit, now we're in trouble, I thought, taking two steps back from the circle.

"Be aware of who you are and the depth of your commitment to the Earth," the voice of Osiris continued. "You are spiritual warriors on a quest, here to perform great work, to embrace all peoples, including your ancient family, for they belong to you and you to them. I and the Spiritual Hierarchy honor you for committing the time and resources to be here now."

Yes, $3,000 and 9,000 miles later, a wicked little voice in me said. I still don't know if that really was Osiris, but I do know that it certainly wasn't Colin. As usual, I was caught between the mystic in me and the rational, analytical researcher.

Afterwards, we filed quietly out of the temple back to the boat. Once on board, Colin complained, "I don't feel so good."

"What's the matter? Channeled something that disagreed with you?" I joked.

"No, seriously," he said. "Look out," he yelled, dashing for the bathroom. He just made it before the entire boat resonated with the sound of this bear of a man losing his dinner, lunch, and everything else.

I knew it. There was something weird about that channeling back there. I went into the corridor and someone asked, "What the hell is going on in there?"

"I don't know. It sounds like Osiris' revenge to me and I ain't going back in there until we have an exorcism," I joked.

Soon, however, I wasn't laughing. Deep down, I was concerned about what we might have eaten. But I couldn't help but wonder about the ceremony in which we had just offered ourselves as lightworkers and our bodies as vessels of light to heal and transform the planet. Were Colin's spasms the result of transmuting negative planetary energies during his channeling experience? Was he experiencing a death of the old self, only to be reborn as a more spiritually evolved being? Or was it really "King Tut's Revenge?"

The next day, we were leaving the boat, ready for our flight to Cairo, Colin dragging his weakened body and heavy luggage through narrow companionways and into the bus waiting to take us to the airport.

Tourist flights through Luxor use the Air Force base and the short bus ride was sheer hell. As soon as I entered the building, violent spasms gripped my intestines, twisting them in knots. *Oh, God, not me! Not now! Please not now!*

I raced to what must have been the most disgusting bathroom in all Egypt. For several minutes, I alternated between throwing up and diarrhea. I had no idea that the human body was capable of such violent convulsions, with fever, sweating, chills, shivering, and aches in body parts I never knew existed.

On the short flight to Cairo, my trips to the bathroom wore out the already thin carpet in the aisle. During the descent into Cairo, I couldn't go, and everything seemed to be in slow motion. The very instant those wheels hit the runway, I was on the run to the back of the plane. The terrified cabin staff watched this crazy, wild-eyed American as my fellow groupies called out, "It's fast, it's fun, it's Egypt!"

The bus to the hotel needed air-conditioning repairs in the worst way and we hit Cairo's evening commute. Four long, miserable hours later, we got to the hotel and I crashed, staying there all day, missing the high point of the trip, the Spring Equinox Ritual of Renewal in the Great Pyramid. The organizer had pulled in some major favors to get private access to the King's Chamber for our group, and I had traveled 9,000 miles only to fall 500 yards short of the pyramids, unable to move. I simply couldn't believe it.

Friday and Saturday merged together into a blur of feverish dreams and hallucinations. I'd been in a high fever for four days, begging for a doctor, but we just couldn't seem to get hold of one. I was a real mess and prayed that somehow I'd make it back to New York alive.

The author and camel

This one needs no introduction

By Sunday, I had just enough energy to climb on a camel that specialized in making uncarthly sounds. The undulating gait of the foul-smelling beast did not help my queasy digestive system but I did manage to stay on long enough to get from the Sphinx to the pyramids—a journey of all of 500 yards.

It's a common misconception that the Pyramids of Giza were burial chambers for the pharaohs when, in fact, they were built as energy devices. One of their many uses was for initiation rituals for those wishing to enter the priesthood. I suppose three days of lying in a sarcophagus in the pitch dark would initiate anyone, assuming you survived madness.

I finally made it up the steep incline to the King's Chamber. The chamber walls were of glass-smooth limestone and surprisingly free of hieroglyphics. I lay in the sarcophagus itself and surrendered to the massive and oppressive energies as I lay at the focal point of this huge energy transformer. And transformed I was. I felt a tight band of pressure around my head as the awesome forces stretched my pineal gland to the utmost. I returned to the hotel, feeling my goal complete. That night, as I drifted into a fitful sleep, I wish I'd known that it was the night of a full lunar eclipse.

As soon as the flight back to New York levels off after leaving Cairo, the captain invites me into the cockpit. He points to the third seat behind the co-pilot and motions me to sit down. This is my first cockpit visit during an actual flight and I'm ecstatic. I look forward and see endless sand dunes, gleaming white in the blazing sun. As I look out the window, I reflect on Egypt, what I've seen, and how glad I am to be going home.

Suddenly the plane shudders once, begins to vibrate, and then shudders again, this time more violently. The plane starts to go down, the angle getting steeper all the time. The pilot and co-pilot exchange clipped phrases and work the controls feverishly as they try to get the plane back under control. The engines are screaming like banshees as the captain tries to pull the nose up. But the desert is coming closer and closer, faster and faster.

I'm going to die. I thought I'd known fear but in that cockpit, my fear level goes off the scale. White knuckles grip the back of the co-pilot's seat. I'm mesmerized by the fast-approaching ground. My thoughts speed up and I suddenly see very clearly who I am and what my life is about. I'm not ready for this! It's not time! Please let them pull up in time.

The plane is almost vertical now, spiraling down out of control. Just as the plane's nose is about to hit the ground, I instinctively close my eyes and hear my voice saying, "It will be all right. I'll be okay." A calm peace overtakes me and suddenly there's nothing. Total stillness, followed by a whoosh. I feel as though I'm a million tiny pieces spread across the sky, like vapor, like I'm a part of everything. So this is what death is like, I say to myself.

A voice asks, "Are you all right?"

I think to myself, I know that voice.

Again, I hear, "Where are we?"

I realize that the voice is mine. Somehow I'm hearing myself. I am a point of consciousness, trying to find some kind of anchor for itself. When you're part of everything, that's not easy.

I see a mist of sparkling, silvery light, which clears to reveal that I'm standing by the edge of a river. The sun is glistening on the water and iridescent sparkles reflect on the surface. I look down to see my reflection and realize I'm alive! Oh, my God, I'm alive. I made it. But how did I get here? There's no wreckage so the plane didn't go down. Somehow they averted the crash and this river is the Nile. No, impossible; there's no plane. So where am I?

I feel fine and begin to walk along the river bank toward some buildings where I see people going about their business. A man walks toward me wearing a black robe with flecks of gold in it. His shoulder-length brown hair shines in the sunlight. Brown hair and blue eyes—I love that combination. My attraction for this guy grows quickly. Who is he?

The man smiles. "Hello, Robert."

I notice that he's able to speak without moving his lips. How does he do that? And where am I? And who are you?

"Think of me as a guide," he says in response to my unspoken thought.

"Where am I?" I ask.

"You've been brought here."

"Where's 'here'?" I ask again.

"This is where we look at the inequities of the spirit."

The thought goes through my mind that inequity means unfair. This doesn't sound good. "What does that mean?" I ask him.

"This is where those things that have not been realized up to this point in one's life are reviewed. Think of it as a review of what you have already accomplished and where you might go from here."

"Have I died?"

"Yes, in a sense, you have."

Again, I'm fascinated by the fact that he isn't moving his lips. But then the truth of it crashes in on me: I'm dead, Oh, God! Everything I wanted to do and now I can't. How I'll miss my friends back on Earth.

I touch my arms, my face. I still feel like me. Then I think, maybe this being dead thing isn't so bad; it just takes some getting used to.

"What is this place exactly?"

"Many souls are brought here, some when they've died, some when they're living and in transition from the old self to a new self. They come here for review. Some who are here realize that they are here and some don't."

I look around at the people walking by and understand that they, too, are souls. Without being told, I simply seem to understand what this means. I look at one man who walks with his head down and wonder what happened to him. Whoosh—my consciousness runs right into him and merges with his. I feel his entire life, his hopes, his fears, the pain of his childhood abuse, the abyss of his horror at abusing his own children. His sense of desolation about his life is so intense that I scream, "I don't like this!" Instantly my consciousness bounces back at me like a stretched rubber band that's released and almost knocks me down.

"You must be very careful how you use your thoughts here," my guide admonishes gently. "You are much different here. You can feel other people's experiences."

He's right. You get things on a deeper level here. All that is inside you—the fear, the love, the anxiety, the hatred, the glory, the depression—all those things that you wear in your emotional body, you wear on the outside in this realm, naked to the world. Everybody knows who you are, knows your deepest fears, your highest hopes.

"Thoughts and the words that express them are very real and powerful," my guide says.

I see a couple arguing and watch in horror as their hurtful words hit their partner's aura like tiny missiles that explode into gray areas. If enough missiles hit, the entire aura turns gray.

I reflect that every thought we have is a tangible thing, sacred and significant. Every thought and word has an impact. We have to be careful how we use our thoughts and what we say.

The guide shows me a tablet with something like hieroglyphics on it. In a way I can't describe, it speaks to me. The tablet is actually talking to me. It is a record of my life. When I look at it, I see silver letters turn to fire. I look into the tablet and see good news. It shows me that, overall, I have lived a good life. I'm not so bad after all. I have lived my life treading gently on the Earth. I have been a generous friend to those in need, a shoulder to cry on when needed, a source of strength to those in doubt. Yes, I can live with myself. That is the biggest question you face in this situation: can you live with who you are?

I also see the inequities, those areas of my life about which I'm not too thrilled. Top of the list is lust. I was so lustful that I used to feel guilty about having those thoughts. But I smile because it all looks so different up here. I see clearly that spirit looks at this with great compassion. Everybody has plenty of petty faults and many are far worse than mine. I am relieved.

My next bugaboo is anger that is translated as indignant outrage whenever people compromise their integrity or code of ethics. Not too much of a fault, I see.

Resentment is next. My habit of harboring grudges is more of a problem because it locks stale, dead energy in my aura. Yes, that's one I must work on in the next life.

Then my fears swim into view: fear of rejection, fear of making mistakes, of not being able to control my emotions. "Trust, Robert. Have faith in your own spirit and in God," my guide telepaths to me.

"Anxiety is a peculiar human condition," my guide tells me in response to the anxiety welling up in me. "It is the background sense of being disconnected from the creator. You yearn so much to feel your intimate union with the Creator and when you don't, you feel forsaken. Trust, Robert. The Creator could never forsake its own creation, its own being."

Wave after wave of love hit me, almost knocking me to my knees. "Robert-the-ego feels bad for having these faults," the guide says, "but Robert-the-spirit feels only compassion for you."

He smiles. An overwhelming burst of love hits me and he explodes into a blinding flash of intense white light. At this point, I pass out.

As I come to, one thought consumes me: LIFE IS A GIFT. Life is the most precious thing there is, a magnificent opportunity to come to Earth, to serve humanity and the Creator, to experience unconditional love.

I begin to hear the thoughts of my guide again. "There are many Earths. The one you know is not the only expression of Earth. This is only one aspect of Earth. Many souls go to alternative Earths, where the consciousness and choices are different."

It becomes clear that we reincarnate into situations that help us see what we gave. We are who we are because we are the result of everything we've been. Most souls are actually millions of years old. We reincarnate into what we have created in other lives. I see a Nazi war criminal reincarnate into a life destined to lead to a concentration camp. I see hunters reincarnate as the hunted. All these Earths make up a huge school, designed to let us experience the outcome of our actions. In review sessions like this, you look at the balance sheet: how much have you given and how much have you taken?

As concepts wash over me, I get them in their entirety. It's like after you've watched a movie, you have the whole movie as one huge memory. But I'm getting the encapsulated memory first, without needing to plod through the entire movie.

My guide answers some of my most pressing questions without my even having to ask them. "The ascension isn't going to happen to you. You see, you are going to happen to ascension. It is just a name for something that humanity and the planet are currently doing: raising their frequency to a new expression. As you move up into it, you will realize what I mean. And then it will become a reality. Ascension is not some impersonal product out-there, but a very personal transition in-here," he says, pointing to his heart area. "Yes, there will be planetary upheaval and land mass changes, but humanity will be around for a long while."

I see the big picture in which the ascended planet and humanity take their place within the great galactic community. What joy I feel at seeing this, but I'm saddened at discovering all this too late to relay it to those still alive on Earth.

Just then I notice three odd creatures, like boxes with faces, waving good-bye to me and congratulating me.

Suddenly my guide says, "It's time for you to go now."

Whoosh! I was staring up at the ceiling, hearing Colin snoring in the next bed. I can't describe how I felt. I had a new lease on life. I'm alive! I'm breathing! I have the gift of life! When you've had it taken away and then given back, you realize how special life is.

What a joy to be alive again. Tears of joy streamed down my face. It's true, life is a gift, the greatest gift we can know. I had embraced the sacred divinity of life and lived to talk about it. A second chance. A second gift. I had met my own divinity and seen the Divine Blueprint. It was within me all along.

Then I thought, I think I've just had a near-death or out-of-body experience. I have to wake Colin up and tell him.

I went over to his sleeping body and shook him. "Colin!" I shouted, "Wake up! I'm alive! I'm alive, Colin, and I'm going home today and I have the gift of life now."

"That's nice," he mumbled, and rolled back over.

I got more agitated. "Wake up!" I shouted.

I stopped myself, feeling guilty at how quickly I could forget the awe and majesty of who we are. "I mean, please, you sacred being."

"I gotta go to Israel today, man. I need some rest," Colin mumbled.

Of course, I thought, nobody can relate to me yet. I'm a newborn being. I put my hand on Colin's shoulder and said quietly, "Sure thing. Go back to sleep."

I walked into breakfast like a zombie. I was not the least bit hungry, but I needed some company. I sat down at our table and a woman looked up at me and smiled. I smiled weakly back.

"Did you dream last night?" she asked, out of the blue.

"You could say that," I replied. "I died last night and went to the other side."

"Oh, my God. What did you find?" she asked.

"That life is a precious gift given to us so we can explore unconditional love. We get to see what works and what doesn't."

She replied, "I'm writing a book called *Born to Say Good-bye.*"

"That title is perfect. We're born here to say good-bye to all the things that don't serve us and hello to all those things that do. That's it. That's why we came to Egypt."

"Ladies and gentlemen, our departure will be delayed about another hour," the disembodied voice came through the cabin.

Oh, no, not more delay, I groaned inwardly. We were already half an hour late leaving. Now it would be another hour. It was one in the morning. I was dehydrated and exhausted. I just wanted to go home.

I dozed off, dismayed at the prospect of a 15-hour flight to New York in an Egyptian airliner. My shallow sleep was broken by another announcement, "There will be a further one hour delay."

No! Please, no more delays. Will I ever see the States again?

Suddenly I was startled into full consciousness by someone shouting in Arabic from the aisle just to my right. I looked round to see a large man hollering at a little boy in the seat right behind mine. The man was particularly evil-looking, with mean, narrow eyes. About six-three, he towered over the boy, whose eyes were wide with fear. He looked so tiny in that airplane seat; my heart went out to him.

Suddenly the man started pummeling the boy about the head with a rolled up newspaper. Wap! Wap! Wap! The poor kid's head was knocked first one way and then the next. He tried to protect his head with his hands, but his tiny arms were useless against those brutal blows.

I'm more tolerant than most, but cruelty and abuse to children and animals bring up a fearsome rage in me. I will not stand by while such innocent beauty is trampled on. In a flash, I'm out of my seat, finger poked in the guy's face. "You hit that child one more time and you'll have to deal with me. You got that?" I growled.

Still in his face, I heard others in my party saying "Robert, don't get involved. It's nothing to do with you."

But I stood my ground, a mixture of rage and fear coursing through me, fear of being knifed right there in the cabin, rage at this insane cruelty. He glared at me some more and rolled his eyes, as if to say, "Who *is* this jerk?"

Suddenly he turned and walked to the back of the plane. Still high on adrenaline, I yelled, "Fuck you!" to his departing back and breathed a sigh of relief. Then I noticed everyone in the cabin open-mouthed and staring at me.

Just then, I spotted the captain up in first class and ran up the aisle as he turned to scurry back to the cockpit. I grabbed his shirt sleeve and said, "Oh no you don't." I looked him square in the face and said, "Listen, there are thirty-seven Americans on this flight and if he hits that kid one more time, we're gonna beat him to death and throw him out of the airplane. Then you can feed him to the fucking Al Jihad!"

The captain quickly motioned to the co-pilot and navigator and these three burly guys went to the back of the plane and cornered the child-beater. Half an hour of intense, animated conversation later, the crew walked up the aisle and Mr. Nice Guy took his seat behind me. Now I would have to deal with *him* right behind me all the way to New York.

After an unsuccessful attempt at sleep, I got up and spoke to a woman in our party who I hadn't had a chance to talk with on the trip. "So what's your most memorable experience?" I asked.

"Thirty-six hours ago, I was throwing up in a trash can, hoping that I would die. Then I looked up and saw an angel looking down at me. The angel said, 'What happened here will not be forgotten and will benefit many people that you will never meet.' "

I smiled and went into my own thoughts. I reflected on my out-of-body experience and why the vantage point on the other side is superior to simply examining our own thoughts. There, we are free of the ego. For example, when I realized that I could live with myself, it wasn't my ego's desire to be a good guy talking. It was my higher self's objective assessment. At that level, we are an impartial judge. Compassionate, yes, but brutally honest. With the ego's need to be liked and accepted, we can never really trust its self-assessment. But when stripped of ego at death, what we encounter on the other side is the truth, the whole truth, and nothing but the truth.

We finally landed on American soil. I dragged my aching, ravaged body through the terminal and found the United Airlines desk. I explained to the clerk that, because of the delay, I'd missed my connection. She smiled warmly. "No problem, Mr. Perala. We have a flight leaving in half an hour. You can just make that."

Oh, thank you. Thank you. Thank you, I said internally. I'll be home in just a few hours.

Ah, the joy of the friendly U.S. skies. That bright, clean United jumbo was a bright, sunny day compared to the dark, stormy night of the Egyptian airline. The food was like five-star fare and the cabin staff were the nicest people in the world. Thank goodness I'm an American. I thought. I had an entire row to myself so I stretched out for the best sleep of my life.

My friend Pamela Millar met me at the airport. Her first words to me were, "Robert, you look terrible. What happened?"

With no shower or shave for three days, wearing dirty, creased clothes, and gaunt from dysentery, I was not a pretty sight. "Oh, I died back there in Egypt," I quipped.

"Oh, you're dead. That explains your appearance," she joked.

Once home, I dropped my clothes in a heap and jumped into the shower. Oh, that wonderful hot water. For almost an hour, I luxuriated in my first hot shower for a week. I was glad to be home!

Afterward, I fell into a deep, deep sleep. Ah, the joys of being in your own bed.

I didn't know what woke me, but soon I became aware of a tingling feeling, like when a leg or arm has gone numb and then the circulation comes back, except that this was over my entire body. I tried to move. Nothing. My body wasn't mine. Who am I? Nothing. I have no identity either. Where am I? Nothing. I don't know where I am or who I am.

Part of whoever I was opened my eyes and I looked from side to side. There was no memory of the so familiar surroundings. I pulled off the covers and looked down at this strange body. Some muscle control had returned at this point and I managed to sit this strange body up.

Who am I? Where am I? Why am I here? As I focused on a chest of drawers, a dim memory lit up: a tiny flicker of the Robert identity now stood alongside the other identity. Then I was *really* confused. Two identities, fully separate, in one body. Our brains are just not designed to handle this.

The visiting consciousness did not try to communicate with me or leave thoughts in our shared mind. It was in strict observation mode. All I felt was its intense curiosity about everything. It didn't seem malevolent, so after about the first hour, I became comfortable about sharing my body with some other intelligence.

In hindsight, I think my weakened and debilitated state so relaxed the fabric of my "personhood" that ingress into my psyche was possible. Some consciousness had decided to take a field trip into my life.

Suddenly it was gone and I was alone, once more sole occupant of my body. The weird thing was that I almost missed the feeling.

The questions came: who or what was that? Another human incarnation from a time so distant that everything was unfamiliar, another incarnation from another planet, or a completely strange energy from God knows where? I may never know.

The next week was doctor-ordered bed rest for me as I shook off the legacy of Egypt, but every night, another part of that legacy came visiting—a procession of Sirian Egyptians. The first night, six of them, three male and three female, woke me up jabbering in some strange tongue, in full-blown, ancient Egyptian regalia right off the temple walls. I couldn't believe it. Full-bodied apparitions, the most solid manifestations yet, so solid I couldn't see through them. I studied them intently, watching how the light reflected off the metallic foil of their robes and the gold and silver in their headdresses.

They talked intently to each other, ignoring me. How rude, I thought. If they've taken the trouble to come see me, why not at least acknowledge me? I also wondered why I could see them. Had they materialized in my bedroom so solidly that anyone could see them? Or are our living spaces always filled with beings just slightly above visual frequency and my psychic sight allowed me to see them?

A friend once remarked, "I don't know about you, Robert. You're always seeing the weirdest stuff!" But ancient Egyptians in my bedroom? That tops it all.

I kept getting the telepathic message, *We're Sirians. We're Sirians*, over and over. After going to Egypt to explore the Sirian connection and failing, *it* comes to *me* once I'm back home.

The funny thing is, I didn't get the impression of them being gods the way the ancient Egyptians did. Yes, they had fine clothes and presumably advanced technology and psychic powers. But gods? No. To a primitive, superstitious race, most definitely. Did I trust them? No. Part of me was even wary in their presence. There was something about them I just didn't trust.

They showed up again the following night, this time in greater numbers. My bedroom was getting really crowded. *Who are you?* I telepathed to them.

We are from the future of the Sirian people, they replied, *and you are related to us.*

I took this to mean that I have some Sirian in my stellar heritage. But these beings were so far removed from the level of my consciousness that when they telepathed pictures of Earth's past and future, all I got was a crazy jumble. They couldn't slow their minds down enough for my poor, linear brain so I'll never know what piece of the Divine Blueprint they held.

I know, however, that one day we'll catch up. One day.

Chapter 10

The Sacred Promise

"And I will show wonders in heaven above, and signs in the earth beneath."

— Acts of the Apostles, 2:19

Wonders in Heaven Above

MILE AFTER MILE OF South Dakota landscape slid by the car windows. Thank God for air-conditioning, I thought as I saw the heat mirages on the road ahead.

I was headed for Wagner, SD, with Dr. Angela Browne-Miller, in a rented car. We were a couple of hours out of Sioux Falls, along Route 281 that leads into the heart of the huge Wagner Reservation, home to the Yanktown Sioux and the site of the Star Knowledge Conference. This particular adventure had blown up out of nowhere a week before with a simple phone call.

"Robert, it's Sheldan. Listen to me carefully. A ship touched down on an Indian reservation in a remote area of New Mexico over the weekend." My friend Sheldan Nidle is a ufologist and co-author of *You Are Becoming a Galactic Human.*

"What kind of ship?"

"Sirian. And big, very big."

That didn't surprise me coming from Sheldan. He'd been channeling the Sirians for years so, of course, he'd be excited about it. And so began a typical conversation for me. Not quite along the lines of, "How about them Broncos last night?" but then I've gotten used to it. I lightly warn attendees at my seminars: "Get used to being regarded as weird in the beginning. After a few years, you won't care but early on your friends will think you've flipped, and in a way you have.

"It's the Blue Kuchina," Sheldan continued.

"What's that?"

"It's a Hopi Indian word. It means Blue Star. It's a mother ship. Oh, by the way, are you going to South Dakota next week?"

"I haven't decided yet. Maybe I'll see you there." I'd heard about this gathering but I hadn't given it much thought. The Star Knowledge Conference was to be a gathering of metaphysical authors, researchers, and the medicine men who lived on the reservation itself.

That was the first act in an amazing demonstration of synchronicity about to unfold. Over the next week I got all kinds of phone calls asking me what I knew about the Blue Kuchina. My curiosity rose. How could so many people be talking about this blue thing, whatever it was?

Something inside me said I would find my answer in South Dakota. I kept hearing how all the top brass in the UFO business would be there, along with hundreds of people from many different countries. The five-day conference would be in Wagner, a place in the middle of nowhere, at the bottom of the state near the Missouri River on an Indian reservation.

Still undecided on Tuesday, June 11, 1996, the night before it was to start, I got a phone call from Tricia McCannon. She had already arrived on the reservation and was to speak on the second day.

"Stop your whining, drop everything, and get on the next plane!" she commanded.

Part of me just couldn't believe I was still in California, but that was about to change. Around midnight, my good buddy Angela Browne-Miller called from New Mexico.

"Robert, as your good friend, I demand that you meet me at Denver Airport around noon tomorrow and fly with me to Sioux Falls. I've reserved a rental car. I'll wait for you at Denver," she ordered, and put the phone down.

Well, what was I to do? I made airline reservations at one in the morning and at seven I was in the air, heading east. I couldn't believe I was doing this. It was crazy but rumor had it that we might have a UFO light show to beat them all. Who am I to turn *that* down?

The Indian reservation was in the breathtaking beauty of rolling plains and gentle hills. The event itself was to be held at the reservation's well-appointed school building.

As Angela and I sat down for first of Thursday's lectures, we were delighted at the roster of speakers; the biggest names in the business were all here together. Heading that list was Bob Dean, the founding father of ufology. Dating back to the Roswell incident, Bob has dominated the UFO scene with the thoroughness and breadth of his research.

The rest of the speaker list read like the *Who's Who* of ufology, ET contact, and abduction, each of them a major player: John Mack, Whitley Strieber, Barbara Marciniak, Drunvalo Melchizedek, Dr. Richard Boylan, Randolph Winters, Dr. Leo Sprinkle, and many more.

Representing the Sioux nation were medicine men Robert Morning Sky, Fast Thunder, Wallace Black Elk, Roy Little Sun, Deerman, and our host, tribe leader and good friend, Standing Elk.

Tricia McCannon opened the conference to a standing ovation. The proceedings had started with a bang. Next, Angela Browne-Miller left her audience with their mouths open when she removed an etheric implant on stage. She regressed the guy back to the implant experience by having him breathe in a special way. Then she instructed him to make certain sounds (very odd sounds), and the implant simply disintegrated. This fascinated me because it was just four years ago that I'd had my implant removed. That, too, had been etheric.

Drunvalo Melchizedek

The next speaker, Drunvalo Melchizedek, made an unusual but effective entrance. With no introduction by the M.C., he stepped onto the stage from behind the curtain, and walked up to the microphone. He looked at the audience for a full three minutes. He must have made eye contact with all 500 of us during that time. His eyes were filled with an odd mixture of wonderment, awe, honoring, gratitude, and God only knows what else. Very few speakers I know could get away with that kind of opening, but it really heightened the anticipation. Finally he spoke:

Good afternoon. You know, I have a confession to make. I've no idea what I'm going to say today. I have no charts or slides to show you. There are so many things we could talk about, so why don't we start with … love.

After three minutes of talking about love, there wasn't a dry eye in the house. Even the most case-hardened ufologists were shedding a tear partly due to what Drunvalo said and partly due to his profound sincerity.

Each of you has made a deep commitment to be on this planet at this time, to serve and to surrender your personal agenda to divine purpose. The fact that so many of you have flown halfway around the world to be here fills me with gratitude and humility.

Let's talk about healing. As way-showers, healing is very important to you. Let me tell you a story about a young woman.

I once took a group of about twenty-four people out to the Bahamas to swim with the spotted dolphins. One of the women on the boat had been crippled with her right arm for about ten or twelve years. It had been slashed under the arm pit, and she had no use of that arm. Every medical doctor she had seen had written this condition off as incurable.

When it came time to swim with the dolphins, she stayed very close to the boat because she wasn't a good swimmer. I was on the upper deck of the boat where I could see all the swimmers in the water with the dolphins. This woman was looking around for the dolphins and didn't realize that two dolphins were on either side of her with their noses in her arm pits. She didn't even know they were there. I called to her to look behind her and when she did, the dolphins quickly swam away,

A few minutes later, she got out of the water and came up to the deck where I was saying that she was very sleepy. She lay down on the deck and immediately went to sleep. We covered her with a blanket so that she wouldn't get sunburned.

I stayed with her to make sure that she was okay. After about two hours, she woke up and stretched *both* arms above her head, saying how happy she felt. I noticed that she had used both arms and said to her, "Look, you're using your injured arm." She looked down at her right arm that was now working perfectly and said, "My arm?" She thought for a long time and said, "Oh yes, it used to be harmed, but it isn't any more." Then she said casually, "I'm hungry. Is there any food?"

It was as though nothing really important had happened. When she was thinking about it, it was like she could barely remember ever being damaged. For the rest of the trip, she never said a word about it, as though it was completely normal for miracles to happen every day.

When we got back to the hotel, we had a closing circle where we talked about our experience on the trip. I figured that when she talked, she would tell her story. She talked about the beauty of the dolphins but never said a single word about her recovery. After she was finished, I reminded her of her arm. Again, I saw how she had to strain to remember her old condition. At last she said, "Yes, it's true. My arm used to not work, but now it's fine." And that is all she said.

When I thought about this after I got home, I realized that the dolphins had not only healed her physically but they had erased her memory of the pain. She could barely remember being an invalid. I've seen many miracles, but never one where the person couldn't even remember being sick or handicapped. Watching this healing was a great lesson for me that changed the way I think about healing. I will never forget.

When Drunvalo finished that story, everyone in the audience was in full flood. Once you accept that healing is your divine right, you open the door to spontaneous healing. Once you set your ego's doubts aside, the love of your spirit can flow through you.

Dolphins are of Pleiadian origin and part of the cetacean family who for millions of years have been entrusted with custodianship of this planet. They are also master healers, using sound and energy. That woman's story inspired each and every one of us there that day.

The next speaker and another good friend was Randolph Winters, who shared fascinating information about Billy Meier, the noted Pleiadian contactee. Meier received his information during several years of physical contact with a Pleiadian cosmonaut named Semjasee. Her mission was to provide the people of Earth with spiritual knowledge about Creation so that we could learn to create the kind of future we want for ourselves based on Truth. (See Chapter 11 for more details of this amazing story, and Chapter 15 for the Pleiadian Blueprint for planet Earth.)

It was sundown when I met up with two other friends who needed a ride out to the sacred spot on the reservation called Sundance. That's where we would meet up with the other members in the conference for chanting, meditation, prayer, and the sweat lodge for purification. Having been told how hot the Yanktown Sioux liked their sweats, I was a little apprehensive about this particular part of the proceedings.

At Sundance, I met up with Tricia McCannon and a fascinating guy called Star Sparks, who knew the way of the Yanktown Sioux, Mayan calendar mathematics, and the secrets of Turtle Island. He traveled from reservation to reservation with his son, Takawa. He explained that the Yanktown Sioux had been planetary record keepers for many centuries, passing the lore down in the oral tradition. That way, it can't get lost or corrupted by outsiders. The only way to be admitted to the inner circle was to be able to flawlessly recite the entire history from memory.

Another part of their training was to develop telepathic contact with each other and off-world visitors. If they had questions, they would hold a sweat and pose the question to Great Spirit.

"So which off-world group do they contact?" I asked as we sat beside the great fire.

"That would be the Sirians. You know, the space brothers," Star Sparks replied, without having to think about it.

How is it that every Native American I meet fully accepts the existence of ETs? Why are they all in on this big secret that our government seems determined to keep from us?

My thoughts were interrupted by an announcement from Standing Elk: "Will all the invited guests and tribe members step forward in a circle. A blessing will be given by someone very special who has come here from Europe."

Standing Elk was introducing Giorgio Bongiovanni, the Italian with the full stigmata, the very sacred and holy signs that were given to him by a female luminous being who delivered a message for humanity to him. She gave him the stigmata on the palms of his hands as a physical sign of the contact. Tonight, he wore white gloves to protect his hands.

Giorgio turned to face us and I had the feeling he truly was a holy man. He knelt and kissed the ground, then stood up. Hands up to the sky, he gave thanks to the cosmic intelligence and asked for the blessings from Jesus Christ, Mother Mary, and the Great Spirit. All this was in Italian and translated into English by his interpreter.

"Now we will begin the sweat for purification," Standing Elk said. "We do this in reverence and humility, to express our gratitude to the Great Spirit and the Great Mother."

It was my first sweat and I was already sweating a little despite the evening chill. But I had heard the chanting and was committed to this purification and transformation.

"Stay low and hold your focus, Robert. Trust in spirit," Tricia had told me.

I was with a group of about eight as we sat inside in the sweat lodge with Standing Elk. White-hot rocks the size of bowling balls were brought in and placed in the pit. Just the heat from the rocks made me sweat. The entrance was closed and Standing Elk began a prayer in his native tongue. Then he began to chant as the first bucket of water was poured over the rocks. Man, it was hot. I kept thinking of what Tricia had told me: *Hold your focus.*

I was just getting used to the heat and steam, when the second bucket was poured. Now I was literally hanging on to my focus and consciousness. After about five minutes, I got used to the heat, when the third bucket was poured. Every fiber wanted to scream out from the wave of pain as steam seared my back and shoulders. I focused on Standing Elk's chanting and that helped me stay grounded.

And then it was over. Full sweats last several hours, but this was the tourist version. I stepped out of the lodge and took one almighty breath. I felt more alive at that moment than I had ever felt before. I went in one guy and came out another. I had never been more present or grounded.

Tricia looked up at me and said, "Well, how was it?"

"I guess Standing Elk was trying to separate the big bears from the little bears. Right now, I feel like a bear cub who's just discovered something wonderful!"

"Come with me, and I will guide you to a place where we can get a real good view of the space brothers," said Takawa, Star Sparks' 12-year-old son, who was tempting me with this impossible-to-refuse offer.

I didn't need to be asked twice. We walked barefoot in the middle of the night to a remote area away from the fires. This kid had razor sharp eyes. Pointing to the sky, he said, "See that blue star? Watch, that one's going to move. When you see it, please make no sound. Many people are meditating or are in the sweat lodges. Let us honor their space, too."

I watched that blue star like my life depended on it. It was slightly brighter than most of the others, but it certainly didn't draw attention to itself. You really had to know where to look. Suddenly, it shot off and made a kind of an "S" movement. Then another streaked across the sky. And another. And another. I wanted to shout out for joy and had to work hard on my self-control. The aerial display was riveting as the ships rolled and tumbled with each other. One did something that looked like a checkmark in the sky at what must have been many thousands of miles per hour. I'm sure that no Earth craft could fly those patterns.

After all the waiting, the rumors, the long search, there they were. The space brothers put on a display for just a handful of the 500 attendees. Thank goodness I ran into Takawa, otherwise I would have missed this performance. With my own two eyes, I saw maybe a dozen ships that night. No one can take that memory away.

After the show was over, I met up with Elizabeth and her friends who'd also seen the display. All the way back in the car, we giggled.

What a night! I didn't care that there were only a couple of hours left before sunrise. Who was interested in sleeping anyway?

On Friday morning, I had breakfast with world-renowned ufologist, John Mack. He had also won a Pulitzer Prize for his biography of Lawrence of Arabia, one of my boyhood heroes. A university researcher, John was a little reticent, preferring to watch, listen, and analyze.

"There's something I'd like your opinion on," I said, handing Isaac's hieroglyphics to him. "Have you ever seen anything like this before?"

After a long silence, he said, "No, never have I seen anything quite like this. Who did these?"

To his rapt amazement, I explained about Isaac, my ET contact.

"Why don't you show these to Michael Hesseman? He's a cryptologist specializing in ET hieroglyphics. Thank you for letting me see them. Very curious indeed."

After breakfast, it was time for Giorgio Bongiovanni to speak again. His interpreter showed us a film of what the stigmata represents. When the luminous woman appeared to him in 1989, two rays of light from her hands struck his hands, piercing them, and forming two wounds from which blood would flow. Medical doctors around the world have studied these wounds, curious about why they never heal, why they bleed at certain times and not at others. The interpreter said the bleeding is a sign that Christ is speaking directly through him.

Giorgio so fascinates the Catholic world that he has had several private audiences with the Pope. The film also showed Giorgio at several places, surrounded by thousands of people who flock to him in the belief that they will be healed and come closer to God.

During his contact with the Being, she revealed to Giorgio the Secret of Fatima. She also told him that the Universe is abundant with intelligent life, and that beings from other planets are visiting the Earth with highly-advanced disc-shaped craft.

Two years later, during a contact with Jesus, Giorgio was again stigmatized, this time on his feet. On May 28, 1992, he was stigmatized on his left side, and July 16, 1993, on his forehead. Since 1989, Giorgio has been bleeding daily. He has direct contact with Jesus during these bleedings.

Finally, Giorgio took the stage and removed his gloves, showing us the stigmata. They looked like a fresh wound, just hours old, but he's had them for a decade. Unlike most wounds, they are slightly raised and a deep, blood red, about the size of a nickel.

Then he removed the bandages that covered the stigmata over his forehead. I was fascinated by the cross burnt into his skin. I'd never seen anything like that before. I was also fascinated by the fact that his aura was so strong he literally glowed.

Through his interpreter, Giorgio addressed us with a short, simple, but incredibly beautiful message:

Earth is on the cusp of great changes and is being visited by many people from other worlds who want to reveal our connection to the rest of the universe. There is nothing more important than loving ourselves because only when you do can you love one another.

I also have a warning. I have seen visions of possible global catastrophe. We are destroying the very air we breathe. However, there is still time to avert these catastrophes if we would only wake up. It is essential that on this planet, we stop our nuclear involvement and take drastic care of our environment. We need to be more conscious of our Mother, Earth. We must take care of her.

It is our duty as way-showers to raise the consciousness as much as possible, so that we might avert our own downfall. As you impart your truth to others, they in turn share it with others, and so on

People in America hardly know anything about Giorgio Bongiovanni but in Europe, he's a household name. Everywhere he goes, thousands in countries like Italy, Spain, Portugal, Hungary, and France line up just to touch this man. As a vessel for Divine Grace, or the Holy Spirit, he has healed untold thousands. I will never forget him.

Next, the German cryptographer, Michael Hesseman, showed amazing footage of spacecraft seen over Europe, including a relatively unknown 1964 crash site in Germany. Michael is also head of the German chapter of MUFON. He presented most of the 45-minute *Alien Autopsy* film and never-before-seen footage of the instrument panel of the craft. It was a device into which you put your hands directly on an imprint. And it was built for a six-fingered hand.

He also showed us the hieroglyphics on an I-beam taken from a crashed ship. The characters were a derivative of ancient Phoenician Hebrew. I had seen these same symbols on temple etchings.

After his talk, I went up to him and asked, "Do you have time to look at something that might interest you?"

What true researcher could say no to that? "Of course," he said, his curiosity pecked.

Michael was a big stocky guy, about 40. He had a beard, and spoke English with a perfect Hollywood German professor accent. He is the author of *The Cosmic Connection*, one of the most authorative books on crop circles (see Reading List).

He studied the Isaac writings for a long time, his eyes opening wider and wider. He looked at me and at the writings again. Finally, he asked, "Where did you get these?"

I told him the Isaac story and he said, "That's fascinating. Some of the abductees I have regressed under deep hypnosis have drawn exactly the same characters. They claim that they saw them on the uniforms of those who abducted them."

Talk about cold shivers and chills. Isaac had casually spoken a language that was found on alien ships. Suddenly, he'd taken on a whole new level of authenticity.

Finally, it was time for the last speaker, the big daddy of ufology—Bob Dean. Bob is one of the most fascinating people in the UFO field, and a wonderfully, sincere human being. Physically impressive, he stands about six feet four, with shoulder-length hair and a white beard.

After a distinguished record in Korea and Vietnam, Bob joined SHAPE (Supreme Headquarters of Allied Powers Europe). There he came across a highly classified program called "The Assessment," an incredibly comprehensive study of global UFO activity. It revealed that "humanity had been under a microscope for centuries by many different species of ET."

More recently, Bob served as a NATO Intelligence officer until his retirement. That explains the feeling that he knows more than he's telling, or is allowed to tell. But now he is lending his vast and invaluable experience to the UFO community. Thank you, Bob, for all you've done for us.

He delivered an incredible 90-minute talk that was powerful, emotional, inspiring, thrilling, and very heartfelt. He ended with a challenge to each of us: "We are caught up in a most extraordinary situation. All of you here today accept certain truths as fact, facts that your government steadfastly denies, while that same government conducts covert operations in the skies and under the ground. My purpose here is not criticize the government but to stress that, in the end, it all comes down to the individual and what *you* are going to do. So what *are* you going to do?"

As the day ended, we all went outside and held hands in a giant circle several hundred feet across. As we began to chant OM, Star Sparks addressed the Great Spirit in his native tongue. After about 45 minutes, I happened to look up and to my complete astonishment, I saw a circular cloud formation hovering exactly over us in the same shape we were.

The cloud circle was bowed in at one point, and when I looked across the people circle, it too was bowed. That cloud formation mimicked us perfectly.

Please indulge me a personal moment. So many people brought so many beautiful teachings to us that they can't all be mentioned here. You were all wonderful. I want to especially thank Marilyn Carlson and her staff members. Many blessings to you all. I love you.

Finally, I want to personally thank Standing Elk for sharing with us the ways of the red man and the Yanktown Sioux. Your people's hospitality will never be forgotten. You and your tribe are the most beautiful, peaceful people on Earth. Thank you for bringing your wisdom to us.

On my return to California, I got a phone call from Sheldan Nidle, who told me that during a telepathic communication from the Sirians, they told him that they were very displeased with some of the technology installed inside Cheyenne Mountain in Colorado. Home of NORAD, the military's nerve center detects and tracks anything that flies over the US. Apparently, they are up to far more than just tracking, and are getting involved in more active pursuits that interfere with the Sirians' free range of the skies.

"The Sirians are going to arrange a little demonstration of their technology to get the government's attention," Sheldan told me. "Keep your eyes open."

"When is this going to happen?"

"The first or second of July."

So I marked my calendar with SIRIAN DEMONSTRATION and promptly forgot all about it. Two weeks later, on July 2, I had an out-of-body experience on waking:

It's early morning and I'm outside a small town, looking over rolling plains, like those in Colorado. It's a beautiful morning and I marvel at the mauve and gold of the eastern sky just before sunrise.

I'm standing with crowd of people who are in total awe and amazement at the sight of dozens of spacecraft hovering over three or four high-voltage lines whose towers march across the plains like giants.

"I'll bet they did it!" someone in the crowd shouts, referring to the fact that the power is out. Apparently the UFOs had tampered with the grid system. Suddenly a UFO breaks away from the pack and hovers directly over us. Many people run off in panic, terrified. I smile, somehow knowing that it's all part of a larger plan.

I woke up thinking, That was neat! But like all visions and dreams, I quickly forgot about it once my day started.

Later in the day, my sister Dennie called. "Robert, you're not going to believe this but we were at the movies watching the premiere of *Independence Day* and halfway through, the entire mall went dark. They told us that half of Idaho had lost power and on the car radio, we heard that several other states had been hit. Do you know anything about this?"

I turned the TV to the news and learned that 500,000 people in Northern California had lost power and that 17 states were without power. Just then, I looked down at my calendar, open at the day and noticed the words, SIRIAN DEMONSTRATION.

I grabbed the phone and called Sheldan. "Sheldan, what the hell's going on?" I demanded.

"I told you so. Quite effective, isn't it?" he gloated, knowing exactly what I was talking about.

Signs in the Earth Beneath

"Do you want to do a lecture in England outside of Salisbury Cathedral?" Power Places Tours, owned by Teri Weiss, needed a group leader on an expedition to England to research crop circles. It was April, 1997 at the San Francisco Whole Life Expo just before I was due to deliver my presentation. "The other leaders will be Barbara Hand Clow, Colin Andrews, Dr. Chet Snow, Rosemary Ellen Guiley, Barbara Lamb, John Michell, George Wingfield, and Busty Taylor." I was ecstatic. It was the sixth Annual International Conference on Crop Circles, Stonehenge, and UFOs (see Resources).

Apart from UFOs, nothing fascinates me more than crop circles, so my answer was automatic. I've always believed that one way to learn more about ETs is to study the signs they leave for us. How brilliant, I often thought that if a superior intelligence was talking to us, what better way to do it than through Mother Nature in the form of patterns in wheat fields? After all, if they're coming from an entirely different star system to interact with another species, such as human, it might be in everyone's best interest if they introduced themselves gently through symbols first, just to get us used to the idea of their presence. Crop circles are like a calling card saying we're here, we're intelligent, and we mean you no harm.

Barbara Hand Clow, associated with Bear & Company, a premier publisher of metaphysical books, is also renowned in the fields of astrology and sacred geometry. She had already led many such expeditions to England's crop circles, and is also the author of *The Pleiadian Agenda*, a fascinating account of the history of planet Earth and humanity from an ET perspective.

Colin Andrews is undoubtedly the elder statesman of circles. Busty Taylor is a jocular, fun guy and also a notable author and tour leader for groups from all over the world. George Wingfield is the epitome of the proper English gentleman; tall, handsome, and speaking with an impeccable English accent. He is also the publisher of *The Cerealogist*, the prestigious magazine for the glyph community. The three of them are known as the "lords of the rings," and without them, cerealogy would not be the respected, scientific, well-researched field it is today. (To contact them, see Resources.)

I met up with the US contingent in New York to begin what was probably the finest flying experience of my life. Virgin Atlantic treats everyone like a first class passenger, and all during the flight, I drooled over the pretty British stewardesses in their jaunty uniforms. Unlike my last trans-Atlantic flight to Egypt, this flight was over way too soon.

Teri Weiss met us at Heathrow and whisked us onto the bus to Salisbury and the delightful Red Lion Hotel. The weather was perfect and the two-hour journey through England's scenery was memorable. Most of the group were women, a broad mixture of New Age thinkers, healers, channels, astrologers, ufologists, and so on.

Our anticipation built during the first couple of days as we covered the theory behind the crop circle phenomenon, the history, the various types of circle, who the creators might be, their reasons for making them, and what they might be telling us.

In 1997, over 300 circles appeared in England alone. In Holland, new circles were appearing literally every other day. However, the circles actually began showing up in the late seventies. Early circles tended to be just that, but over two decades, they have progressed to more complex forms such as DNA spirals and graphical representations of mathematical formulas. For this reason, the term "glyph" is often used instead of the word "circle."

Buddhist monks claim that their complex mandalas are actually graphical representations of the sounds of their chants, suggesting a link between sound and geometry. This may explain why certain glyphs have a profound effect on us—we know what they mean at a subconscious level. While our conscious mind marvels at the clever designs, the real message is being decoded and acted upon many levels deeper where language is irrelevant.

Oddly enough, Colin Andrews reports hearing a trilling sound in the air around circles. Researchers speculate that the increasing complexity of the glyphs may be related to the increasing resonant frequency of the planet over the last two decades (more in Chapter 13.)

Researchers study how the stalks are laid down. In circular glyphs, the stalks are bent in either a clockwise or counterclockwise direction. In straight lines, the bending is uniform, running the length of the line. But in odd shapes, the stalks are bent in layers of flattening in different directions.

Not only are the stalks not broken, they are bent in some way and even genetically altered at the bend. Researchers have noted a malty smell when the stalks are cut at the bend, suggesting that they've been "cooked" from the inside. The only way researchers have been able to reproduce the unusual cell enlargement is with rapid heating in special ovens, like super-powerful microwave ovens. But how the true creators bend stalks without breaking or splintering them is still a mystery.

Crop circles are seasonal, starting every spring in late March and lasting until September. They've been appearing in the same places, thought to be energy vortexes or dimensional doorways, such as Stonehenge and Silbury Hill. But they're not limited to England. They're

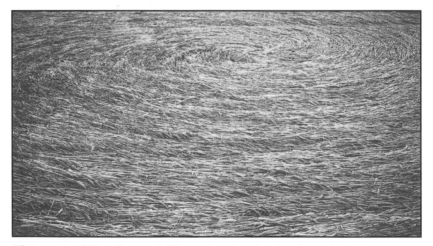

The center of Woodborough Rings, showing the circular swirl of the flattened crops at the center

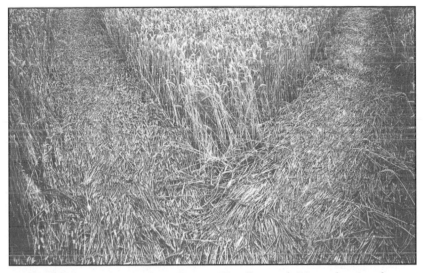

One of the intersections of two lines at Woodborough Rings showing the layering of bent stalk when two lines cross

appearing all over the world now, even in places accessible only by helicopter. In the early 1990s, the average Englishman in the street was very skeptical, dismissing them as hoaxes, but since 1996, the patterns have become so complex that people are beginning to accept them as authentic but unexplained phenomena.

We reviewed the types of glyph and how they've changed over the years, from the thirty or so relatively simple circles in 1975 when they first began appearing to about 500 that looked more like coded messages by 1990. But even in 1975, the circles were cleanly delineated (like a "cookie-cutter," according to Colin Andrews), and demonstrated the careful stalk bending that allowed the crop to continue growing. By 1990, the circles had evolved to the point where the term "pictogram" and "glyph" came into use.

In the mid-nineties, the patterns got very interesting. Many fascinating glyphs appeared in 1995, notably the "Missing Earth" formation showing Mercury, Venus, and Mars in orbit around the sun, but not Earth, hopefully signifying ascension rather than destruction. This glyph raises so many questions, such as why Earth is missing, the meaning of the single circle off to the side, and the code contained in the outer ring of large and small circles.

Another notable in 1996 (7/8/96) was the so-called Julia Set, a glyph of a complex mathematical concept. Close to Stonehenge, this glyph

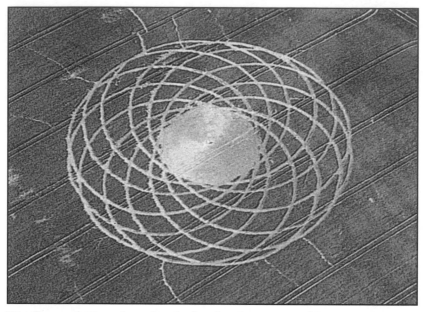

Woodborough Rings from the air, showing the center and intersections seen in detail on the previous page. [Photo courtesy of Ruben Uriarte] (To contact Ruben, see Resources.)

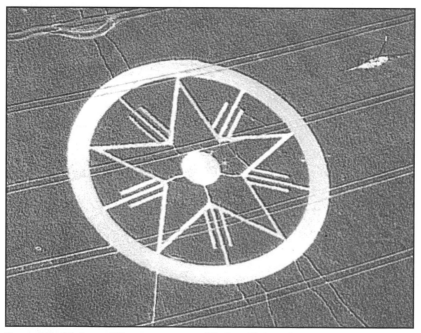

Star of Bethlehem [Photo courtesy of Ruben Uriarte]

prompted researchers to speculate on whether coded energy was somehow being pumped into the Earth's grid system. Busty Taylor dowsed the formation and detected a very powerful energy field. (Dowsing is the age-old practice of using wood, copper, or just your hands to detect energy changes. Its best known use is probably by well-diggers for the location of water.)

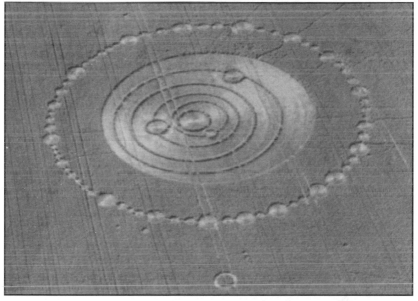

The Puzzling Missing Earth Glyph [Photo courtesy of Ruben Uriarte]

Crescent Moons, aka Spinning Crescents [Photo courtesy of Colin Andrews]

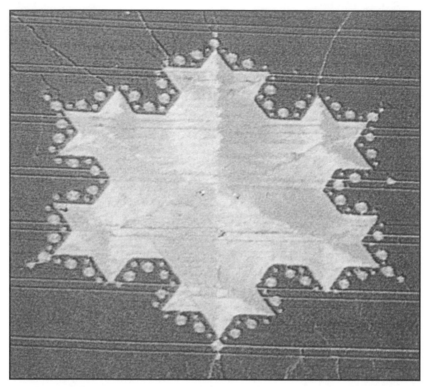

The Fractal Star of David, showing the damage from sightseers
[Photo courtesy of Ruben Uriarte]

DNA Glyph [Photo courtesy of Stephen Alexander]
(Stephen has many images available spanning 1994 – 1998.

By August, 1997, we already had some of the finest examples yet, such as the Snowflake (400 feet in diameter), Spinning Arcs (160 feet diameter), the Goddess (90 feet long), and the Star of Bethlehem (150 feet in diameter). One of the best of the early 1998 was captured by Stephen Alexander at Trusloe: a five-pointed star within arcs (see below).

Among the language elements used in the circles, we have seen sacred geometry, like the Flower of Life (which consists of 19 inter-locking circles), genetic codes, math symbols, and sacred symbols of ancient cultures such as Egyptian, Celtic, and Native American. If these are the words used, what's the message?

Field watchers note that complex patterns have appeared within sec onds, quite silently and in total darkness. However, Stephen Alexander has talked to many hoaxers who claim that they could achieve the same result with boards and garden rollers in complete darkness!

Once we got out in the field, I interviewed a landowner at his farm near Swindon. His farm has had one or two circles every year for many years and he's come to expect them. In 1996, a new circle appeared and he vowed to plow it under to avoid the crowds that swarm over his fields, trampling them down. When he drove his tractor into the circle, the electrics went dead. He towed the tractor out and it started right up again. When he drove it in again, guess what? "Looks like the circle stays for a while," he said ruefully.

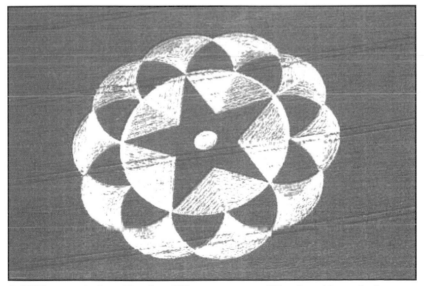

A 1998 crop circle at Trusloe [Photo courtesy of Stephen Alexander]

I wondered about the role of the so-called "authorities" in all this. Their official position is that the circles are of no consequence, so they leave the research to private groups and individuals "who are crazy enough to waste their time on something so obviously unimportant." But if the circles are so unimportant, why do Army helicopters buzz over every new glyph. And why are those helicopters invariably outnumbered by mysterious unmarked gray helicopters? Who's flying them and why did they seem to be more interested in us than the circles themselves?

Finally it came time to visit our first circle: Woodborough Rings. My first impression was the enormity and majesty of the thing. It was on a gentle slope and from the roadside you could see the whole circle. It was astonishing. All the hours of theory were forgotten. In front of me was undeniable evidence that we're not alone in this time and space. I couldn't figure out why everyone on the planet wasn't here, witnessing this amazing evidence. *We are not alone* kept going through my head.

Who or what could lay this vast, complex pattern gently into a field of wheat? I turned to Colin Andrews and remarked, "You know that reference in the Bible to signs in the earth and signs in the sky? Well, here's one half of the equation."

Chills swept through both of us. Think about it for a moment. Suppose you wanted to contact the inhabitants of a planet who were so primitive they hadn't even formed a planetary government, couldn't even control the weather or earth movements, and still died horrible deaths from disease. You knew they'd be terrified at your arrival, even though you were there to help them. What would you do to gently announce your presence?

You would leave puzzling signs in plain view, made by a technology they didn't have. Then they would know that someone with more advanced technology was there, someone who obviously meant them no harm. The first step would be to get the locals used to the idea of your presence. Notice how unobtrusive you've been. Cloud circles in the sky would have freaked out primitive Earthlings, but you laid your message gently in the Earth herself, thus honoring her and demonstrating your relationship with her as a living entity.

The next step you'd probably take is to convey information to the primitives in a language they understood—their rudimentary understanding of math and science. You would probably also elicit the aid of the Earth's consciousness and the devic realm (the elementals who oversee all natural life). That day, one of these signs was right before me, and I became a believer.

As I stood in the center of it, I was amazed at how exact it was. The barley was laid over in a carefully calculated pattern. It's impossible to grasp any of this until you actually see it. Each formation I entered gave me the same chills down my spine, plus that wonderful feeling that we're not alone in the universe.

I carefully laid down in a circle at Cley Hill, just west of Warminster, and meditated. I asked my guides to reveal to me what this was all about.

Hard work, this research

What they had to tell me was very interesting:

"As the earth reaches the end of the precession of the equinoxes, the planet readies herself to be birthed into a new expression. Because of the nature of humanity's position at this time, a language for the new millennium is being brought forth, a combination of frequency symbols and geometrical shapes for man to recognize and decipher. Hints are placed along the way, also in the form of ancient hieroglyphs, sacred geometry, and Celtic symbols. Just as the prophecies say in reference to the last days before the return of the Spiritual Hierarchy, "There will be signs on the earth and signs in the sky.

"These symbols are not just produced by Mother Earth or by the extraterrestrials but rather by both. You see, both ETs and angelic realms have a closer relationship with Mother Earth than you understand. They cooperate on a vast scale. You will learn more of this relationship in the near future, as humanity's consciousness gains higher levels of awareness, which is beginning to happen now."

Then I believe I heard the Earth herself saying, "Recognize me. I am the foundation of your reality. Know this: Great changes are coming and you are entering a New Age."

I sat in many other circles, including "The Bicycle Spokes" and "The Harlequin Circle" in Wiltshire, three miles north of Avebury in Winterbourne Bassett. The two that moved me the most were "The Star of Bethlehem" in Bishop Cannings and the famed "Snow Flake" next to the 5,000-year-old man-made pyramid in Silbury Hill—six perfect six-pointed Stars of David woven together. What amazed me about the Snow Flake is that farmers and pub owners say that bright lights were seen buzzing all over the area when it was created. They told me in that blunt way that only English country folk have, "Make no mistake about it, mate, the extraterrestrials were here that night!"

Who Creates Them?

A curious thing about the glyphs is that many who actually enter into one undergo subtle changes. They may develop telepathic ability, increased insight or intuition, or their thought processes speed up. The effect is even more pronounced if you actually eat some of the grain. But this is not their main purpose, researchers say. Most of them agree that their main purpose is to reach us on a subconscious level. Souls incarnating on this planet have a rich stellar heritage, and different symbols are significant to different people, triggering certain deeply-laid patterns. It's like a cosmic alarm clock going off.

If this is true, then who's setting the alarm? Although the ET connection is researchers' first choice, there may be other explanations, not instead of, but in addition to. Another view is that the glyphs are the work of Earth's consciousness and the devic kingdom. She is a lot smarter than we give her credit for and she could be providing us with the proof.

In view of the wide variety of styles and techniques that have been found, maybe there's more than once source. Here is an alternative from Merlin, received telepathically by my friend and co-author, Tony Stubbs and first published in *Eagles' Wings* magazine:

This is the Merlin. I have often told you that your spirit will find many avenues to communicate with your conscious mind. And one of these avenues is currently staring you right in the face, but is being ignored by all but a few. Most of those folks who do pay attention are not recognizing the medium for what it is. I'm talking about crop circles, glyphs, or pictograms, as they're now being called. They are speaking directly to the deepest levels of your consciousness—your cellular DNA. So who is talking and what are they saying?

With a few exceptions, the circles are messages from your future selves that have already passed through the fourth dimension and are currently in the fifth dimension. Your future self knows exactly what needs to happen with you today because it's already been here, so it's a message worth heeding. And what is the future you telling the current you? WAKE UP AND REMEMBER WHY YOU'RE HERE!

So, how is the future you using crop circles to wake you up, and what is being woken up? There's something that's been dormant for millennia, tucked away in your cells, and it's time to activate it. Cellular memory holds awareness of the entire species' history and purpose and until now, it's been hidden from you, otherwise the knowledge would spoil the game of hide-and-seek that you've all been playing with your *true* identity of divine co-creator with the Source. But now, as you know, that's all changed. It's time to remember why you came to this party in the first place, what's it's all been about, and what are the next steps. And as we'll see, the patterns within crop circles do just that.

Why peculiar patterns in wheat fields? Think about it for a moment. There are hundreds, if not thousands, of folks running around channeling beings like me and most people are so skeptical that they wouldn't believe in us even if we bit them on the nose. So your higher selves decided to use another approach that even the most hardened skeptic could not dispute. Not only does this approach get the job of cellular awakening done, it tells your mental body—the great doubter—that something is definitely going down on planet Earth, something your mental body cannot dismiss, explain, or analyze (although lots of people are trying).

Your scientists are convinced that the phenomenon is real and that the circles are produced by ways that cannot be explained, but some are reading more into them than is actually there, and in the process, missing the entire point. Yes, they contain sacred geometry, and yes, sacred geometry is a universal language. But their purpose goes far beyond some ETs showing off their prowess in universal math and stalk bending. Don't get confused between the message and messenger. Pay attention to the message. WAKE UP AND REMEMBER!

Ignore the scientists who talk about series and progressions within the circles and among groups of circles. This is a distraction. These are messages directly from your higher selves who have already ascended— future aspects who know what it took to get there. And remember, ascension is supposed to be accomplished with grace, ease, and fun—

not pain and anguish—so why wouldn't you make it easier for yourself and leave some tantalizing clues along the way?

One of the most potent meditations you can do is to ask a future self, "What do you know in your time that you wished you'd known in my time?" Well, one of the answers is emblazoned daily across wheat fields all over the planet.

But why crops? Because the message is also intended for the Earth's consciousness and the plant kingdom. They get it first, and then you.

The patterns were intended as a semi-permanent yet undeniable message—one that the scientific community could not dismiss as "new age psycho-babble." A public witness of billions of people on this planet tells a story that cannot be ignored. Yet it is. Why? Because of narrow-mindedness on the part of scientists, politicians, and the media. But the grandest wake up call of all time is before you right now so don't let it be trivialized by skepticism, or denied TV coverage, pushed out by the soap operas. Call the investigative journalism program producers and demand coverage. Ask questions of everyone you meet and quietly inform them of your truth. This is a global phenomenon, not just weird local events in odd corners of the world.

Each of you, as an individual, rightly chooses what you let into your awareness. I urge you to let the pictograms become part of your reality. But before that, your mental body may need some more feeding as to their meaning.

There are a number of soul groups currently incarnated on this planet and by definition, if you are incarnate today, you are a member of one of them. Each soul group has its own 'insignia,' a characteristic geometrical pattern. You saw during 1996 and 1997 a pictogram for each soul group, a call to action to bring that group on-line, to mobilize the members of that group. When you see your insignia, it will appear to be the most beautiful thing you've ever seen. You may break down in tears over its beauty because it reminds you of your far distant home and why you came to this planet all those millennia ago.

Other pictograms will leave you cold, or even instill a little fear. That's okay—they're not for you, so ignore them. But whatever you do, do not invalidate them or the effect they have on others. To those of the other soul groups, they are as meaningful and important as your pictogram is to you. I just ask you to honor the fact that everyone's path is sacred to him or her.

How are these phenomena created? First, remember that at the soul level, you operate freely across the timeline. So the future selves of the members of each soul group get together and decide when and how to manifest their insignia, and come back in time to our 'tomorrow.' There your future selves create an etheric pattern of the insignia and impress it on tomorrow's crop field using techniques that are infinitely too complex to describe here (but know that each of you can do this, because you have already done it in the future). Of course, the pattern doesn't show up today because the event hasn't happened yet. With me so far? But when linear time catches up with tomorrow, boom—the pattern 'just appears' instantaneously out of nowhere.

Why, you might ask, are UFOs so often seen around crop circles, especially those little blue glowing spheres? That's because our alien visitors are fascinated with this process and want to know how you're doing this, and why. And those little spheres are simply probes, measuring and analyzing, just like human scientists do. Advanced though alien technology may be (after all, they've had a few millennia head start), Earth humans are actually a far more advanced species than most ET species. Just because ETs have more sophisticated toys doesn't put them any closer to the Source. In fact, Earth humans are probably the most complex species in the galaxy. Remember that you took on the greatest challenge of any species—to cut yourself off from all memory of the Source and then try to claw your way back to unconditional love. No other species would be that courageous.

So that's why UFOs hang out around crop circles—not to create them but to investigate them and their creators. Why does ability of your higher selves to move around the timeline simply by intent fascinate the ETs? Because they need complex technology to do the same thing. Of course, to fully appreciate the compliment, you must identify with your spirit and not that puny flesh-and-bone "earthsuit" your spirit is currently wearing.

What does all this mean to you? Open up to the pictograms and see which one calls to you. Try to view as many photographs as possible. Use photographs rather than those line drawings that investigators make of them, because the latter don't capture the energy of the pattern. When one sticks out, commit the pattern to memory and meditate on it, holding the image in your mind's eye. Visualize it often and let it work on you at deep, deep levels. As the thought-form of the pattern assimilates in your energy fields, the cells will respond by unlocking the ancient memories locked in your DNA. In fact, the purpose of the vast majority of those tiny spirals is to retain the species' holographic memory.

What will this do for you? It will trigger a remembering of why you and your soul group chose to come to Earth. You came here with a mission but as part of the deal you had to forget your mission until the "alarm clock" went off. Guess what? It's ringing, so wake up. Get with the program and do your thing, whatever that is. Only you and your spirit know what that is. Some groups are here to educate, some to heal, some to wake up other humans, some to urge to action, and some to navigate us all through ascension. Whatever your mission, the next few years are critical so be on the alert for others whose mission aligns with yours. (Responding to the same pictogram is a good clue.) You will feel an immediate comfort level with these folks because they're old buddies and you've worked with them for eons. Blend with them, unite with them, align with them in service to the Source. We're all going home, folks, along with Gaia, who's pretty tired by now. So follow your spirit in every moment and with every breath.

Live Heaven, The Merlin.

No metaphysical foray to England would be complete without visiting the ultimate mystery: Stonehenge. Built thousand of years ago by God knows who, Stonehenge taunts us with as many "who, why, when, how, what for's" as do the pyramids and the Sphinx. And despite just as much speculation, we know just as little.

However, all the questions melt away when you're there, encircled by those sleeping stone giants. I could feel the unmistakable energy of a major vortex (or focal point of energy), and could sense the ley lines spreading out like the spokes of a wheel. But beyond that, I was in silent awe.

Our visit was capped by a wonderful channeling of the Arcturan presence around our planet:

"We honor you for your service to this planet, and to humanity, and we wish to remind you to constantly reaffirm your vows of service."

Just a few months earlier, I'd heard the same message delivered in the dry heat of the Egyptian desert. Today, I was in the cool, lush green fields of England. It really is a small planet, I thought.

The channeling concluded with:

"Rejoice in your connection with this beautiful planet, your home, and with your extraterrestrial neighbors. We are here to serve you."

All this intriguing information reminded me of the wealth of communication that flows between the Earth, the ETs, and each of us. Just the very thought of it sent chills up and down my spine. My Divine Blueprint was alive and receptive. I had found what I came here for—the Sacred Promise. Need I say more?

Chapter 11

Teachings of the Extraterrestrials

A Giant Leap for Mankind

Tʜɪѕ ᴄʜᴀᴘᴛᴇʀ ᴄʟᴏѕᴇѕ Pᴀʀᴛ One by taking a look at what the ETs are saying to us as we come to the close of the millennium and prepare to enter a new and exciting phase of humanity's evolution. Why should we listen to them? Because they've been doing it longer than us, have made their share of mistakes, and now want to help our fledgling species as we stand on the edge of our nest and prepare to take flight for the first time.

Some ETs are here because they know that the next step in our evolution depends on helping another species make this spectacular leap into the future. Others are here to discharge a species-wide karmic debt so vast that it will take planet-sized good deeds to pay it off. And, yes, other less altruistic ETs are here out of opportunism.

Who's Here?

First, let's create an ET *Who's Who*. It's important to know who's here, why, and who's friendly and who's not, although I'm assured that any self-serving ETs are closely watched by those here to serve humanity, and the latter will keep the former on a short leash if they start getting out of hand. In this section, I'm going to draw on the wisdom found in *The Extraterrestrial Vision* by Gina Lake, an astrologer and the conscious channel for a higher-dimensional teacher for Earth named Theodore.

The reason for drawing on Theodore's wisdom is simple. When I first read *The Extraterrestrial Vision* in 1995, Theodore was saying exactly the same things as my Pleiadian visitors did in the summer of

1992. Although Theodore isn't (to my knowledge) Pleiadian, he had their teachings down to a T. But then I figured, why shouldn't they all talk to each other during their celestial coffee breaks? So it is with the blessing of Theodore, Gina, and Oughten House Publications that I recycle some of this timeless wisdom. (Please read *The Extraterrestrial Vision* for yourself; I've just scratched the surface of the wisdom here. See Resources for how to contact Gina.)

Incidentally, in addition to *The Extraterrestrial Vision*, Gina also brought us *ET Contact*, in which the Galactic Federation of Planets briefs us on what life will be like after contact, especially in the fields of education, science, medicine, politics, the media, and religion. They conclude by recommending what we can do to prepare ourselves for post-contact integration.

Pleiadians: the first visitors to Earth according to most sources. Because of our shared Lyran ancestry, they look very much like Caucasians except for slightly larger eyes. The greater age of their cultures means that they're more developed mentally and spiritually than humans. Improved mental prowess means more advanced technology, but after millennia of fierce civil wars, peace has finally prevailed. Their spiritual development means that they have overcome the dominance of the ego over the soul and now serve their higher selves. For example, open relationships are common with them since they are no longer ruled by jealousy and limited notions about the purpose of relationships.

Their home system consists of seven major stars, six of which are visible to the naked eye, yet oddly native folklore has always referred to all seven. Their home world, Erra, shares its star with eight other planets, four of which sustain life.

A large task force of Pleiadians has been orbiting Earth for centuries in a huge mothership just outside the third dimension so as to avoid detection. They are here to monitor, prepare, and plan for contact and as we shall see later, the fact that Pleiadians look so "normal" will play a vital role in first contact. First contact with beings with tentacles and eyestalks would not go as smoothly, no matter how evolved they were.

Also, the visitors who appeared to me in the summer of 1992 identified themselves as Pleiadians and confirmed that they were preparing humanity for first contact.

Sirians: a fifth-dimensional race from the star system of Sirius, or the Dog Star, who can materialize at will. Up until now, they have been most involved with the evolution of humanity, especially during ancient

Egypt when they were worshipped by primitive Earth people as gods. According to Theodore, they incarnated at key points in Earth's history, such as during the great Greek civilization, appearing as Pythagoras, Socrates, Hippocrates, and Plato. When they withdrew from active involvement, our planet went into the Middle Ages in which no real advancement took place. Sirians have been behind most of our technological advancements, such as atomic weaponry, air flight, and space travel by implanting thoughts telepathically in the minds of inventors.

For background, Sirius, or Dog Star, is the brightest star in the sky and has long played an important role on our planet. It was so revered by the ancient Egyptians that they built temples so that the light of Sirius reached the inner chambers. Sirius is bright because it's one of the closest stars to Earth, only 8.7 light years, or 51 trillion miles, and it's much hotter than our sun. In 1862, it was found to be actually two stars— Sirius A is circled by a white dwarf, Sirius B, a fact long known by the mysterious Dogon tribe in Africa, whose legends speak of visitors in spacesuits and helmets appearing to them in ancient times.

Most Sirian influence on Earth has been positive and inroads by those whom Theodore calls "service-to-self" Sirians have been few, usually limited to influencing secret societies and mystery schools, and individuals like black magicians and self-proclaimed "satanists."

Arcturans: Dr. Norma Milanovich is probably the expert on Arcturans, thanks to a series of telepathic conversations she had with them in 1985. She documented all this in her book, *We the Arcturians*. The group of Arcturans who contacted her describe themselves as fifth-dimensional beings, about three feet tall, wispy, and slender, with large almond-shaped eyes. These sound nothing like the Arcturans who visited me, but when you drop from the fifth to the third dimension, you can take any shape you like, so they may have manifested as seven foot giants to get my attention.

Norma's contacts told her that they ascended long ago and are here to help planet Earth and its inhabitants through the same process. Having seeded human life on this planet long ago, they see themselves as stewards and protectors of Earth. Their mission also includes waking us up to our true identity by increasing the frequency of our bodies so that we inherit the wisdom that is already ours. One of the most significant things Norma was told was that the fate of the planet is in our hands. We must rise to the occasion and become our own stewards, taking on the responsibility that this implies.

Orions: according to Theodore, most Orion influence has been negative, but usually working in the background, appearing occasionally as the infamous Men In Black (MIBs). Their intent is to create doubt in contactees' minds about the government and to acquire information about contactees' experiences. These "service-to-self" Orions have actually traveled here from Orion's past. Present-time Orions are much more highly evolved and are also appearing on Earth. They regret the role played by their ancestors but honor the free-will nature of our planet.

According to Randolph Winters in *The Pleiadian Mission*, Orion was colonized over 230,000 years ago. It happened as a result of a devastating war that raged in the constellation Lyra that drove millions of Lyrans to flee their home worlds in order to survive. A fleet of thousands of great spacecraft carried the ancient ones to new homes in Hyades, Orion, and the Pleiades. Our visitors today from these distant worlds carry the legacy of their tragic past and hope that we, their younger brothers and sisters, will learn from their mistakes and come together in peace.

Zeta Reticuli: these small, gray beings with large eyes are relative newcomers, answering the call that went out when humans discovered nuclear weapons in the 1940s. According to Theodore, they are interested in humanity because we have the genetics to take them back to the time before they cloned themselves and because they want to warn us not to follow the same tragic path they did. They are here to collect genetic material to reverse millennia of damage to their DNA and made soul agreements to conduct the necessary abductions. Because they simply do not "get" emotions, they may seem cold and clinical in their interactions with us, but actually they have great love and appreciation for us.

The Zetas' goals and intentions are honorable and when their work is complete, they will return to their home world, which cannot be said for the Greys, their negative counterparts. Following an intense nuclear civil war that rendered the surface of their planet uninhabitable, the two factions had to live underground, and over many millennia, their spiritual evolution took very different paths.

Greys: the epitome of service-to-self, they see Earth and her inhabitants as resources to be exploited and enslaved. They, too, conduct abductions, although with none of the care of the Zetas. Since our first encounter with Greys during the Roswell incident, the Greys, according to Theodore, have traded technology with our governments in return for power and the freedom to conduct abductions without official opposition. Having been in league with them for over fifty years, our government has very few options and the Greys want to keep it that way. The last thing they want is for the American people to learn about them because their power lies in being able to coerce the government behind the scenes.

Evidence of ET Influence

Many people ask me at my seminars, "If what you say about ETs and our planet is true, how come we don't have any evidence?" And I usually reply, "We have tons of evidence but science brushes it off, religions are scared of it and try to cover it up, and governments deny it."

So what is this evidence? Let's take a look.

Crop Circles

Every summer, hundreds of pieces of evidence turn up in our fields that almost certainly is the work of extraterrestrials. And each summer, I'm amazed at how they're ignored by the "authorities," who should be issuing university grants to go out and study the things instead of denying them. In fact, they spend more money debunking crop circles than they do studying them. This vital task is left to private individuals like Colin Andrews.

Ancient Mysteries

Archeological evidence abounds of ET involvement on this planet for millennia, even millions of years. Researchers like Brad Steiger and Tricia McCannon have brought critical information to light, such as complex electronic circuitry found *inside* rock formations that are many millions of years old. How did they get there? Who put them there?

Unfortunately, evidence such as this is so "far out" that any serious researchers who even ask these questions promptly and mysteriously get their grants cut off because the fuddy-duddies in academia can't see beyond the bifocals perched on their scholarly noses. Research seems to move at the speed of a glacier, and sudden "shocks" to the academic system are to be avoided at all costs.

Consider the mysterious lines etched in the ground at Nazca in Peru. Built to a vast scale, they portray the outlines of animals and are, some argue, paths for meditative walking to emulate the energy of the particular animal, while others argue that they are landing markers for arriving UFOs.

Consider the remarkable Sumerian tablets, dating back to about 3000 BC and painstakingly translated by Professor Zecharia Sitchin, that tell a remarkable story of how *Homo sapiens* emerged on this planet around 24,000 BC, courtesy of the genetic engineering of a species of ET called the Nefilim. In his book, *The 12th Planet*, Sitchin translates ancient Sumerian tablets that reveal that until about 50,000 years ago, Cro-Magnon Man was the pinnacle of Earth's native life. But around that time, *Homo sapiens* suddenly emerged with the ability to use tools, build structures, and farm the land. After millions of years of Neanderthal stagnation, this new species emerged almost overnight. Why the sudden discontinuity in evolution?

Sitchin's admirable work reveals that a planet the Sumerians called Marduk, or Niburu, periodically enters our solar system on its long, 3,600 year elliptical orbit around the sun. Coincidentally, the lineage of Sumerian god-kings reveals a 3,600-year pattern, as though the arrival of Marduk signaled a "changing of the guard."

The tablets name the godly inhabitants of Marduk the Nefilim, along with a subordinate race, the Anunnaki, who appear to serve as overseers of the native peoples of Earth that were co-opted into the Nefilim mining operations. The texts reveal how the Nefilim brought the skills of agriculture and cattle raising to the planet, but were faced with a mutiny among the Anunnaki who objected to the hard manual labor involved.

The Nefilim undertook to create a new "worker race" from the already existing *Homo erectus*, and fashion it *in their image*. This meant, according to the texts, that not only did the new race have Nefilim DNA, but was also able to host their souls. To do this, the Nefilim fertilized *Homo erectus* ova with their own genes and implanted them in female Nefilim to await birth. They early hybrids were infertile but after more genetic work, they could procreate among themselves. This created problems because the Nefilim males began their own unofficial "breeding program" with the hybrid females.

Eventually, *Homo sapiens* emerged from the experiments with mental and emotional "hooks" able to host higher dimensional beings. The newly emergent species worshipped their creator-gods, toiling long and hard—exactly what they had been designed for. The Nefilim "gods" ruled Mesopotamia for millennia, while the new "thinking man" spread out to many parts of the world.

The texts tell us that around 11,000 BC, the approach of Marduk coincided with the end of the last ice age and brought tidal waves and devastating weather changes but, after its passing, that region of Mesopotamia enjoyed unparalleled growth and civilization. For the Nefilim, however, their culture declined, and these once omnipotent gods became no more than local rulers, overlords, and priests. Soon they were assimilated in Earth's cultures, but what a legacy they had brought to planet Earth. According to Barbara Hand Clow in *The Pleiadian Agenda*, this legacy also includes a planetary grid that has been controlling our emotions and perceptions of reality. She goes on to say that using this "Net," the Anunnaki have controlled the planet from the fourth dimension ever since. But under pressure from other ETs, they have agreed to dismantle the Net and cease their control. Again, time will tell.

For another fascinating story of ET/native contact, consider the ancient legends of the Dogon tribe in Africa. To this day, they revere carvings of people in "flying suits" who they believe come from a *binary* star system which turned out to be Sirius. All this long before astronomers discovered only in the fifties that Sirius is, in fact, a binary system. Some anthropologists dismiss this evidence, claiming that the Dogon people were "polluted" by inexperienced researchers who planted the evidence.

The Sphinx and the Pyramids

What about the theory that the primitive peoples living in ancient Egypt about 4,500 years ago (the current archeological dating) built structures incorporating advanced math, using methods that defy even today's civil engineers? The hand of ETs is no more clearly evident anywhere than in these amazing structures and here's why.

When you look at the pyramids, you see the absurdity of science trying to prove itself to itself, talking itself into thinking that it has all the answers. Current official thinking among Egyptologists is that the pyramids were built by King Cheops around 2750 BC by primitive peoples just out of the Stone Age, in order to house their dead king. For a primitive people to even bury their dead is remarkable, let alone build incredible monuments that we can't even replicate today.

Built allegedly in the 4th dynasty (2900-2750 BC), these pyramids alone remain, while 3rd and 5th dynasty monuments are today just piles of rock. If this is true, where did the necessary skills suddenly come from and why did they vanish just as quickly? Traditional Egyptologists don't like these kinds of questions and brush them aside as irrelevant.

If the Giza pyramids are just tombs, why is it that the ratio of their circumference to height is *exactly* the same as the ratio of the Earth's circumference to its diameter? The official line is … coincidence. How did these primitives even know the Earth was round, when science wouldn't discover that until 400 years later? And how come they're aligned *perfectly* to the cardinal compass points? Again, coincidence. How did they manage to get the 750-foot sides accurate to within five inches, or lift 200-ton stone blocks hundreds of feet up?

How were hard granite blocks so expertly carved out to make a sarcophagus when even today we can't do it? And what about those curious "air conditioning" shafts into the King and Queen's chambers that run in straight diagonal lines with a machinist's precision? And how come you can look up through them to see *exactly* where Orion and Sirius would have been 12,000 years ago? Again, coincidence, says the official line. (Orion and Sirius were the reputed homes of Osiris and Isis respectively, two dominant names in Egyptian lore, and believed responsible for bringing civilization to the Nile Valley.) Coincidence? I don't think so.

Why is the third, smaller pyramid offset from the diagonal connecting the two larger pyramids? Researcher Robert Bauval pointed out in 1993 that in the three stars making up Orion's belt, the third star is offset *exactly* as is the third pyramid from the diagonal, except that the match is perfect *only* if we go back to 10,500 BC. How did the early Egyptians even know what Orion's Belt looked like in 10,500 BC, let alone care?

There are only two possible explanations. First, the pyramids were built around 2750 BC using stellar maps and building techniques inherited from a much older culture, now long forgotten. But why? Or second, this ancient culture actually built them much earlier as monuments to their civilization, their wisdom, and possibly their home world. Were they, perhaps, telling us where they came from? But the pyramids may be much older than even that according to researcher Larry Hunter. He contends that the stones used in the pyramids weren't quarried but *poured* using some long forgotten technology in the same way we pour concrete today. According to Hunter, for reasons he cites in his book, *Project Gateway to Orion*, co-authored with Alex Knott, the pyramids may, in fact, be several million years old (see Reading List and Resources).

As to that date of 10,500 BC, Hunter points out that every 26,000 years, the stars repeat their configuration, so the pyramids could have been built any multiple of 26,000 years before then.

An equally baffling puzzle sits right alongside the pyramids—the Sphinx. The feline body and human head are carved out of a huge natural rock outcrop. The Sphinx is officially dated around 2750 BC but evidence suggests that it, too, is much older, according to researcher John Anthony West. West points out that the head is much better preserved than the rest of the body, but is much smaller than it should be, suggesting that the head was recarved sometime later than the original carving. Much later, in the 4th dynasty, according to West and Hancock, the ruler Khephrin recarved this already ancient monument with a human face, thus obliterating the original lion's head. Was it to look like the pharoah who ordered the facelift? West asks this and many more questions in his books and tapes (see Reading List).

In 2750 BC, the sun rose in the zodiac sign of Taurus, so why would a king, asks Graham Hancock, West's co-researcher, carve a statue of a lion? Only in the 11th millennium BC would the dawn sun break over the horizon directly into the face of the Sphinx and under the constellation of Leo. Was this the builders' way of telling us when they carved this magnificent monument? But again, this same circumstance would repeat itself every 26,000 years.

West heaps on even more evidence. The erosion of the body of the Sphinx is caused by *water*, not wind-blown sand as Egyptologists claim. Only thousands of years of torrential rain could have worn rock as we see on the Sphinx. But when in history did torrential rain fall in the Nile basin? At the end of the last Ice Age, about 12,000 years ago!

According to geologists, during the last Ice Age, the northern hemisphere was covered in a layer of ice up to two miles thick. This all ended "in the blink of an eye" in geological terms, creating havoc in planetary weather patterns—hurricanes and rain for thousands of years. And just as suddenly, the lush, fertile Nile region became the arid desert we see today.

Why, I ask, would the authorities of Egypt dismiss such overwhelming evidence and the theories of Hancock, West, and Hunter? Because to accept their ideas would take credit for these major monuments away from the Egyptian people and give it to a much older civilization, probably extraterrestrial, long departed by the time the primitive tribes of the Nile Valley formed the ancient culture of Khem, today known as Egypt. So in the face of such nationalistic pride, we are denied thorough and exhaustive research into what is truly both a gift and a challenge to humanity as a whole.

Drunvalo Melchizedek, a guest on my May 6, 1998, radio show told my stunned audience that in 1996, Larry Hunter and other researchers had discovered a vast network of tunnels under the Giza complex spreading out great distances. And apparently the authories are hushing this up.

Larry Hunter was also a guest speaker at a workshop in Oakland on May 23, 1998 in which he gave more details about this and even more staggering discoveries. For example, he revealed that this network led out from a huge underground "city" 450 feet down and 12 stories deep, covering an area of 6½ by 8 miles. Hunter believes that the complex was some kind of planetary nerve center serving many functions. We were left with the certain conviction that the pyramids were certainly not burial markers for the pharoahs.

Larry Hunter also talked about Bauval's theory of a correlation between the three Giza pyramids and the Belt of Orion. Apparently, Bauval couldn't quite make his theory work. Larry discovered a mistake in Bauval's calculations and went on to show that the correlation actually applies to more than just the three central stars.

If the Orion constellation (corrected for time and declination) is superimposed on a map of the area, every star corresponds to an ancient sacred site. Often all that remains of the structure are stones strewn about the desert, but the stone is of the *exact* same type used in the Giza pyramids. The fact that often local buildings use the stone suggests that some of the sacred structures were demolished at some point for building materials.

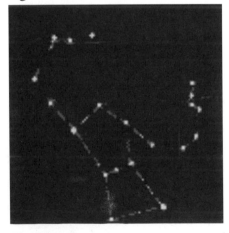

The Orion System

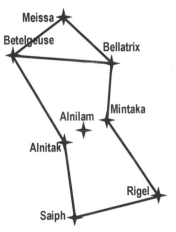

Stars of Orion (corrected)

The stars Rigel, Saiph, Betelgeuse, and the three stars of the Belt relate to established sites, but the theoretical locations of the Bellatrix and Meissa counterparts led Hunter to the telltale white stones.

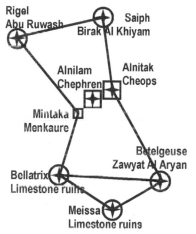

We can only speculate as to why these ancient builders deemed it important to recreate the Orion constellation on the Egyptian landscape. Was it perhaps to recapture the energy of home?

In the same presentation, Hunter astonished the audience by talking about a vast chamber inside the Great Pyramid that he has named The Hall of Osiris. Soaring hundreds of feet up from below ground level to just under the King's Chamber, this room is one of Egypt's best kept secrets. According to Hunter, from this room, a vertical shaft at the exact center of the pyramid drops down thousands of feet, on its way intersecting with the network of underground roadways beneath the Giza Plateau.

In order to get the word out to the world, Hunter has disclosed incredible detail on the websites at www.amargiland.com and www.hall-of-osiris.com. Who do we believe? The Egyptian establishment with everything to gain by claiming national ownership of these vast monuments or mavericks such as Hunter with nothing to gain or lose by revealing the truth. Only time will tell.

Physical Evidence

UFO folklore abounds with amazing stories such as the famous incident at Roswell, NM, on July 2, 1947, in which the Air Force immediately issued a press release announcing the crash of a "flying saucer," as they were called then. This story was soon replaced by another press release claiming that it was really a weather balloon—a very common piece of equipment. This weather balloon was quickly bundled on to an airplane and flown under great secrecy to Wright Patterson Air Force Base (then called simply Wright Field), home of the Army/Air Force Foreign Technology Division. Some weather balloon!

To add insult to injury, the Air Force later dismissed claims by many of the locals that they'd seen the actual bodies of the ETs by telling them that all they'd seen were crash dummies.

One person who is infuriated by the government's cover-up is this country's leading UFO researcher, Bob Dean (see Chapter 10). On the Art Bell Show on May 7, 1998, Bob reported that the British Royal Air Force allegedly routinely tracks battleship-sized UFOs which fly at speeds of over 30 times the speed of sound, or about 25,000 mph, and can change shape in mid-flight. According to Dean, a senior RAF officer has gone on record to say that these craft have been logged by the RAF's state-of-the-art phased-array radar system in North Yorkshire, England as they zigzag at these incredible speeds.

When Art asked if Bob had any specific evidence of UFO existence, Bob said that he could fill a truck with memos and photographs, and that if Congress could summon up the courage to hold formal hearings, he could fill the room with eye-witnesses who were willing to risk everything to reveal what they knew.

Bob talked specifically about two little-known incidents. The first allegedly occurred in the sixties at Timmensdorf, Germany in which a UFO crashed killing the crew of 12 Greys. The British recovered the craft and their findings were documented in the legendary "Assessment" report (see Chapter 10).

Reportedly prepared between 1961 and 1964, the Assessment is said to conclude that: (1) ETs have been studying planet Earth for centuries for some reason unknown; (2) at least four species of ET were involved; (3) their intentions are probably not hostile, because if they had been, their superior technology could have made short work of mankind; and (4) there's not a single thing we can do about it, so why worry.

Bob also revealed astonishing details of an alleged 1981 incident over a North Dakota Minuteman missile silo in which ETs scrambled a missile's navigation system and melted down its ten-megaton warhead. When a security team arrived, they found the UFO still hovering over the silo and the 20-ton silo door lying about 30 feet away. They began firing on the UFO and distinctly heard their rifle bullets ricochet off the craft's outer hull. This demonstration apparently threw the Pentagon into a panic out of which came the Strategic Defense Initiative, or the Starwars program, under President Reagan.

Bob concluded the Art Bell interview with the observation that he regarded the incident as an ET warning to humanity: We are watching you.

Sightings

Dozens of sightings are reported every day—just browse the Internet—but the rash of sightings in recent times began in 1947, the year of Roswell. For example, a very credible witness, search and rescue pilot and deputy federal marshal Kenneth Arnold was flying past Mt. Rainier en route for Yakima on June 24, 1947. He saw a formation of nine saucer-shaped craft flying at what he later calculated as over 1,000 mph. One inventive reporter would call them "flying saucers." The term stuck.

Explanations abounded but the one selected by Dr. J. Allen Hynek, who headed the government probe, was "mirage." Arnold, an experienced pilot, contested this, but the controversy was swept aside by the daily stream of newer sightings. Behind the scenes, however, the military was on alert. Humanity was not the only species on this planet with technology.

Another credible sighting came a year later, courtesy of Lt. George Gorman of the U.S. Air Force. On October 1, 1948, over Fargo, ND, Gorman reported that his P-51 Mustang followed a UFO for several minutes, narrowly missing a midair collision with it. Just before impact, the other craft shot straight upwards at incredible speed. Official explanation: weather balloon.

The first casualty of the great UFO chase came on the afternoon of January 7, 1948. Captain Thomas Mantell led four Air National Guard P-51 Mustangs dispatched to investigate a sighting over Godman, KY. As the UFO climbed, Mantell reportedly ignored standing orders (and commonsense) to fly no higher than 15,000 feet. Intending to level off at 25,000 feet, he apparently passed out, lost control of his aircraft, and was unconscious when it spiraled down to earth. Why an experienced pilot would do this without oxygen is still a mystery. Hynek's first conclusion was that they had been chasing the planet Venus (at 3 p.m.!), but he revised this in 1952 to … guess what? A weather balloon!

As a goverment spokesman and the official "debunker," Hynek was in a difficult position. He was the one who had to come out with these outrageous explanations that would fool no one with an IQ higher than a houseplant. However, once he had left government service, he could "come out of the closet" and reveal what he knew. With Jacques Vallee, in 1975 he wrote *The Edge of Reality: A progress report on unidentified flying objects*—the very book I was reading in 1977 just prior to my abduction. That book disappeared during the abduction and, curiously, it was not until I was writing this book in April, 1998 that I found a used copy in a bookstore.

The reports of sightings climbed steadily in number over the next few years, culminating in July, 1952, when several UFOs flew over the White House. Fighter jets scrambled to curb this infraction of forbidden airspace, only to find that the UFOs wanted to play cat-and-mouse with them. Hoards of reporters besieged the military for answers and got them: a meteor shower. At least it wasn't those pesky weather balloons up to no good.

Probably this country's most notable recent sighting occurred on March 13, 1997 in the night skies over Phoenix. Seen by thousands of people and recorded on untold numbers of video cameras, a formation of several bright lights moved slowly across the sky, starting at around 7:30 p.m. over the Superstition Mountains and ending around 2:00 a.m. over Rainbow Valley. Witnesses disagreed on whether it was one huge craft or several smaller ones. Media response was patchy; some reported it and others totally ignored it. The "official" explanation? Flares dropped from an Air National Guard plane.

The mystery of one craft versus several was solved when the famous lights returned on the nights of January 12 and 13, 1998. They took a variety of configurations that would be impossible for lights on one large ship, thus proving that there were about seven separate craft involved. (For more information on these events, see the website: www.phoenixlights.org.)

Contact and Abductions

Abduction stories began with the famous Betty and Barney Hill story of September 19, 1964. They reported that their car was pursued by a high-speed "weather balloon" and they stopped to look at it through binoculars. They were able to see about a dozen occupants (a weather balloon manned by crash dummies?).

When they got home, the Hills found that they couldn't account for two missing hours. Under hypnosis, it came out that the occupants took them into the craft and subjected them to a variety of clinical tests. They told the Hills that they came from Zeta Reticuli, even pointing out their home star on a star map. (No dummies!)

The crash dummy explanation wore even thinner in 1975 when Travis Walton was abducted by more Zetas in Arizona, witnessed by the six other members of his logging team. They saw the beam of intense blue light strike Walton and knock him down. They fled the scene but returned later to find Walton missing. Suspicion that the six had murdered him was averted only by Walton's reappearance five days later.

Under hypnosis, Walton described many of the hallmarks of the classic abduction experience that would surface over the next decade. Made into the movie, *Fire in the Sky*, the story publicly aired the whole abduction issue, but even that was eclipsed by *Communion*, the Hollywood version of Whitley Strieber's experience. But unlike Walton, who resisted his terrifying memories, Strieber welcomed them as "shock therapy" that blows apart our limited pictures of reality and replaces them with something much larger. Following the phenomenal success of *Communion*, Strieber went on to write *Transformation* and *Majestic*.

In August 1976, four men were night-fishing at Allagash Lake in the wilderness of Maine when a bright light appeared over their canoe and a beam of light shot out of the object. The next thing they remember was being back on land, finding their roaring camp fire burnt out. Tired and dazed, they didn't question the missing three hours until much later. It was not until 1978 that the four would begin having *identical* nightmares of having the same medical procedures performed on them in some unknown place with large insect-like faces looking down at them. Regressive hypnosis revealed both interlocking details and a shared terror. What happened has never been satisfactorily explained.

The Out-of-Body Abduction Syndrome

Abduction ... the ultimate mind-blower. Over the years, countless abduction cases have been documented around the world. But there is a phenomenon that involves far more people, one that's not talked about—the Out-of-Body Abduction Syndrome, or OBA. Of course, most of the *reported* abduction cases involve physical abduction but my research has uncovered that far more cases are non-physical, or out-of-body abductions, in which people's consciousness is literally pulled out of their bodies and taken who knows where.

During my lectures around the country, many attendees report having weird dreams in which strange-looking people enter their bedroom and take them to some kind of vehicle. Without speaking, the abductors communicate with them, teach them, maybe show them some form of hieroglyphic writing. Does this sound familiar to you?

Serious research on this phenomenon is still lacking. According to my good friend and colleague, Dr. Richard Boylan, author of *Close Extraterrestrial Encounters*, as many as 60 percent of abductions could be out-of-body, leaving only 40 percent physical, and even the vast majority of the latter are written off as just "bad dreams."

To understand this syndrome fully, we must realize that with ETs, we are dealing with inter-dimensional phenomena that do not conform to our limited three-dimensional science. When we try to squeeze these into concepts such as height, width and depth, we inevitably run into trouble.

Contact, Abduction, and Possession

When dealing with out-of-body encounters with ETs, there are some obvious warning signs, and repeated encounters call for some form of spiritual protection. For example, each night, I ask for the guidance and protection of my angels and surround my house with the Christ Light. There is no set procedure for this; do what feels intuitively right to you.

A pioneer in this field is my good friend, Jim Downey, spiritual healer, psychic, and clinical hypnotherapist. According to Jim, the Out-of-Body Abduction Syndrome (OBA) can take one of three forms:

- *Conscious Out-of-Body Abduction (COBA)* which most commonly occurs without warning. People suddenly find themselves in totally alien settings, most commonly on a spacecraft, surrounded by unfamiliar objects and instruments. All reported abductions begin while people are conscious, regardless of what they were doing, their attitude, or their frame of mind at the time of abduction.
- *Altered State Out-of-Body Abduction (ASOBA)* which can occur while a person is using mind-altering drugs, including anesthetic and extreme intoxication, while chanting or meditating, or while asleep.
- *Unconscious Out-of-Body Abduction (UOBA)* which can occur when a person receives a blow to the head. Since such accidents are rare, so are UOBAs.

Regardless of the type, an OBA experience usually leaves the person with various degrees of fear, anger, confusion, and anxiety. The residual effects may cause the person difficulty in grounding, focusing, meditating, holding down a job, and even functioning within society.

Anyone who believes that they have been, or are, the target of OBA should seek a holistic healer who emphasizes spiritual intervention.

As for possession, just about every culture, religion, and society on the planet acknowledges some type of this phenomenon. In his professional practice, Jim has encountered and released countless cases of spirit attachment, which usually fall into one of three types:

- *Alien, extraterrestrial, and non-human.* These may have interdimensional origins, or come from planets in other systems. These beings are usually results-driven and relentless in their obsessive desire to obtain data from what they see as their "assignments." This may involve implanting etheric or physical probes in their human subjects. Most non-human attachments stem from bioengineering experiments dating back to Atlantis, about 14,000 years ago. The products of these experiments were treated as "freaks," and often either tortured or enslaved. This mistreatment may have caused them to remain trapped in the earth plane.

- *Human.* In general, human attachments come from a spirit who, at death, did not make it to the Light. Often termed a "ghost," if the entity wanted to experience physical sensation, it would attach to a living human, usually without that person's knowledge or permission. Someone who is particularly vulnerable may have many such attachments, which can mislead a therapist into thinking the client has Multiple Personality Disorder (MPD). The target of possession experiences confusion, interference, and often physical pain.

- *Demonic.* This is the most well-known and talked about type of possession, and originated from God's battle with Lucifer (see Revelation 12:7–12). Lucifer is also known as Satan, the Devil, and the Lord of Darkness. There are various levels of demonic possession, with diabolic (the Devil) and satanic (Satan) being the levels of greatest risk and danger.

Jim recommends that anyone suffering from possession or attachment deal with this compromise of spiritual sovereignty as soon as possible.

Billy Meier

In 1975, Swiss-born Billy Meier announced to the world the truly breath-taking tale that he was in weekly contact with a Pleiadian named Semjase from Erra, the Pleiadian home planet.

According to Randolph Winters in *The Pleiadian Mission*, Earth has been observed and gently guided by the Pleiadians for close to 230,000 years. But it was our more recent past that caused them to take a more personal interest. It began during a war between Atlantis and Mu which threatened to end all life on Earth. These two great civilizations who had lived together for so long as friends had turned their mighty weapons of mass destruction against one another, causing the Earth to tremble and the oceans to leap from their shores and wash over the lands of its people. Millions died as the war came to an end in the year 9498 B.C. The atmosphere of earth was filled with the dark debris of death that would leave no room for life for 50 years. Earth fell into a dismal period that did not see the return of civilization for many thousands of years.

The Pleiadians, who have watched over Earth for countless millennia, are still concerned about our development of technology without the requisite spiritual wisdom to use it. Without actually intervening to prevent our species from self-destruction, they vowed to periodically feed us information that would cause us to question our headlong love affair with self-destruction. This was beautifully confirmed by my Pleiadian visitors in the summer of 1992.

The Pleiadians watched, knowing that the same situation would recur in the distant future. They enlisted the aid of a very advanced being who would periodically incarnate in a human body to guide humanity. One such appearance was as Gallileo Galilei (1564-1642) who challenged the Church's position that the sun rotated around the Earth. This cost him his freedom but took science irrevocably into a new future.

Another incarnation of this ancient spirit began on February 3, 1937, as a son born to a Swiss farmer and his wife. Named Eduard, the boy led an ordinary life until the age of five, when a Pleiadian teacher began to coach him and unlock his ancient memories. This coaching went on until his late teens and then ceased so that the young man could set up a normal life. This sojourn ended, however, when a long-predicted bus accident robbed him of the use of his left arm.

Enter Semjase, a Pleiadian researcher and teacher, who jumped at the opportunity to work with planet Earth and its inhabitants. Before leaving Erra, her home system, she learned German from their archives. Unfortunately their archives were out-of-date and she learned 16th century King's German, the equivalent of someone today talking like Shakespeare.

On January 28, 1975, Semjase telepathically contacted Billy (an adopted nickname after his boyhood hero, Billy the Kid) and asked him to go to a remote mountain area with a camera. A silver "beamship" appeared and Semjase stepped out into the afternoon sun. Dressed in a gray flightsuit, she was totally human in appearance, with a self-assurance and poise that matched her beauty.

All the years of Billy's preparation paid off and he quickly entered into a lengthy conversation with Semjase. Her agenda was to inform humanity that: (1) Pleiadians have long observed us; (2) they look just like us; (3) being a much older culture, they have more advanced technology and psychic powers; (4) being human, they are "on our side" but cannot directly interfere in how we run our planet; and (5) this was to be the first of many meetings in which she would convey to Billy a body of knowledge approved by the Pleiadian High Council.

Before leaving, she told him they would meet weekly on her ship and that he should bring his camera to record undeniable evidence of her existence. After each meeting, Billy was to type up his notes and eventually publish them, along with the photographs. But Billy's famous *Contact Notes* were received with a mixed reaction, ranging from avid fascination to outright ridicule. Fortunately, a small group of believers quickly formed around him to help handle the enormous workload.

The photographs taken by Billy of Semjase's craft have been thoroughly analyzed. Their clarity is unparalleled but supporters claim that Billy's detractors have tampered with genuine photos to make them look fake in order to discredit him. Billy explains that the Pleiadians allow the controversy so as to let us make up our own minds. Truth or convenient excuse? That's exactly what the Pleiadians want us to decide for ourselves.

After three years, 115 meetings, thousands of photos, and 1,800 pages of notes, Semjase suffered a fall and had to return to Erra. This interrupted contact and the High Council decided that enough information had been relayed. Following their last meeting on October 19, 1978, many fine books have come out of Billy's meetings but probably Randolph Winter's account of the history of Billy Meier and the information given by Semjase in *The Pleiadian Mission* is the best place to start for any-one interested in this fascinating story. We will return to the teachings of the Pleiadians in Chapter 15, but for now, I heartily recommend Randolph's book (see Reading List).

The Great American Cover-up: "ET-gate" in the making?

In what may well end up being "ET-gate" or "UFO-gate," our gov-ernment, in common with most other governments on this tiny planet, is keeping a monumental secret—the truth of UFO/ET contact—from its citizens, i.e., you and I. The ironic thing is that a 1997 CNN/*Time* poll revealed that 80 percent of the U.S. population believes that *the government is hiding knowledge from us*. When four out of five people believe their government is lying to them, that's a country in deep trouble.

Any concerned citizen trying to get to the bottom of this by citing the Freedom of Information Act is given the run-around between vari-ous government agencies such as the National Archives. If a document *is* released, just about every word is blacked out. If there's nothing to the whole UFO/ET business, why the cover-up?

I must stress that this is not meant to be critical of the government; I'm just enjoying the absurdity of the situation. The current administra-tion has inherited its plight from the late days of World War II when UFOs, nicknamed "Foo Fighters," buzzed planes of both the Allied and Axis air forces. Both sides assumed that the craft were secret weapons of the other side. As WWII gave way to the Cold War, paranoia stepped up and both sides buried the whole issue under a national security blan-ket, safe from the prying eyes of curious citizens.

This was a reasonable precaution on the part of a government trying to protect its citizens, but when both sides of the Cold War 'fessed up to each other about being in the dark, why didn't they both come clean? Possibly because if our countries' military forces admitted that they don't have air superiority, then why do we need trillion dollar defense budgets for the promise of keeping our skies safe.

Yes, the UFOs are out there, but the government can't admit to having lied to the citizens of the United States, so they *have* to perpetu-ate the lie just to cover up the lying. Damned if they do, and damned if they don't. Hence the Great American Cover-up.

With each new presidential inauguration, I hope to hear the words, "Citizens of the United States, I have something to tell you ...." I'm not holding my breath but the Great American Cover-up is getting harder to maintain. Repeated appearances of UFOs in known hot spots are building expectations of more sightings in the near future which *no one* could deny. Already citizens of Mexico City go out on their roof tops expecting sightings, and they are not disappointed. For a startling photo of a UFO over Mexico City on August 6, 1997, see Art Bell's website: www.artbell.com and make up your own mind.

Cover up or not, ETs are in our skies, on our land, and beneath the ground and they seem to have no intention of leaving. If they won't leave, our governments have little alternative but to bow to the inevitable and admit that they are here. So let's take a look at how First Contact might go.

First Contact

Everyone on this planet is at a different level of acceptance of ETs and UFOs. Some people are tuned into ETs and eagerly await their arrival, whereas others are still terrified of "little green men from Mars." So how is this going to play out?

Slowly, in order to avoid any sense of something being done to us. The one thing *we* must do on our end, however, is to be free of fear. Suppose you wake up on a strange planet or find a bunch of ETs in your bedroom. If you accept that either you consciously asked for the experience or your soul did, so what? There's really nothing to fear. But for those still afraid of ETs, it's another matter.

ETs know that society is a fragile thing that could be torn part by a mass landing. If the population was suddenly faced with an overwhelming presence of ETs, angels, or whatever, how would we react? We might demand that the Air Force blow them out of the skies, but our weapons are no match. Without military superiority, the government is helpless. So the citizenry takes to the streets in the biggest civilian insurrection ever. How would that serve?

My feeling is that the sporadic sightings will continue amidst widespread cover-up and denial. Meanwhile, the media does its work, preparing a whole new generation which, within a decade, will have a strong voice ... and the vote.

Unlike the bug-eyed monsters of the fifties and the "Greys" commonly seen in the media, what is not widely known is that many species of ET look just like you and I. This is not surprising since it's now widely accepted by many researchers that our species was genetically engineered and brought here to "seed" this planet. Where did the DNA, or genetic blueprint, for our bodies come from? The genetic engineers themselves so, of course, we look like them and they look like us. It's highly likely that our first major contact will be no more shocking than watching a bunch of tourists getting off a tour bus.

I once made this point in a very dramatic and effective way. I was part of a panel discussion with Ruben Uriarte, Tricia McCannon, Angela Browne-Miller, and Whitley Strieber. At the end of my presentation, I asked the audience if they would like to see a full-length image of a bunch of ETs. Of course, they loudly cried, "Yes!"

"Okay, then," I said, and propped up a six-foot high, mystery object in front of them, covered by a blue satin cloth.

"Ladies and gentlemen," I announced, "I will now reveal the images of the ETs!"

With a flourish, I whisked the cover off a full-length mirror! The audience went wild at this simple truth. "You are they; they are you; we are one."

So, if you want to see an ET, look in the mirror.

Take the Pleiadians, for example. The Pleiades is a group of a few thousand planets rotating around a few hundred stars, seven of which are visible to the naked eye. Many different lifeforms have developed there, some of them descendents of our common ancestors, the Lyrans, and they are physically *identical* to us, except for slightly larger eyes.

Why are the ETs so much more advanced than us technologically and psychically? Look at the advances our science has made in just the last one hundred years. Think what science will achieve in *five hundred* years, or *one thousand* years. Now imagine where we'll be in *one million* years, which isn't really all that long in our planet's history. That's the kind of head start the Pleiadians have over us, so it's no wonder they've solved problems we don't even know we have yet. And in the distant future, I'm sure that we'll be helping out some primitive culture on some planet we haven't even heard of.

According to Theodore in Gina Lake's book, *The Extraterrestrial Vision*, human contact with ETs has already occurred many times and each time it was not accepted for what it was because people refused to believe what was before their eyes. Most who do remember are traumatized by their memories and laughed at or persecuted. Since contact under these circumstances only causes problems and pain, the ETs will not contact us until we are ready. They want to avoid mass denial and repression because this would cause undue pain and delay the achievement of their goals.

Theodore foresees three possible reactions to the appearance of ETs here on Earth:

1. The media ignores the announcement or the government or military try to cover it up.
2. The media treats the announcement as a joke, dismisses it, and then buries the story.
3. The world takes the announcement seriously and open, honest dealings begin between national governments and ETs under public scrutiny, much like the proceedings of the United Nations.

The role of the media is obviously key in the first official contact. ETs have always seen it as a powerful force for good that can be used for education and improved understanding between nations.

First contact, Theodore says, is likely to "stop the world temporarily" as news spreads and is processed by each person. People will react differently, depending on how rigid their beliefs are, and how well they've been prepared. For example, the *Star Trek* generation will take the news a lot differently than, say, a fundamentalist Christian in the mid-west, who might see ETs as Satan's emissaries. Some will adjust readily and eagerly, but others will feel that their lives have just been upturned, as did the Aztecs on the appearance of the 16th century Spanish Conquistadors. Theodore warns us that our meeting with extraterrestrials will be no less upsetting than that. Once such a meeting is made, however, history is changed from that point forward. ETs want it to be a positive experience, not a fearful one.

Another warning from Theodore: Not only will we find intellectual differences between us and the ETs, but differences in spiritual evolution. The enormous love, acceptance, peace, and wisdom exuded by ETs will make many feel as if we are meeting gods. Some will want to worship them, but the ETs will have none of it, stressing instead our own godhood. They do not want power *over* us, but want us to embrace our own power. They see this as a "family reunion," not a hostile takeover.

As far as appearances go, Theodore tells us that some species of even the most highly evolved ETs might appear hideous according to our narrow idea of what constitutes beauty. Eventually we will come to see that physical beauty is only one form of beauty as even these "hideous" creatures will evoke our love and respect. But, because we're not there yet, human-looking Pleiadians will be the first emissaries.

The Pleiadians, however, will not be alone. We will be approached by less positive ETs, who will try to pressure us with hype and promises. "Beware of sales pitches," Theodore warns. The positive ETs will not be pitching anything. They'll offer advice and solutions when asked, without insisting that we follow them.

Working with ETs will prove challenging. We already have difficulty with cross-cultural dealings such as when Americans and Japanese sit down at the negotiating table. Sensitivities can be easily bruised, even with the best of intentions. Imagine dealing with beings from other planets. However, Theodore stresses that we should focus on our shared concern for planet Earth and the welfare of the human race. This will help us overcome our differences.

Theodore is clear about how contact will *not* be made. "We will *not* disrupt the air waves and make a statement. This would be too sensational and controlling. We will *not* take control of anything in order to gain your attention, because this sends a message of aggression and dominance. The last thing we want to do is have you feel you are being taken over. For the same reason, we will not appear spectacularly on the White House lawn. Drama and splash are not our style."

Theodore affirms that, "We will contact the President of the United States because this is a matter of state, an official greeting on our part to your head of state." This will be followed by intermediaries setting up a private meeting with the President, undeniable proof of the Pleiadians' identity, and a program for informing the public. All the details have already been worked out. Now it's just a matter of how quickly John and Jane Citizen out there can get ready. Are you ready?

Life After Contact

According to Theodore, after contact and some integration time, the world of the future will see two forms of integration: the first, personal, and the second, societal, including racial, bearing in mind the variety of extraterrestrial races we'll be living with.

What will this personal integration feel like? We will have accepted our dark side, our shadow, and will love all our "nasty" emotions for what they are—pointers to our needs. "Denying your needs leads to depression, anger, resentment, and outbreaks of violence," he warns.

"Denying anger creates a backlash of violence and hatred, which fuels the cycle of negativity on Earth ... But a cycle of *love* also is possible in which love begets more love."

Acceptance goes hand-in-hand with forgiveness—acceptance for every member of society and forgiveness for those who make mistakes. We will accept and revere our racial differences because we understand their contribution to society's evolution and richness, to its ability to survive and thrive in an ever-changing world. A world in which we rub shoulders with ETs will emphasize racial integration where we relish acceptance and peaceful co-existence. Our ET teachers will show us how we and our neighbors can benefit each other and live peaceably." Rather than blame others for our ignorance and poor decisions, we will take responsibility for them, learn to make better choices, and organize our lives better. Then, we will not find it so hard to get along with each other.

Teachings of the Extraterrestrials

So what are they teaching us? After having read countless accounts of what ETs have revealed to abductees in person and to those able to receive messages telepathically, here's what seems to have happened.

Earth has been visited on and off for many millions of years, most notably by the Lyrans, ancestors of the Pleiadians. They co-existed with the primitive animal lifeforms of Earth, just as we do, leaving them pretty much alone. Interference was limited to the occasional genetic experiment or interbreeding that would produce interesting hybrids.

A few hundred thousand years ago, colonization was stepped up and more extensive genetic experiments produced a species more suitable for heavy manual labor as we have seen, possibly by enhancing *Homo erectus* to engineer Cro-Magnon man, and later *Homo sapiens*.

However, all sources point to something remarkable happening when the 26,000 year long Mayan calendar runs out at the end of the year 2012. For 26 millennia, this amazing timetable has governed and predicted events on Earth and it expires in just a few short years. What does this mean?

Most ET sources agree that it marks the shift of this planet and her inhabitants to a higher dimension. Some call it the fourth dimension and others the fifth, but what is certain is that we're leaving the third, with all its veils that block us from knowing the Truth, the Divine Blueprint.

In this Truth, old male-dominated stereotypes will fall away as every man, woman, and child comes into perfect balance. Long-buried emotions will have surfaced and will have been cleared, allowing spirit to move through us unimpeded.

This will require some action on our part, even if it's only to relax our rigid beliefs a little to allow this reality in. More likely, however, is that when people wake up to the awesome reality unfolding before them, most will rush into the streets to proclaim their truth to whomever will listen.

There's no question that we'll have all the ET help we can handle but WE MUST ASK! The ETs can't just barge into our lives; we must ask for their help and guidance. I suggest you ask silently in your heart as often as the thought crosses your mind: "Help me play my part in the Divine Blueprint."

A Message from Theodore

Let me close this chapter by turning to Theodore, who brought this message through Gina especially for the readers of this book. My thanks to Gina and Theodore for their tireless work in service to Source.

In the following passage, Theodore brings us some timely advice:

Extraterrestrials have been involved with you for eons. They are actively engaged with you now because you are moving into a new age, an age of greater enlightenment and peace. Before you can experience this, a cleansing will be necessary. Just as in your own lives, you experience difficulties intended to shift your consciousness, so Earth is experiencing difficulties as it shifts to a new order. Breakdown is often necessary before a new equilibrium can be established. Adjustments are being made now in the earth's mantle, which will initiate many changes, including a monumental shift in consciousness.

Extraterrestrials and nonphysical beings like ourselves are overseeing and facilitating this planetary shift. We work with your energy fields if you allow us to in order to help you heal, which is so essential in raising your own personal consciousness. We work through many healers, as well, both energetically and by intuitively guiding them. Many healers are now remembering and applying the healing technologies they developed in other dimensions before coming here.

We work with each of you in your dream state, and sometimes you travel with us to other planets or to spaceships where much of our work on your behalf is being carried out. We are performing experiments to better understand Earth's condition and its future needs. Your climate and other geological features are changing and will continue to change somewhat dramatically, and we are here to monitor that. We observe events on Earth, including the actions of your governments, to ascertain how your choices will affect the planetary changes and how we can best assist you.

We are taking special interest in you now, though, because you are at such a critical juncture and change is happening more quickly than at any other time in your world. We are here to help you through these changes, but first we must understand them ourselves.

Another way that we work with you is intuitively and psychically and we communicate with you more than you realize. Many of you are developed enough to receive our communications intuitively and psychically. The rest of you receive messages in the dream state.

Those of you who are able to receive our messages intuitively usually act on them because you are pre-programmed, if you will, to respond to suggestions that resonate with your mission. Many of you incarnated now to carry out specific tasks for Earth. Consequently, you have a certain inborn receptivity toward anything that relates to those tasks. When you pick up a suggestion intuitively and it resonates with you, then you more readily act on it. As a result, many of you are already doing the work that needs to be done to help Earth.

Be aware that many advanced beings have incarnated with the intent of creating disruption and chaos. Their high intelligence and technological know-how have been developed in other dimensions to undermine our efforts to help you. These individuals, however, are few compared to the numbers working for the good of the planet and they are not nearly as powerful. We allow them to do what they are doing because it is not for us to interfere with their free will. We are able to repair and counteract much of the damage they cause. You will have to handle what we can't repair; this is your lesson in all of this.

You must choose to fight evil yourselves. We are in this together. We can only do so much. We need your participation and we need you to invite us to help you. If you are choosing evil either by doing nothing or by not asking for help in overcoming it, then we will let you make that choice, for we have the deepest respect for your free will.

Let us outline our agenda for Earth. Above all, we want worldwide peace for you. For you to live in peace, you will have to share your resources. Until you are willing to do that, and to see every person as equally valuable and worthy of Earth's resources, there will be war. This is a tall order but we can help you unite your world through the many individuals working toward peace and love in your world.

Your future can be bountiful. There is no reason why you cannot all live in peace and abundance. We will show you how. Your population cannot continue to grow as it has, however, nor will it. Many natural factors are at work now to keep your population in check. Overpopulation is probably the biggest threat to your planet, but it will take care of itself, and you will have to accept nature's way of doing that. Earth will reclaim itself from you in certain ways which will be tragic for you but necessary. Learning to deal with these tragedies is part of your spiritual growth and a means for raising your consciousness. You will develop your inner resources and become stronger as you face these challenges. You will no longer be tempted to place materialism and other superficial goals above humane values.

You are part of a wonderful plan which includes not only you on Earth but many whose home is your galaxy. These are momentous times when you will come to know yourselves as galactic citizens and part of the evolution of something greater than just Earth. You will be asked to open your minds and your hearts in the times ahead. As always, we will be here to guide you. We have always been here but you will come to know us more intimately now. We are your galactic brothers and sisters, and we have come to welcome you into your larger family. We will show you around and teach you new ways. We are deeply grateful for this opportunity to speak with you so directly. But know that we can hear you whenever you address us and that your capacity for hearing us is greater than you realize. Blessings!

Part Two

What Does It All Mean?

Chapter 12

Where on Earth Am I?

We Landed On a Therapy Planet

Therapy: The treatment of illness or disability [Greek: therapeía]

"**P**lanet Earth is a therapy planet!" That opening to many of my seminars usually gets the audience's attention mainly because of how we typically define therapy, the treatment of dysfunction. I have a very different take on the subject. Most, if not all, mental conditions requiring therapy seem to me to be caused by conflict—conflict between parts of the person or between their reality and that of other people. Conflict in moderation is not a bad thing. Out of conflict comes change, and out of change, hopefully, comes growth. Where there is no conflict, there is no stimulus to change anything, so nothing changes and nothing grows.

If my car hits your car, we have conflict. Hopefully, I change by becoming a better driver; I have grown. How you choose to deal with the event is up to you. Hopefully, you will extract some growth or understanding from our conflict.

The ultimate conflict is between your ego and your soul. Your soul's one and only purpose in incarnating as you is *growth*. That's why anything, anywhere exists—to increase in learning, understanding, and wisdom through growth. The reason you-the-soul incarnates as you-the-ego is to set up a scenario where you can grow as quickly and effectively as possible. Of course, you're still growing between Earth lives but very few experiences are as conducive to rapid growth as life this side of the veils.

Let's begin with the plan. What do you need to know or understand? Do you-the-soul have any karmic debts from other lifetimes that you want to clear? Any behavioral patterns to break?

Next, you choose the gender, nationality, historical period, and DNA traits of your new incarnation-to-be. All this leads to your choice of parents and the imprinting you will receive. You carefully weigh all these factors and put together the package that will best serve you-as-soul.

Finally, the big day arrives. It's time to "drop in" on your new body. You say your good-byes to your soul family and you're almost ready. There's one last thing to do, the one thing that will make all this work. Your guides tell you, "You won't remember us and you won't remember this place. But we will be watching over you, nurturing you, guiding you. In fact, once you've squeezed into that tiny body, you won't remember a thing about who you really are."

Sure I'll remember; it can't be that hard, you say to yourself. How can I forget all this? you ask, looking at your guides, your buddies, the celestial temples, the angels. Of course, I'll remember! Whoosh! You're in a tiny little body, squeezing down the birth canal. It's dark. Your head hurts. Suddenly a blast of cold air hits you. Bright lights dazzle you. A sharp smack starts your breathing. Ouch!

WHERE ON EARTH AM I?

You're on your own, kid. Well, not quite alone. For several years, you'll be in conscious contact with your guides until someone tells you that big boys or girls don't have imaginary friends. By puberty, your hormones will become the dominating factor in your life as your body clock's alarm goes off and you'll have forgotten all about your guides.

Your guides never leave your side while you wallow in the Grand Illusion that you are separate from everyone and everything else. Even your connection with your own soul is forgotten, and when your closest soul buddies show up in your life disguised as lovers, bosses, colleagues, and so on, you don't even recognize them. Fortunately, our guides are still able to get through to most of us intuitively, and they do what they can (through the subconscious) to influence us to make choices that will be in keeping with our soul's plan.

The term "therapy" usually implies that you're broken and need fixing, that you've "lost it" and need help. The inner and outer conflict you experience is thought to be dysfunctional. Let's turn that around for a moment. Suppose we look at therapy like a research project in which we study not how various chemicals react with each other, but how the various parts of our being interact with one another and sometimes subvert each other. Therapy, then, would be an exciting journey into new truths.

We come to Earth, our therapy planet, to explore how emotions, thoughts, and physical sensations interact within us, and between us and other people. We are learning about our minds and emotions, relationships, the physical world, and how to manifest our desires. We are learning about being human and we are learning to be creators. Because we're not given the answers, our therapy planet is also a great mystery, which we have to solve.

Unraveling the Great Mystery is the greatest adventure we can have on this planet because as we dispel ignorance, we come to faith. In a world where uncertainty lurks at every turn, we want to find a place where we can feel safe and secure. That place is one of spiritual values and universal truths that are found externally in the great religions, and internally in the human heart. Our search is for that core of common values with which we all resonate. We are all searching for that which will bring us more hope, charity, love, and compassion. It all comes down to one thing: the relationship you-the-ego has with you-the-soul, which requires sincerity, humility, a willingness to learn, an open heart, and a passion for the truth.

I'd like to share with you some of the understanding that Theodore, the nonphysical being channeled by my dear friend, Gina Lake, has given her about the Divine Blueprint. The following is taken from an unpublished manuscript by Gina Lake called *Sojourn* and reproduced with permission.

The following myth is one conception of the story of Life, which shares many similarities with other creation stories from all over the world. It describes the state that we existed in before our incarnations on Earth and helps us appreciate the purpose of life on the physical plane.

In the beginning, was darkness and the Void. All That Is existed as undifferentiated energy, infinite and all-inclusive. Then, the Light was born and shined upon the Void. With the Light, came awareness of being, and the Divine smiled. This gave rise to an urge to further differentiate and explore that which is differentiated. Thus, the physical universes were born. The Divine breathed life into them by sending a portion of Itself into matter. This way, the Divine could experience life through the perspective of matter. Each new experience fueled the Creator's desire for further experience and differentiation. While encased in matter, we, as part of the creation, still know the Creator and long for the unity we have lost.

This desire to reunite with the Divine, to return to the primeval state, is the energy that fuels evolution. When evolution is complete, the Creator recalls that portion of Itself back unto Itself and sends forth others. The energy of creation is constantly in motion, moving from unity with the Creator to enmeshment in Its creations. In and out of creation, the creative energy moves, all the while expanding the Creator's understanding and love.

This is an allegory and shouldn't be taken too literally. The fact is that we are encased in forms that are temporarily incapable of grasping the truth of our Being and our origin. This should not and does not prevent most of us from trying to understand our origins and purpose for being here, however. And, fortunately, there does come a time when our intellectualizations about this are overshadowed by the experience of our Being. When this happens, we know we are not far from Home. For those who are yet unable to experience their Being fully, intellectual understanding or faith will have to suffice.

As the myth describes, All That Is differentiates and sends a portion of Itself into the myriad physical forms on our plane to experience this plane's diverse possibilities. The Creator breathes Life, or a portion of Itself, into matter. This Life expresses itself on many different levels: human, animal, plant, and mineral. These are the various kingdoms of matter, but of them all, humankind stands alone in its ability to contemplate its reality. Although we are instinctual, we also have free will. This is what separates us from other creatures. No other creation on Earth can think rationally, make choices, and learn from those choices the way we can. Our will, guided by our intellect, is what differentiates us from the animal, plant, and mineral kingdoms.

We use our free will not only while we are part of the physical world but in between those physical lifetimes. With our guides and Higher Self, we participate in choosing our next life's circumstances. We choose where we will be born, when, and to whom. We also choose our gender and our appearance. By choosing the moment of birth, we are choosing the astrology chart, which imprints us with certain personality traits and drives. By choosing our parents, we also are choosing our genetic makeup, which will play a large role in our future experiences but will by no means predetermine them. Our entire soul's plan, in fact, is encoded in our genes and it includes our life purpose and our karmic and other lessons. This plan, however, is general and broad and encompasses many possibilities. The details of this plan are determined by us through our free will. For example, it may be part of our plan to meet a particular person and marry that person, but how we meet, how that unfolds, whether we actually marry, and how we behave in that relationship is totally up to us. This is our story, our creation. Yes, we do in large part create our reality, but we must do it within the plan our soul has set or we are likely to experience considerable pain. Life has a way of keeping us on track. Still, we are always free to go against it. Fortunately, there are many ways we can fulfill our plan, many paths we can take and still be operating with this plan. Furthermore, the plan is sometimes modified if need be during the course of our lives. The soul must improvise as it co-creates with us since because of free will, the variables are so numerous.

To understand how this all works, we need to understand a little about reincarnation. Reincarnation states that we live many lifetimes in many different bodies with a period of review between lifetimes. It holds that we are spirit traveling through the world of matter, which is like a school for us. The lessons of the physical universe are many and varied, therefore demanding a variety of body types, historical periods, environments, people, cultures, and challenges. They also allow us to experience life through the ever-changing lens of our evolutionary status. Thus, a young soul will learn from a situation something different than an old soul in the same situation. So, not only do circumstances change as we evolve but also what we bring to them.

"But, why bother?" you may ask. "Why have all this pain and struggle?" The answer to this cannot be fully appreciated from the physical frame of reference. But once we are out of the body, why we bother is eminently clear: we choose to. Our soul eagerly embraces all experience and the opportunities these experiences afford for growth. When we quiet ourselves long enough in meditation to experience our Higher Self, or soul, we know this. We know our existence to be purposeful—and glorious.

Contrary to what many think about reincarnation, we are not on an endless treadmill or wheel, returning to life to make amends, only to reincarnate again in another imperfect form. No, we are here to evolve beyond the physical dimension. For that, perfection is not required, since human beings can never be perfect. For that, only understanding and love are required. When we have finished with the lessons of the physical plane, we move on to another dimension and its lessons. Just as certain lessons can only be learned on the physical plane, others can only be learned on other planes, which are not physical at all. Life is a progression; the wisdom gained in one lifetime is carried into the next and built upon. And this continues indefinitely in other dimensions.

We are continually evolving, as is the Godhead, of which we are part. We are not entities apart from God as much as aspects of God, which continually expand God. We don't have to become God—we already are God (or part of God)! This explanation is simplistic but useful. It may be all that we can hope to grasp of our greatness while encased in the physical body and limited by the mind and senses.

Like reincarnation, the concept of karma is often misunderstood. Some think that their problems are punishment for something they did in a former lifetime. This couldn't be farther from the truth or the spirit of karma. Karma is the means by which we receive the lessons that we need to evolve. Our karma is the situations we create to teach us these lessons. These teachings come in many forms, some painful and some not. Actually, many of our challenges are not karmic at all but are chosen by our souls to speed our growth. Challenges are the means by which we evolve and become conscious of ourselves as Spirit, as something beyond our personal self—not proof that we did something wrong in a former lifetime. Difficulties are part of the natural process of evolution on the physical plane.

The nature of life is to evolve and this sometimes necessitates pain. Blaming ourselves, others, or God for our misfortunes is a waste of energy and a misuse of our will. And yet, we are free to choose blame over acceptance, although this will lead to stagnation and pain rather than wisdom. Although we may not be able to choose whether or not we will evolve (but we all eventually do), we do choose how we will evolve—slowly or quickly, through pain or through acceptance. Accepting everything that comes to us is the joyful choice.

Karma is an impartial and wise teacher. Furthermore, we participate in choosing our karmic circumstances. They are chosen through a cooperative decision-making process entered into willingly by the souls involved—not meted out by an external judge. We choose the circumstances that will teach us to make better choices, and the Godhead is expanded by experiences our personal self and our soul freely choose.

The best news is that we are never alone on this journey. Many advanced beings guide each of us daily. Our soul, or Higher Self, and our guides speak to us intuitively and through dreams and other people. They plant ideas and inspiration in our subconscious. We only need to heed these thoughts and turn away from those that do not serve us. That's where free will comes in once again. We choose what we will think, what we will believe, and what we will do about it. Both high-minded thoughts and lower ones bubble up from the unconscious. We must become conscious and choose only those thoughts that are in the highest good of all.

Betty Eadie

Another person who has done so much to reveal the Divine Blueprint to me is Betty Eadie in her book *Embraced by the Light*. Betty tells of how, during an NDE (near-death experience), her guides told her that death is merely a change in state in which the spirit slips quietly from the body. In cases of trauma, this usually happens before any pain is felt. The spirit often hangs around to comfort those left behind while, at the same time, meeting those who have gone before and other old soul buddies who stayed in the higher dimensions. Betty's guides stressed the importance of knowing all of this before death to minimize confusion during what her guides called "graduation." What she experienced in her four-hour NDE has stayed with me every waking (and dreaming) moment since I first read her book. No one tells it better than Betty.

Reading Betty's book was a major emotional event for me because it dispelled any fear of death and included a heart-touching scene about Jesus. I firmly believe that humanity owes Betty an enormous debt of gratitude for bringing us this book and it should be required reading for every person on the planet, especially wayshowers. I am convinced she should be inducted into the lightworker's Hall of Fame for her service.

I'm going to borrow from the experience of Betty, who described the third phase brilliantly in *Embraced by the Light*.

After an operation, Betty left her body and looked down at it, noticing that it looked 'dead.' She felt no fear, just a little sadness because there was still some use in it—a bit like losing a fairly new coat. "My new body was weightless and extremely mobile ... I was whole in every way—perfect. And I thought, 'This is who I really am.' "

Then three robed men appeared and told her that they'd been with her "for eternities." As scenes filled her head, she saw that death was actually "a rebirth into a greater life that stretched forward and backward through time." The guides told her that she had died prematurely, and her thoughts turned to her family. In an instant she was home, watching her children prepare for bed. Suddenly it became apparent that they were not *her* children but individual spirits in their own right and she had just been taking care of them. She flashed on their futures and saw that they and her husband would be okay without her. Instantly she was back at the hospital where the three guides awaited her return. Suddenly she was engulfed in a tornado-like energy and was whisked into a warm, dark tunnel.

Betty's story is classic textbook NDE stuff: momentary disorientation, looking at your own body with tenderness, relief of any pain, checking up on loved ones, meeting with guides, and off into the tunnel. Let's follow Betty to what waited at the other end.

She sees a figure glowing more brightly than any light source imaginable, a huge impossibly brilliant aura into which she is drawn. She is overwhelmed at the waves of unconditional love that pass through her. "I am finally home," she says to herself. She knows who this being is— Jesus Christ—and realizes that she has known him before.

Jesus tells her that it's not her time yet but she aches to stay with him. Questions flood through her and Jesus answers them as fast as she can think them. Why so many different religions? Why are we here? Are Jesus and God the same?

One thing that surprised Betty and delighted me was the amount of interaction between the spirit realm and the mortal realm. She was shown that we are constantly fed ideas and inspiration, that each great invention *here* began as an idea *there*. She also saw that each of us is here with a mission and that we draw our fellow souls around us to assist us. But once we are here, we play the game according to our beliefs. The spirit realm can only intervene directly *if asked*.

Betty saw that our earthly selves are but temporary roles we play, our true nature being infinitely richer, more creative, and more loving. No matter how despicably we might act here, over there we are powerful entities, full of love, light, and truth. The only *real* purpose, Jesus told her, for incarnating here is to be of loving service, that *true* growth only comes through service to others.

The ultimate truths that Jesus revealed to Betty were that "love is supreme," and that we must judge no one. I've always felt that, with our limited human understanding, we can never know why anyone really came here, so to judge another's actions is probably the highest form of arrogance.

Betty also learned the importance of loving our enemies, how holding grudges and resentments damages the soul's growth. But above all, she saw clearly the perfection of the plan, the unconditional love of God, the love that Jesus holds for humanity.

Betty also had an insight that matched my own during my Egyptian out-of-body experience: that our thoughts are as real and potent as our words and deeds. "If we understood the power of our thoughts, we would guard them more closely ... Thought is the key to reality ... We are to create our own lives, to exercise our gifts, and experience both failure and success." Further, Betty saw that it is our powers of imagination and creativity that make us most God-like.

As to the power of prayer, Betty saw the Earth from a distance with sparks shooting up from the surface. These were sincere, heart-felt prayers, Jesus told her. She saw angels rushing to answer them. Above all other prayers are those of a mother for her children. The more we thank God for our blessings and abundance, the more we open the way for more. The ultimate blessing to be grateful for is the opportunity to serve, for it is through service that our souls grow.

Betty's sojourn with Jesus was interrupted by a summons to the "review committee." Her life flashed before her as an incredibly fast collage of holograms in which she relived her words, deeds, thoughts, and emotions, *plus* the emotions of all the other people involved. She cringed at having let others down and grieved at how her short temper had hurt them. Whenever she couldn't take any more guilt, the review council swamped her with their unconditional love. She realized that the council wasn't judging her, *she was judging herself.* When she saw what she called "the ripple effect," her self-judgment went off the scale. The harm you cause others often causes them to harm others, who harm yet others, and so on. Pretty soon, one mean act affects hundreds. Poor Betty was distraught until Jesus stepped forward to show her how her acts of kindness also rippled out and helped hundreds.

The review ended with one of the council telling Betty that she had to return to Earth, that she wasn't done yet. She threw a tantrum right there in front of the council. It took Jesus showing her what her mission was to change her mind. But she was told that on her return to Earth, she wouldn't remember her mission.

After many other adventures, Betty's farewell was attended by thousands of angels and the most beautiful music imaginable. After tearful good-byes, she was back in the hospital room looking at her body, seeing it as a cold, heavy encumbrance that she must put on again. She rebelled but, remembering her promise to Jesus, she slipped into it. I, for one, am glad she had the courage to come back to tell her story.

Chapter 13

The Ascension of Planet Earth

The Photon Belt
and the Zero Point Factor

Ascension

Let's begin by defining what ascension really is. According to Tony Stubbs, author of *An Ascension Handbook*, ascension is basically a change in frequency of the Earth's elecromagnetic field, of our very cells, and in the focus of our consciousness. Tony talks a lot about energy as the "stuff" behind everything that combines in indescribably complex ways to form everything everywhere on every dimension. Energy has two main qualities: amplitude (with sound, this equates to loudness), and frequency, the rate at which it vibrates (with sound, its pitch.)

We each possess four bodies: the physical body with which we're most familiar, plus our emotional, mental, and spiritual bodies. Each of these bodies is made up of energy of different frequencies. This energy, plus the energy behind what we call matter, is even higher frequency energy. It's not detectable by scientific instruments because they, too, are made of matter, and no instrument can detect frequencies higher than the frequency from which it's made.

This higher frequency energy is the energy of the Source, the ultimate origin of *everything*. It is the energy from which third-dimensional energy such as light is derived and the energy that congregates as subatomic particles that make up atoms. The most amazing thing about this energy is that it is *conscious*. It voluntarily agrees to participate in things like the cells of your body. We repay the debt to this energy by providing a means by which it can express itself and its creativity. Yes, the universe is creative at all levels.

Our physical bodies, emotions, thoughts, and spirits (or souls, if you prefer) are all made of this stuff, blended in ways that make us each unique in the universe. Because the energy making up our physical bodies has frequency, we can change it. As we do, our physical bodies become less dense. Eventually, we'll be vibrating above the level of the physical plane and be free of its limitations. In fact, we're on our way to becoming fifth-dimensional beings. Once there, low frequency energies such as fear and limitation will have fallen away and we'll be one with spirit. At this point, we'll also be one with Christ Consciousness and with the spirit of everyone else. That's what ascension is.

If there was anyone left on the physical plane, they would no longer see you. Your energy would be too high a frequency for their physical eyes to see. However, there'll be no one left. Ascension is not just a personal thing — the entire physical plane is ascending, along with the planet, too. This is what I was shown by my Pleiadian visitors in the summer of 1992 and this is what all the fuss is about. It's the most exciting thing to have ever happened on this planet and it will happen within the lifetime of most of us.

Is this just talk or is there substance behind it? Let's look at some actual phenomena that are pointing the way.

The Photon Belt

In 1992, my Pleiadian visitors showed me a vast cloud of intense energy into which our planet was headed. For a year, I had puzzled about that and the other visions but couldn't make sense of it. The Pleiadians told me the same information was being given to others. A year later, I got the confirmation I needed.

I learned that the vast energy field I was shown is called the Photon Belt, a huge mass of light-energized space. Our planet's entry into it would herald the much-acclaimed ascension of planet Earth when we will move from the third dimension to the fifth. Let's take a look at what the Photon Belt could be.

A photon is a particle of light energy that registers on the eye when it strikes the retina. Photons are emitted from atoms when an electron changes orbit when energy is applied, like flipping a light switch to allow electricity to flow through the filament. Electrons bounce between orbits when the juice is turned on, and photons are emitted. Some of them strike the retina directly and you can see the light bulb. Other photons reflect off things in the room and you can see them, too.

Imagine a huge cloud in space made of nothing but photons, pure light energy. Now imagine our planet going into that cloud. It's bound to have an effect on us, right? That energy will fill our cells, change our DNA, alter the way our senses work, change the way we think, and allow us to see in the higher dimensions.

This so-called Photon Belt is a huge doughnut-shaped area of space close to the Pleiades, a cluster of 400 to 500 stars about 415 light-years from us, out towards Taurus. The cluster was originally named the "Seven Sisters" by the ancient Greeks because they could only see seven stars with the naked eye.

According to some sources, our solar system is already in the outer reaches of the Photon Belt. We can't see it because it is not emitting yet. The photons cannot yet get out to stimulate our retinas, so we can't see it. But once we're in it, we can expect some interesting phenomena. For example, we'll see an increase in paranormal experiences. Our dreams will change. Lucid dreaming—when you wake up inside your dream and realize that you are dreaming—will increase. By the way, lucid dreams are an excellent place to meet your guides or extraterrestrial visitors.

In order to maintain the Belt's shape, the outer boundary of the Belt is very dense. In Fred Sterling's book, *Kirael: The Great Shift*, Kirael tells us that when the Earth passes through this outer perimeter, we'll encounter the most densely compacted part of the field. The photons are so tightly packed that they will shut out the light of the sun and we will experience three days of utter darkness.

To experience total darkness in the presence of dense light energy seems like a contradiction in terms, but my scientific friends assure me that, in theory, it could happen. It's never happened in modern recorded history so we just don't know for sure.

Kirael confirmed what my Pleiadian visitors told me in 1992, that going through this outer boundary of the Belt would take about three days. This also ties in with the Biblical prophecy of three days of darkness. In the following, The Book of Revelation might mean the Photon Belt:

"… and the sun became black as sackcloth of hair, and the moon became as blood. And the stars of heaven fell unto the earth." [Revelation 6:12–13]

"The sun shall be turned into darkness and the moon into blood." [Acts 2:20]

"And there shall be signs in the sun, and in the moon, and in the stars." [Luke 22:25]

"And then shall they see the Son of man coming in a cloud with power and great glory. And when these things begin to come to pass, they look up and lift your heads; for your redemption draweth nigh." [Luke 22:27–28]

When interpreting the words of ancient prophets, we must remember that this was 2,000 years ago and folks back then had no vocabulary to describe their visions of life today. How would someone around the time of Christ describe a helicopter, a camcorder, a microwave oven, or even the simple match? It couldn't be done. They could only describe their visions in terms they already knew.

My visitors showed me that the Earth would also become very cold and that electricity would no longer operate because electrons would no longer be able to move along wires. That won't really matter because our spirits will put us in a kind of suspended state much like hibernation.

Apparently, this boundary holds such intense energy that little if any three-dimensional energy could survive passage without significant change. For this reason, the energy fields of this planet must be dismantled before that happens. This is why the Earth's magnetic grid is slowly being taken down. It's a matter of public record that weird things are happening to the planet's magnetic field. Airport runways designated by degrees from magnetic north are being renamed. Animals that rely on lines of magnetic force for their migratory patterns are getting confused, whale pods are beaching themselves, and so on.

Another side effect of hitting the boundary would be a tremendous strain on the Earth's seismic structure, and the stability of the tectonic plates will probably suffer. On the bright side, there might be swarms of moderate earthquakes rather than a few devastating shakers. We can also expect a high degree of volcanic activity. Already we've seen weird things happen: Mt. St. Helens, the island of Monserrat, and Popocatepetl to name just three. Weather patterns will be a thing of the past. The weather will follow no discernible pattern. Already we are seeing dramatic shifts in weather and we should prepare for much more climatic disruption.

During my radio show on the May 6, 1998, Drunvalo Melchizedek confirmed that the Earth's magnetic field has been haywire since 1996, sending birds and cetaceans widely off-course during their migrations. Major fluctuations during 1996 even caused problems for aircraft as the magnetic poles wandered.

Drunvalo also said that our brain cells contain tiny amounts of magnetic material, which makes our memory dependent on the planet's magnetic field and therefore, if the field intensity dropped to zero as part of the upcoming polar reversal, our memories could be wiped clean!

February 26, 1998 saw a planetary event Drunvalo called the "Quickening" that marked a dramatic acceleration in our personal growth, as forecast by just about every native legend on the planet. So if we think the pace of change is already fast, hang on because there's more coming.

Drunvalo is a pioneer in a whole new field called Zero Point technology, an inner dimensional arena that operates in the realms behind our three-dimensional reality. He is instrumental in bringing a number of remarkable devices to the world, such as free energy sources and atmospheric cleansing devices. The transition to Zero Point technology, he warns, will not be smooth since it may well destabilize the economies of many countries and alter the balance of power, which largely depends on planetary energy sources.

Many experts confirm the timeframe of around 2012 as was given to me by my guides. According to the Mayan calendar and the astrology for that period, it's going to be a very interesting time, well within the lifetime of most of us. Some entities predicted that we would go through the Three Days of Darkness as early as 1995. That didn't happen, which tells us that beings outside the third dimension exist in simultaneous time and not in linear time so, to them, in a way, this has already happened. Neither do they comprehend our reliance on linear time, or our obsession with dates and times. These are two very good reasons for any channel to take timeframe predictions with a few grains of salt.

What will life be like after this incredible event, assuming we survive it? The Book of Revelation predicts that after the three days of darkness, the atmosphere will lighten up and return to normal, with the sun becoming visible once again.

In a major shift, consciousness will change dramatically. Some people will find themselves waking up as though they were waking from a dream. Their energy centers will open up and they will become fully conscious entities, meaning that the veils will be removed around the body and the planet. People will begin to know who they really are and what their soul purpose is. Their psychic senses will be greatly enhanced and they will know what's happening the return of the Christ Consciousness to the planet. Many, on the other hand, will be in confusion and even denial. The day of the way-showers will have arrived and the task of supporting and coaching the others will fall to them.

The Spiritual Hierarchy will return, which includes the extraterrestrials. The Earth will possibly have changed in its cosmological alignment. Stars and constellations will appear different. Could this explain the reference "and I saw the stars fall from heaven," or could it be how the ancient seers interpreted ships landing?

Maybe "your redemption draweth nigh" refers to the dimensional frequency shift that will take place. The veils that surround the planet will drop away to such a degree that visitors who seeded this planet and are part of this process from other planets will re-emerge here and establish a whole new civilization and incorporate a whole new paradigm of reality.

The Zero Point Factor

Almost three years after I first heard about the Photon Belt, Gregg Braden delivered his first book, *Awakening to Zero Point*, to an eager world. Working in earth sciences and the aerospace industry equipped Gregg with the understanding and vocabulary to describe with scientific precision many of the phenomena that were shown to me in 1992.

Gregg illustrates two major changes occurring simultaneously, very different, but complementary, in what he called the "Magnetic/Frequency relationship."

Let's look at frequency first. The Earth has a resonant frequency that would sound like a low-pitched hum if we could hear it. For eons, this frequency, the Schumann Resonance Factor, has been around 7 hertz (cps), confirmed by paleontological evidence. According to Gregg, since the mid-1980s, this frequency has risen dramatically and stands at around 11 hertz in 1998 and will likely peak at about 13 hertz within a decade. This unprecedented increase in the Earth's frequency suspiciously mirrors the higher energy frequencies in our bodies, which tells me that something big is happening.

The significance of this lies in the return of the Christ energy to this planet. If you define "resurrection" as the conscious increase of body frequency, we are well on the way. This is important because if we somehow migrate from the third dimension, then we would become invisible to those still in the third dimension, even though we were standing right next to them. We could still be able to see them, as well as all the neat goodies in the higher dimension.

On the other hand, some critics insist that the planet's resonance has remained faithfully at 7.8 hertz, so who are we to believe? Something unprecedented is certainly happening to our bodies—we all know that— but exactly what is it? Maybe the other side of Gregg's equation—planetary magnetics—has something to do with it.

On the question of magnetics, one of the side effects of the Earth's relatively strong magnetic field is that it blocks us from experiencing the full realm of our own consciousness, even though everything that happens 'out there' is a result of our thoughts (the you-create-your-own-reality syndrome). The magnetic field slows things down so that there is a time lag between having a thought and actually experiencing it. This is actually a very good thing because some of us have some pretty unsavory thoughts. To actually manifest something in your reality, you must hold a thought consistently and with great clarity, something few of us can do.

A side-effect of the ETs reducing the Earth's magnetic field, however, is that this time delay is being dismantled. Gregg points out in *Awakening to Zero Point* that "as planetary magnetics are decreasing rapidly, without lag time buffering, you are beginning to experience nearly instantaneous consequences of your thoughts." He goes on to say that "at the same time, each cell of the mind/body/spirit complex is striving to maintain resonance with the Earth—a resonance that is moving through an unprecedented shift into a higher band of frequency!"

The shift has already begun and each individual, without exception, is participating in the process. Gregg predicts that when the Earth's frequency hits 13 hertz and the magnetic field approaches zero, an *outside* observer of the process would most probably see the following:

1. A reduced rate of planetary rotation (longer days and nights), followed by a sustained electromagnetic null-state for approximately three days (i.e., the Three Days of Darkness)
2. Gradual increase of planetary rotation, accompanied by the increasingly stable magnetics of a *reversed polar field*. Earth's base resonant frequency will stabilize at a new minimum of 13 hertz
3. Unusual activity within other bodies of the solar system, such as sun spots and solar prominences of record magnitude
4. The radical shift / breakdown of energetic systems of balance:
   - geological—record-setting seismic activity accompanied by new types of faults, fault zones and earthquakes
   - meteorological—unusual weather patterns, winds, ocean currents accompanied by extremes of record rainfalls and flooding

- social unrest—the appearance of chaos evidenced as "pockets" of unrest expanding and overlapping into other systems, such as political and economic.

If the above is what an outside observer would see, how will it feel to us on the inside? How will our daily lives change? Gregg forecasts the following:

1. A drastic change in the manner with which individuals, corporations, governments and nations perceive themselves, others, their lives, jobs, careers and family

2. The radical shift / breakdown of the systems forming the infrastructure of technology/society (social, political, economic, military, agricultural, industrial)

3. A perceived increase in the passing of time in which events feel as if they are 'speeding up' due to the body's attempt to match the Earth's increasingly rapid resonance rate

4. Intermittent loss of memory concerning 'trivial' information. (birth dates, anniversary dates, ATM codes, etc.) with episodes of a feeling of 'un-reality'

5. Odd sleep patterns with periods of 'null' sleep, e.g., waking up physically exhausted, feeling fatigued and tense, occasionally with sore muscles, followed by consecutive nights of vivid, prolific and *meaningful* dreams

6. Difficult challenges as we draw into our lives our worst fears to be balanced and healed

7. During the shift itself, the majority of us will experience the three days of darkenss in an unconscious state, essentially an out-of-body experience. Those who have learned to remain conscious within these new parameters will experience it consciously and facilitate the process for others.

These changes have already been underway for some time now. It is only recently that pioneers such as Drunvalo Melchizedek and Gregg Braden have come forward to expand our knowledge of the Divine Blueprint. Thanks to them, as we reach the controversial zero point, we'll have a greater understanding of these events. Millions of people already know that something is happening but don't quite know what or where it's coming from. As scientific evidence meets ancient prophecies, it creates a crossroad, and we, as way-showers, have the opportunity and responsibility to share this vital information with everyone we meet.

Chapter 14

Return of the Spiritual Hierarchy

First Contact; The Masters Return

"Let your soul stand cool and composed before a million universes."
— Walt Whitman

HAVE YOU EVER LOOKED up at the night sky, at all those billions and billions of stars, and wondered, "Who's out there? How are they like us, and how are they different?

To me, it is inconceivable that there's no one out there. What a waste of space that would be, and I don't see the Creator as wasteful.

This was proven on a December night in 1977 when I put out that call that was picked up by three extraterrestrials—my angels in spacesuits. I called out in love and service and the call was answered. I spent the next 20 years trying to understand that experience, a search that would take me to many corners of the world, and even the galaxy. It has taken me into the depths of human emotion and the heights of the soul.

A wise man once said, "If you want to know the mysteries of the universe, go into your garden." So I did. I sat quietly, watching and waiting. After maybe 30 minutes, a whole other world came into view, a world of elementals watching over plants, trees, rocks, birds—all living things. But more than just watching over physical things, I saw that the physical bodies were *expressions* of the elementals. The higher consciousness of the elementals manifested as the bodies of trees, plants, rocks—even my cat as he dozed in the afternoon sun.

If everything in the physical world is a manifestation of a higher entity, is it conceivable that man is the only exception? Of course not. Our physical bodies are also a manifestation of a higher entity—one we call "soul." The burning issue in my mind is why we don't accept this, why we don't *know* that we have a soul, just as we know we have eyes and ears.

If an individual rock is watched over by a higher order being, what about the planet, the solar system, the galaxy? According to the age-old principle, "as above, so below," everything from a galaxy to an atom has an "overseer." The sum total of these beings, from a wood nymph up to the consciousness of an entire galaxy, is what I call the Spiritual Hierarchy.

In the distant recesses of our history, humanity was in full, unquestioning contact with the Spiritual Hierarchy but over countless millennia, we lost contact. Everything from elementals to gods was relegated to the weird fringes of folklore. A few groups, like the pagans, went underground to keep the old truths alive, despite the searing heat of the Inquisition's fires. These truths are slowly reemerging into the daylight of the mass consciousness. Slowly, these ancient truths are surfacing and fueling what's been dubbed "the New Age," ironic because the truths predate all recorded history.

The Spiritual Hierarchy never left our planet but they did leave our conscious awareness as organized religions struggled to abolish all contrary thought. But today, the Hierarchy is coming back into focus.

My visitors showed me scenes of a major leap in the evolution of our planet—not the usual timeframe of millions of years—but an event that was to happen almost instantaneously, an event they called "ascension."

You and I and the guy down the street are not skilled or experienced in ascending entire planets so obviously we're going to need help in this ascension business. That's why the Spiritual Hierarchy has to reveal its presence once more. They need our conscious cooperation in this so they have to come forward to tell us who they are and what they want us to do. In other words, they have to *return* to our awareness after a long absence. Remember, they never left; they've just been working in the background, coming forward occasionally to nudge us in the right direction, the way Jesus did about 2,000 years ago.

Who makes up the Spiritual Hierarchy? We've already encountered the "terrestrials"—the elementals who "run" the planet and her lifeforms. The Hierarchy also includes those extraterrestrials who, physical or not, have come here in service to planet Earth and humanity.

The list also includes beings from dimensions higher than our physical planet who may never have taken physical form, such as Kryon speaking through Lee Carroll, or Kirael speaking through Fred Sterling.

The Angelic Kingdom is also prominent, headed up by archangels such as Michael, Ariel, Uriel and Gabriel (the list is endless), who perform specialized functions having to do with space and time, and the integrity of reality as we experience it.

How is this Return going to happen? It's already underway. Probably nothing so blatant as a mass landing in Central Park or on the White House lawn but we can't rule anything out. More likely, an increase in the frequency of telepathic messages and visions (as with me) and an increasing number of people who receive them. These won't be crystal-toting, bead-draped New Age remnants of the sixties but respectable "mainstream" doctors, engineers, business people, and even ministers. (Imagine the Almighty speaking directly through the clergy. Won't they be in for a surprise.)

Since the mid-1980s, the movement has been quietly building. Every town of any size boasts a metaphysical bookstore, 900-number psychic hotlines compete with the less savory 900 services, and conventions and conferences bring words of wisdom to those eager to hear them. The media jumps at every opportunity to spread the Hierarchy's message, whether through programming about ETs or with commercials.

The Hierarchy's approach must be subtle. Universal law prohibits any entity from wading into a free-will system like ours and changing it without being asked. It is up to us to raise our consciousness to the point where humanity as a whole knows: 1) that we need help, 2) what kind of help, 3) who to ask, 4) how to ask, and 5) how to use the help when it arrives. The task of the Hierarchy is to prepare us for this before we blow our planet to pieces with nuclear weapons, render it uninhabitable with "toys" like HAARP, or destroy ourselves with runaway biological weapons.

You'll notice that I've left one big question hanging: *Who, if anyone, is in charge of the Spiritual Hierarchy?* Is it a free-wheeling, haphazard deal where any ET, angel, or whoever just pitches in wherever they want? Or is it a carefully-planned, well-orchestrated effort involving dedicated, highly-trained specialists drawn from every corner of creation? You'll be relieved to know that it's the latter. But who, if anyone, is in charge?

It is my belief that the organizing force behind all this is the Christ Consciousness energy. The hierarchical structure in turn takes its direction from yet another source—the Christ Consciousness that pervades everything, everywhere. This is coherent energy, of a particular set of very high frequencies. As we increase our personal frequency through meditation and clearing old stuff like fear, we can approach the frequency of the Christ Consciousness. The other important prerequisites are intent—you must *want* to tap into that energy—and an emotion of strong, consuming desire.

Emotion is the important energy structure that allows us to access the Christ Consciousness and this, curiously, is behind the abduction phenomenon. Apparently, the little gray ETs—the Zeta Reticuli and their close cousins, the Greys—have evolved so as not to have any emotions. This, they have discovered, is an evolutionary dead-end. Having developed their minds at the expense of their feelings has proven to be a monumental mistake which they are trying to reverse.

Another important aspect of tapping into the Christ energy and becoming aware of the Spiritual Hierarchy is living in harmony with the planet. Every atom of your body was once a part of the Earth and we are tied to her in ways we cannot begin to imagine. This is why the rising frequency of the planet is so important—we have no idea *how* it will change us but intuitively we know that it will.

One of the most frequently asked questions at my seminars is, "If the Spiritual Hierarchy is all around us, how come some of us see them and others do not?"

Let me answer that with a dream I had in 1986 while in Las Vegas, of all places:

A Native American guide I've never seen before wakes me up from sleep and takes me outside. We are on a long, lonely stretch of road in front of a gas station, which I know symbolizes energy.

He asks me, "What is it that you desire to know?"

"I want to know how the Spiritual Hierarchy might manifest to us and what ascension will look like."

He waves his arm in a half-circle and suddenly the night sky opens like a curtain being pulled back to reveal the most amazing sight. I see thousands upon thousands of beings, mostly human-looking, moving freely but purposefully, as though they have business to attend to.

The sky is also filled with geometrical shapes: three-dimensional triangles, spheres, and shapes I can't name, all glowing, translucent, and moving through each other. Shafts of pure energy shoot across the sky to and from enormous spacecraft. From one horizon to the other, the entire sky is lit up and vast, colored rays of light slice through everything.

At this point, it suddenly becomes clear to me that the Christ Consciousness isn't a being but a vast, all-encompassing energy. It is all around us; we just don't know it, like the radio and TV signals that continuously flood our houses and bodies. But because our bodies can't detect them, we don't know they're there.

I watch in awe for what seems an eternity. I turn to thank the guide for showing this to me and for his patience while I drink it all in. Then I notice three colleagues from work: Patrick, Joel, and Rick. "Just look at all that," I say to them, in total excitement and awe.

Then a *really* weird thing happens. As I study each of them in turn, my consciousness actually merges with theirs and for a moment, I become them, seeing what they see, feeling what they feel, knowing what they know.

Joel is almost pure intellect; if something cannot be logically deduced, it doesn't exist for him. Joel looks up at the sky and says, "What? I don't see anything except a few stars." Being inside him, I know it's true—he is looking at a perfect night sky. I look at the guide and he smiles a knowing smile back at me.

It's the same with Patrick. Inside him, I see only sky and stars but feel his curiosity about what I'm wildly pointing at.

Then into Rick, who can see some of the brighter shapes and says, "Yeah, I think I can see something."

Wham! I'm bounced back into my body, knowing that a certain openness is necessary to see beyond the mundane. First you need emotional openness to even receive the vision and, second, an open belief system that allows you to process what you're seeing. If the belief system can't accept what you're seeing, you simply won't see it—it would be too overwhelming. This is exactly what Dr. Wayne Dyer conveys with the title of his book, *You'll See It When You Believe It*. Most of our religions operate on a faith basis, yet require that we believe first and experience second.

To really form a relationship with the Spiritual Hierarchy, something more formal is needed, like regular meditation, alone or in a group. The first step in any work like this, however, should always be protection. Surround yourself in Light. Just the simple statement like, "I surround myself with the Christ Light" works well if spoken aloud and with focus.

Next, state your intent. What *is* your intent? An earnest desire to serve others by requesting healing, say, or an ego-driven desire to dabble in the supernatural? It should be obvious that the latter will, at best, do nothing and at worst, create a whole bunch of trouble as a mischievous astral entity has some fun with you. It's apparent to me that purity of intent was imperative for my angels-in-spacesuits experience to occur.

Once you've clarified your intent, clear your head, take a deep breath, and speak it clearly to the universe: "I request that my mother/father/son/daughter/dog/cat/whatever, be healed if it is in accordance with the will of their higher self. And so it is."

Two things to note here. First, the person may not *want* to be healed. Remember that experiencing illness is one of the reasons a soul incarnates here, and your aunt's condition may be part of her plan, so make sure you don't interfere where you have no business. Second, "And so it is" tells the universe that you *know* you've set something into motion and that you *expect* results. At this point, leave well alone. Don't keep opening the oven door to see if it's done yet.

You might state your intent as, "I wish to serve the Spiritual Hierarchy in the highest capacity possible. Please give me clear guidance as to what to do next. And so it is."

Then wait. You might repeat your intent twice more but basically you wait until they contact you. How might that happen? Dreams, visions, ideas dropped into your mind out of nowhere, chance meetings with strangers or old friends you haven't seen for years. One thing's for sure: *expect* the unexpected. When you bump into an old friend after ten years, don't dismiss it as coincidence. It's actually a phenomenon called synchronicity at work [syn = same; chron = time] and the masters had to work hard to get both of you on the same street corner at exactly the same time. So ask your friend, "Why do you think this happened? Do you have a message for me?" Of course, you'll be more subtle about it, unless your friend blurts out something like, "I've been meaning to call you. I'm writing a book on animal healing and I need your help."

When this happens, immediately kick into gratitude mode. Thank the universe for this clear sign, and for being astute enough to recognize it. "Thank you for this sign. Now tell me how else I can serve. And so it is."

It's *essential* that you know that this is how the universe works. *There are no coincidences.* Everything that happens is just part of the big plan unfolding, so look for clues in everything. Be conscious of your environment, of your impulse to drive a certain route to work rather than another way, of all the little details we hardly notice in our hurry to get to the next thing.

I think that's why all the weird stuff happens in my life, because I go looking for it. The trick is to dovetail your intent with the overall intent of the universe. You won't be shown the entire plan—it's simply too vast—but you can certainly ask to see your part in it.

You will probably not get it all at once, either. You really only need to know what to do *next*. If you're contemplating a job change, you don't need to know how that will affect you in five years. You need to know what to do *next*—sign on with a job search company, read the Help Wanted ads, or check out the Internet. The important thing is to *follow your impulses*. A sudden impulse to go to the Italian deli round the corner may mean your next employer is unknowingly waiting for you. Or it may just mean that your body wants a bologna sandwich. That's the delight of the Great Mystery.

Finally, watch your dreams. This is the best time for contact because your ego and conscious mind are off-duty and not running the show. At last, your higher self can get a word in. It can, however, work both ways. Suppose you want guidance with a thorny matter, say, whether to break off a troublesome relationship or hang in and try to heal it. Before you go to sleep, call for your higher self's input; "I call for guidance on my relationship with _____. And so it is."

You may need to repeat this for a couple of nights but wait and watch your dreams. Your higher self may use standard dream symbols, like a snake means wisdom and being bitten by one means imminent enlightenment. The death of someone rarely means physical death but usually a transformation of some kind. (There are plenty of dream interpretation books out there.) Who knows? You might have a visit from members of the Spiritual Hierarchy itself, with a direct message specially for you.

This process of becoming an active, conscious player is what I call *integration*. The task facing the Spiritual Hierarchy is so vast that they need as many conscious players as they can get here on the physical plane. The pay may not be great, but the fringe benefits are knowing that you're on the team about to win the ultimate Super Bowl of all time.

One of the cornerstones of the major religions is that their followers are the "chosen ones." To them, I simply say, "CHOOSE YOURSELF!" Step up to the plate and sign on. No one will be turned down, even if he or she has no skills. Maybe your loving heart energy is your contribution, or even just the way you tend your garden.

What's truly important is that *you're on the team,* offering to let the Spiritual Hierarchy use you according to whatever agreements your soul made before you incarnated. I use the phrase "use you" very deliberately because this is how it will feel to your ego when it surrenders to your soul's purpose. But then it's always been that way. Your soul has *always* run the show. Anything the ego does is either instigated *by* the soul or allowed by the soul. So you see, you-the-soul has always been in charge. The only difference is that you-the-ego now consciously acknowledges it, and agrees to work with you-the-soul.

If you're on the team, what's the game plan? It is said that when the Earth enters the Photon Belt, the compacted energy will obliterate the sun and three days later, we will leave the densest energy and the sun becomes visible once again, with a strong red tinge. At the same time, since the Earth has been literally relocated in space, we will see different stars in the sky.

As Earth emerges, we would find ourselves in a higher dimension, where telepathy, compassion, and soul wisdom prevail—truly heaven on earth. As we become adept in that higher dimension, we will encounter those who hang out there—the Spiritual Hierarchy.

At the threshold of the new millennium, we sense that great change is in the air. If the Mayan calendar is accurate, we can expect this shift around 2012. That gives us the schedule that the Spiritual Hierarchy is working on. Expect steadily increasing preparations between now and then.

What can you do, apart from paying attention? Watch your dreams— they are another "branch" of your consciousness. They are you, not just something happening to you. You can program your dreams to deliver your own "Book of Revelation." Everything you need to know is within you—your own personal Divine Blueprint—and dreams are a major way of exploring that knowledge.

Another thing you can do to listen to yourself and your inner wisdom is to meditate. I don't mean hours of lotus position like those guys in the East. I mean just sitting quietly, without the TV or stereo on, and letting thoughts come. At first, your thoughts will be the superficial stuff: *Why was the phone bill so high this month? Why was the supermarket checkout clerk so rude? I should have my teeth cleaned next week.*

Gently nudge these thoughts aside and wait. The good stuff should come: *If my boss moves to Chicago, I'll be in line for her job. Maybe I should start preparing.* And then the great stuff: *I don't want her job. I really want to coordinate metaphysical conferences.* And then the awesome stuff: *If the Creator made me out of its thoughts, that makes me a part of it. I'm part of the Creator! Wow! I'd never thought about that before!*

Every night, I go outside (weather permitting), raise my hands to the sky, and say with all the intent I can muster, "Help me integrate my own wisdom so that I can better serve the Spiritual Hierarchy in the evolution of planet Earth and work more closely with my guides." This earnest request opens the door to help from my guides and the Hierarchy.

One final thing: Know that you are loved and that you have your personal mission, your piece of the Divine Blueprint.

Tricia McCannon: The Age of Aquarius

Let's conclude this chapter on the Spiritual Hierarchy with my dear friend, Tricia McCannon, who wrote these touching and inspiring words especially for this book. Tricia is an internationally renowned clairvoyant, contactee, speaker, and the author of the book *Dialogues With the Angels* and the newly released *Beings of Light, Worlds in Transition.*

To understand the vast and sweeping changes coming to our planet in the next few years, we must begin as students of history. Not a hundred- or a thousand-year span of history, but to gain any real understanding, we must go back further to include a larger viewpoint, to the Procession of the Equinoxes, with its 26,000-year long cycle, and its twelve 2,160-year phases. This is the key to everything.

Within this perspective, our Earth's history begins to make sense. What was obscured by the Dark Ages' wholesale destruction of millions of sacred books becomes clear once again when we realize that Earth and all of humanity actually move into degrees of greater or lesser density with the change of every new age. The cyclical rise and fall of matriarchal and patriarchal empires, institutions and religions, indeed of the very consciousness of the people themselves, begins to make sense as we see these repeating patterns of dark and light in the perspective of time.

How does this impact us now, standing at the end of the 20th century, the end of the Age of Pisces and the beginning of the Age of Aquarius? How does this relate to the reported appearance of UFOs in our skies, angelic encounters in our bestsellers, and the slow but continual increase of mind/body co-creation in our world today?

For the better part of 4,000 years, we on planet Earth have been asleep. Our genuine knowledge of our Divine connection to the Cosmos has slipped from us, and our memory of who we truly are and where we came from is amnesiac. In fact, until the advent of the Scientific Revolution in the last 400 years, ignorance was actively cultivated by our churches, and those who showed an exceptional connection to the Source were burned alive.

Each age, however, brings its gifts and its hardships. The Age of Aries, from 2000 BC to 0 AD, took us on a backward slide in evolution. The leading Earth cultures went from the late Egyptian dynasties and early Greek cultures, both of whom were conversant in sacred geometry, the phi ratio, and advanced arts of healing and astronomy, to a morally bankrupt Roman police state, smitten with the desire to conquer the world. Yet it was in that Age of Aries that we last recognized a connection with the "gods." In that connection lie the clues to our genetic seeding and our own cosmic lineage from the stars. By eliminating the awareness of these "gods" as real, we left behind any possibility of rediscovering the map to our own identity. These higher dimensional intelligences are, of course, part of those we now call extraterrestrials.

The Age of Pisces took us down yet another notch in consciousness. Much of Pisces was dominated by the Christian and Moslem theologies which insisted on such strict monotheism that we forgot that the Ancients also knew there was only One God behind the many. They were clear that the "gods" were merely aspects of the One, and that most of these off-world teachers who came to visit them brought the arts of agriculture, astronomy, writing and architecture. And by their very high dimensional nature, they seemed to live immortal lives. But then we must remember that our own Earth lives were shorted from the 1,000 years of Methuselah documented in the Bible, to our own brief spans of 80 years. Such short lifetimes hardly allow us time to learn from the mistakes of our own history.

Monotheism replaced the tolerant, secular reverence of the gods with a life of strict adherence to rules, punishable by excommunication, death and eternal damnation. Not a pretty sight. Thus did our Age, the Age of Pisces, the Age of our ancestors and our ancestors' ancestors, seek to turn us from connecting within ourselves to Source directly. We were told by the new religions that we could only connect to God through certain prescribed intermediaries—priests, rabbis, bishops and, of course, Jesus. And in the doing of this, we lost the core of the message that Jesus had to bring: "The Kingdom of Heaven is within."

The truth is that we are all connected to the Source by virtue of even being alive. The Source runs through us and through all living things. This Divine Intelligence permeates the Universe. Thus we are all sacred beings—stars, moons, animals, plants and, of course, one another.

In the same way that Columbus was called a madman for believing that the Earth was round and Galileo was imprisoned for suggesting that the sun was the center of the solar system, many of us who know about the existence of extraterrestrial beings lead the vanguard of world consciousness today. Some of us have been called crazy. Some have been ridiculed, fired. and discredited. Yet all us who know, who truly know that the Universe is a wide, sweeping multi-dimensional presence with infinite variety, are the pioneers. Those of you reading this book are part of that wave of awakening that will change everything, allowing us to finally take our place at the table of the galactic family.

We as a people, stand at the brink of a new age, an age that is already bringing sweeping changes. The theme of these changes is Unity, the Age of Aquarius, the consciousness bearer. Thus we see advances all around us; in holistic medicine, a rebalancing of racial issues, a rehonoring of women as equals, and a slow but sacred movement towards remembering that the Earth herself is a living presence.

We also hear about the presence of many extraterrestrial visitors, from the benevolent to the threatening. And while we are trying to separate truth from fantasy, let me give you a clue: The Universe is a hologram. All things are contained within the Self, from the highest spiritual presence to the darkest parts of our own nature. These visiting extraterrestrials merely mirror ourselves. The Greys, those aliens who so heartlessly abduct and traumatize humans without their consent, are genuine enough. They are here, as are the Draconian reptilians. Some even take human form. Yet their cold and unfeeling natures are only a reflection of the same destructive consciousness that gassed millions in Auschwitz during World War II, and have experimented on human beings for twenty years at Montauk Point, Long Island, and Dulce, New Mexico. Are the monsters we see in them really any different from the dead eyes of men who work in slaughterhouses in our own cities? Or the hunters who kill animals who are now almost extinct for their livers or their tusks? I think not.

By the same token, we are also the Light beings. They, too, take human form. They, too, have chosen to incarnate into our world disguised as mothers and fathers, teachers and writers, scientists and poets. And are the luminous light beings who live in the sentient plasma ships and visit people like Giorgio Bongiovanni, Carlos Dias, and myself also real? They are. They are drawn here because they, too, are within us.

Each of us has a light body that corresponds to the frequency we come from, whether we know or not, whether we activate it or not. For every "miracle" that the higher dimensional ETs produce—levitation, telepathy, and healing—do we not also have humans who have shown those same exalted qualities? We have.

Within us lies the potential of the Universe. Dark and Light, good and evil, involution and evolution. It is our choice, each and every day. Are we takers or givers? Do we run our lives from ego and power or from the higher heart aligned with Divine Will? In this Age before us, we must choose, because the Age itself will not support denser levels of consciousness. Those who do not enter the Domain of the Heart, the Christed Self, will not be able to handle the frequencies of vibration.

The Divine Blueprint is returning. Our remembrance of ourselves is returning. All time as we know it will change in the next thirty years. The new grids are being activated. Let us stand before the Truth of Love and know its name.

Chapter 15

Blueprints for Living

If a man does not keep pace with his companions,
perhaps it is because he hears a different drummer.
Let him step to the music which he hears,
however measured or far away.

— Thoreau

Throughout time, mankind has searched for some kind of blueprint for living, the way, the purpose, the meaning of life, an explanation of his place in the universe, the "Holy Grail" if you will. Every religion passes its doctrines down through the generations, hoping they will sustain their truths as the centuries pass.

Many factions have held tightly to the belief that "our religion is right, therefore everyone else's must be wrong." This has unfortunately produced the oldest war of all, the religious war, in which each side's priests would beseech their deity to protect their departing soldiers and bring death and disaster to the soldiers of the opposing side, assuming that *their* god was their god *only*, and really didn't care too much for the so-called "enemy."

Religious doctrines have helped, supported, and enlightened humanity while at the same time causing untold world suffering, separation, and division from the original intent—becoming one with the creator. Theologians, scholars, researchers, and students of religious and esoteric sciences have all found pieces of the puzzle in their search for a Divine Blueprint that explains it all.

Each of the major religions believes that it embodies or embraces the plan, so let's take a brief look.

Religions and Their Blueprints

Religion can be defined as a way of life or belief based on how you relate to the universe or a deity. If we narrow the term down to "faith in a divinely created order of the world, with salvation for each individual who adheres to that faith," then we've got Judaism, Christianity, and Islam since each involves faith in a creed, obedience to a moral code, a special class of intermediaries (or priests), and some form of participation with a group of like-minded followers. But if we expand the definition, we could include Buddhism, Confucianism, Hinduism, and Shintoism. Each of these is expanded in Appendix A.

In the first group, the followers pledge themselves to three things: (1) a creed of beliefs, (2) a code of behavior, and (3) worship. Underpinning this group is the notion of a central deity, and the creed is a declaration of faith in the deity that gave it; the code is the system of human laws and morals that govern interaction between the followers; worship involves ritual by which the followers acknowledge their deity, such as with prayer, sacrifice, and song.

The whole point of getting the deity's attention and pledging conformity to its will is the hope for survival beyond death, or salvation, while non-believers perish.

Each of these blueprints has a built-in assumption: that man, by nature, is unworthy of salvation. Original sin, committed by the first man and woman, Adam and Eve, means that salvation is impossible without divine assistance. So a particularly important ritual calls for the followers to repent their shortcomings. Then the deity offers salvation to the undeserving faithful.

In Christianity, the followers can implore the services of a mediator, Jesus of Nazareth. According to the New Testament covenant between Jesus and the followers, Jesus incarnated and died to take on their sins. This then is the Christian blueprint: that followers are intrinsically flawed and must call on Jesus to petition God for forgiveness and admission to heaven upon death.

A more formal contract, or covenant, exists in Judaism between God and followers, in which God acknowledges the Jewish people as "chosen" in return for them obeying His laws as handed down through Moses. Islam, too, stresses an omnipotent God who will preside at Judgment Day and judge men according to their deeds.

The search for a centralized deity is, I believe, a response to the need for "someone to be in control" and ultimately responsible for the apparent randomness of worldly events. The veil that we so cleverly draw at birth hides us from the truth of who we really are and, therefore, we need to invent a conceptual deity to fill the gap. We therefore deny ourselves our true role in creation and instead credit some entity that we invent with the accolades that rightfully belong to us.

The second group of world religions are less focused, if at all, on a central deity. Hinduism and Confucianism are more systems of social values, while Buddhism focuses on personal development. Shintoism deals more with nature, and Taoism takes this to the limit—that the purpose of life is to transcend its superficial trappings which camouflage the hidden mysteries of the Tao.

The Scientific Blueprint

Up until the days of Copernicus and Galileo, religious leaders also dictated scientific thinking, so when the Pope said the sun moved around the Earth, it did. But the 17th century saw the scientific approach split from the religious dogma of the day and ever since, science and religion have been uncomfortable bedfellows. But what *is* the scientific blueprint?

Science (from the Latin *scientia*, from *scire*, "to know") is the pursuit of systematized knowledge in any field using standard methods to acquire objectively verifiable sense experience. By definition, it is the antithesis of religion, which is based on subjective intuition, faith, and divine revelation, so it's no surprise that they don't get on.

Galileo was the father of the modern scientific method, repeatedly verifying results using objective, systematic methods. By the 18th century, the scientific discoveries of Newton and Descartes had reduced most of the mysteries of life to equations and chemical reactions. Gone was the notion that man was somehow a divine spark of God. Now he was just an organized collection of chemicals that interacted in neat ways, living in a vast stellar machine of orbiting planets and galaxies, with no more importance than any other piece of cosmic dust floating in space.

In 1859, the final nail in the coffin of man's divinity was driven in by Darwin in *On the Origin of Species by Means of Natural Selection*. Looking for a direct genetic line of evolution from the primeval ooze to mankind, scientists saw what was not really there, and although Darwin called it a *theory*, it is taught in schools today as scientifically verified fact.

While the scientific blueprint, with its emphasis on verifiable results, is laudable, many scientists make the mistake of denying the validity of subjective experience. I say "mistake" because they are out of their element and are not qualified to tear down someone else's blueprint just because a second person could not exactly duplicate the experience of the first.

Fortunately, many scientists are waking up to the fact that, for example, thought *does* change the nature of an atom. But since the thinker of the thought is human, part of the experiment is still subjective and therefore cannot be replicated *exactly*. One day, I hope to find that the leading edge science is *inner science*, whereby we use the power of the mind to heal the body and manipulate the outside world. Now just how *did* those pyramid builders do it?

The Astrological Blueprint

Widely dismissed by science as meaningless drivel, astrology is an ancient form of divination based on the theory that movements of the celestial bodies (stars, planets, sun, and moon) influence human affairs and events. Believed to be originated by the Chaldaeans and Assyrians as early as 3000 BC, its practice was arrested by the rise of Christianity. To Christians it was unacceptable, although it was still widely practiced through the Middle Ages. It regained popularity during the Renaissance and the practice has continued in the West. In fact, during World War II, Hitler relied extensively on astrology in planning his campaigns, and Allied intelligence consulted astrologers to second guess German strategy.

Today, it has enjoyed a come-back, and even Wall Street brokers hired astrologers in the 1980s to predict the market. After the 1981 assassination attempt on President Reagan, Nancy Reagan consulted an astrologer about the timing of major events such as important speeches, surgery, and signing treaties. And today, even the most hardened skeptic knows his or her sun sign. "What's your sign?" is a cliche of social conversation, often leading to instant character analysis such as honest Sagittarius and neat and tidy Virgo.

Astrology (Greek astron, "star"; logos, "discourse") studies the positions, movements, and relative juxtapositions of the sun, moon, and planets. Astrologers claim that the various planets have a certain energy associated with them which influences your personality and your destiny. Particularly important are the planetary positions at the time of birth. Each planet lies in one of 12 signs of the zodiac and one of 12 houses which govern such aspects of life as marriage, career, parents and children, money, romance, travel, death, health, and personal growth.

Despite many attempts, proof of the scientific accuracy of astrological predictions remains elusive since results depend so much on the

individual astrologer's interpretive skill and intuition. But many satis-
fied clients can attest to the fact that a good astrologer does have an
uncanny insight into a client's personality and life.

The positions of the planets are represented on a chart such as the chart
shown for May 3, 2000. What's remarkable about the heavenly configuration for this particular date is that even expert astrologers have no real idea
what it portends. Jeanne Johnson, an astrologer friend in Denver, has this
to say about what some are calling the "Millennium Configuration."

The chart shows that on May 3, seven of the ten planets lie together
in one sign—Taurus—the most grounded and unchangeable sign. With
the Moon conjuncting them all, Venus at 3 degrees and Mars at 29, plus
Mercury, Sun, Jupiter, and Saturn in between, we are seeing one huge
conjunction. According to Jeanne, each of their energies goes to make a
very powerful energy cocktail: Mars' warrior energy, Venus' loving en
ergy, Mercury's communication skills, the Sun's driving force, Jupiter's
benevolence, and Saturn's structure and discipline.

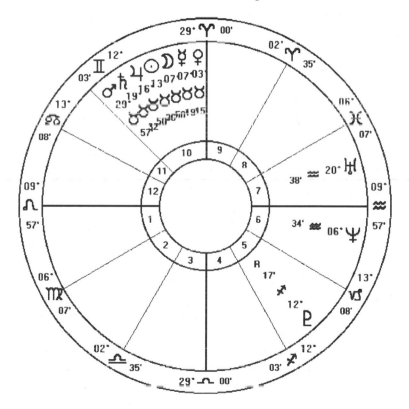

Astrological Chart for May 3, 2000 [Chart by Halloran Software]

Jeanne goes on to say that Pluto is inconjunct to the group (i.e., at a 150 degree angle), an aspect that can bring about a major crisis and/or major change that is usually not in anyone's control. Pluto rules things deep below the ground as well as the mass psyche. This will magnify the energy of all the planets in the cocktail and, most wonderful of all, can truly deliver a miracle.

Neptune squares the group (i.e., at a 90 degree angle), a powerful aspect with a lot of challenging energy. Neptune is a planet of very high vibration and pure spirituality but its lower energies of deception and delusion tend to trap humans both individually and in groups. Neptune also has the ability to wipe out people, places, and things, but in such a way that the damage or erasure is not noticed right away. It can also create a feeling, real or imagined, of isolation.

The first thing Jeanne warns is to "watch your back." Pluto in the 7th house of the U.S. and Neptune in the 9th house suggests a long distance or overseas, so we could be faced with a totally unexpected crisis of some sort involving a foreign power that could require the U.S. to respond rapidly. 2000 is also an election year and the 9th house governs religion and philosophy, so the conservatives or religious right could surprise everyone.

Pluto rules the masses, so this could mean riot or revolt. Pluto also rules big government so maybe our government could be doing something behind the public's back. This could keep any conspiracy theory fans busy.

Jeanne told me that the last time this configuration happened was on February 4, 1962 which puts the two charts about 38 years apart. To astrologers, this period is known as the Uranus opposition, or the time of "mid-life crisis." Jeanne sees our country in a sort of mid-life crisis the likes of which have not been seen since the industrial revolution so maybe we are due for some kind of shake-up or major change. (To contact Jeanne, see Resources.)

My friend Art Martin adds that this portends a three-day period (May 3 – 5) which marks the end of the transition from the Age of Pisces to the Age of Aquarius. It is also the beginning of the period 2000 – 2011 during which each of us must choose whether to continue with ascension or stay behind to evolve in the third dimension. Those who prefer to leave altogether will be able to choose from natural disaster, epidemic, or accident as their means of exit. Those living in peace, love, and harmony will come into their power, while the fear-mongers and power-brokers will find their power bases being eroded as the higher frequencies coming onto the planet will no longer support their fear-based strategies. (To contact Art, see Resources.)

Flower of Life Blueprint

The Flower of Life is a symbol that mysteriously appears in ancient drawings on cave and temple walls around the world. It is treated as the emblem of sacred geometry—the study of shapes and angles that underpins creation itself.

The name of Drunvalo Melchizedek is synonymous with modern day teachings about the ancient science of sacred geometry and he maintains that everything that has ever been, or will ever be, created is based on the Flower of Life. Every living thing goes through these geometrical shapes as the newly fertilized egg divides and divides, and petals on flowers unfold.

Made up of 19 interlocking circles and numerous arcs, the Flower of Life contains the geometry of creation.

The 13 major circles from the Flower of Life give us the Fruit of Life, the basic pattern of female energy on which all male-oriented linear geometry can be superimposed (see over).

If we join the center of every circle, we form what is called Metatron's Cube, from which every building

The Flower of Life

block of creation can be derived, such as the cube and the star tetrahedron (see over).

For more information about this fascinating blueprint, see the website: www.floweroflife.com.

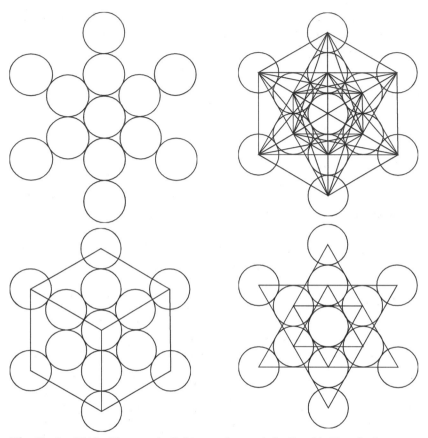

The Fruit of Life, Metatron's Cube, a cube, and the Double Tetrahedron

Tree of Life superimposed on the Flower of Life

Tree of Life

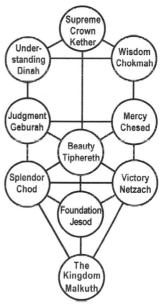

Also known as the Kabbalah or Quabbalah, this is a pattern of ten circles and connecting lines that represent the down-flow of spirit from its pure, non-manifest state until it manifests as matter and the animating force behind it. The three columns in which the circles are arranged represent the Pillar of Severity (female, material, passive, negative), the Pillar of Mercy (male, spirit, active, positive), and the Pillar of Equilibrium, or balance. The lines joining the circles represent the development of mankind on our way back to our state of spirit.

The ten circles of the Tree of Life, another ancient geometry from the Cabalistic tradition, fit perfectly over the Flower of Life.

The Phi Ratio: Nature's Blueprint

The natural universe uses several different building blocks in its creation, but none more prevalent than the Phi Ratio, which is found in the structure of all living things. (A ratio is simply one number divided by another, such as length divided by height.)

Suppose we draw a square, A and draw a vertical line down its center. Then we draw a diagonal, D, and rotate D until it's horizontal. Curiously, the ratio of A/B, and C/A are exactly the same, i.e., 1.6180339.... This ratio is known as the phi ratio.

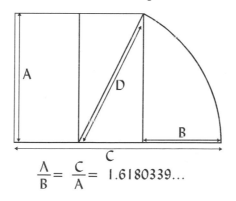

$$\frac{A}{B} = \frac{C}{A} = 1.6180339...$$

Next, let's enclose the arc made by D in its own rectangle. We now have two adjoining rectangles whose sides obey the phi ratio, and together, they make up a Golden Mean rectangle.

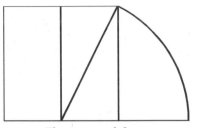

The original figure

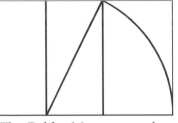

The Golden Mean rectangle

Now draw another square inside the smaller rectangle; we have a second Golden Mean rectangle. And we keep on drawing squares inside the smaller rectangle until we can't get any smaller. We could also work out, reversing the process.

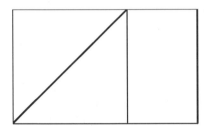

The Golden Mean rectangle

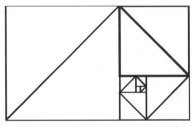

Five Golden Mean rectangles

If we draw in the diagonals and measure their lengths, something very odd happens. We find that the lengths follow a pattern called the "Fibonacci Series" (named after the Italian mathematician who first found it). Each number in this series is simply the sum of the two previous numbers:

$1 + 2 = 3, 2 + 3 = 5, 3 + 5 = 8, 5 + 8 = 13, 8 + 13 = 21$, and so on to infinity. In our diagram, the ratio of the lengths of the diagonals are: 1, 2, 3, 5, 8, 13, 21 … Curious, and it gets better. If we draw in all the arcs as shown in the diagram, we find one of the most common structures in Nature. This is exactly the pattern many crustaceans use when growing their shells. How do you suppose they know the math to follow this complex blueprint? Or is it just so deeply embedded in Nature that it comes naturally?

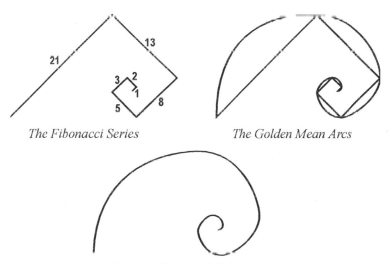

The Fibonacci Series   *The Golden Mean Arcs*

One of Nature's Favorite Blueprints

But it doesn't stop there; the phi ratio also applies to you and I. In "Proportions of the Human Body," Leonardo da Vinci demonstrated his knowledge of sacred geometry. He showed that we can draw a circle and a square around the human body when the arms are straight out and the feet are together. The circle and square meet under the feet. And the ratio of the circumference of the square to the circle? According to Drunvalo, it's the phi ratio.

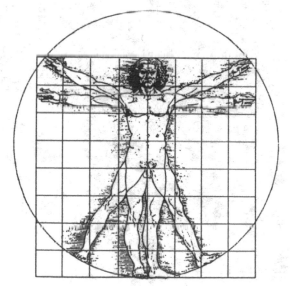

"The Proportions of Man" by Leonardo da Vinci

According to Drunvalo and his colleagues, this ratio and its spiral forms govern the formation of galaxies, the cells in our bodies, cell division during the first few minutes following conception, and even how the pyramids are laid out on the Giza Plateau. Now that's a blueprint!

There are many, many other blueprints: Mayan, Celtic, Druidic, Native American, Aboriginal, and so on—too many to recount here. And, of course, each species of ET has its own blueprint. That's a whole other book, but let's take a quick look at some key points of the Pleiadian blueprint, as related to Billy Meier and reported by Randolph Winters in *The Pleiadian Mission*, following his many visits with Billy in Switzerland.

The Pleiadian Blueprint

According to the Pleiadians, our universe is only one of 10^{49} (that's 10 followed by 49 zeros) that make up the "Absolutum." The Absolutum is spiritual energy, or pure spirit, and is a living, learning, evolving entity, constantly growing in complexity as it "tries out" different forms. The *only* way for it to evolve is to create material forms that also learn, grow, and evolve. These forms are the material universes that comprise the Absolutum.

A newly formed universe begins a journey of evolution that will last for trillions of years. It starts with the task of learning how to create matter. As its education continues, it then divides itself into seven bands of spiritual energy that resemble the rings we might see in a tree trunk. Physical matter begins to manifest itself in the fifth ring out from the center. It is here where all lifeforms begin their cycles of evolution and start on their own journey of knowledge that feeds the Creation.

Slowly, the central intelligence of the new universe creates progressively denser thoughts of matter—electrons, protons, neutrons, and so on. First, hydrogen forms, followed by increasingly complex atoms. Next, time is introduced to the material band as a pulsed energy against which motion can be measured. "Clocking" subatomic particles to the time pulses creates the sense of solid matter. Time pulses several billion times a second, and this "strobe" effect synchronizes our senses to atomic motion so we get the sense of matter being stationary when, in fact, it is in constant motion and far from solid.

According to the Pleiadians, the complete cycle of creation for our universe will be 311 trillion years. Our universe was formed 47 trillion years ago, complete with the spiritual energy that would later become the planet Earth about 626 billion years ago.

The main purpose of the material band is for spirit to learn through experience. The Pleiadians stress the importance of knowing that *we are spiritual being*s who just happen to be associated with a physical body for a short time, and that the force that drives your spirit is the search for truth.

They lay out a schedule for evolution with seven major phases, each with seven steps, making 49 steps in all. The following is reproduced by kind permission of Randolph Winters (see Resources).

Phase 1: The Beginning

1.1 **Development of the intellect**: Spirit is physical for the first time and has to "figure it all out."

1.2 **Spiritual life emerges**: after many purely physical lifetimes, primitive spiritual explanations for life may be formed.

1.3 **Development of Reason** based on many lifetimes and millions of years of experience, in and out of physical bodies.

1.4 **Use of Thinking** allows us to predict and plan for the future. Our spirit is also able to help the ego by feeding it with hunches.

1.5 **Reasonable Action**, in which we are still pretty self-centered, but slowly begin to think about others.

1.6 **Thoughtful Action**, in which we begin to cooperate with others and form social units like primitive tribes.

1.7 **Awareness of Reason**, leading to symbols and languages and more sophisticated communities like cities and, ultimately, nations.

Phase 2: Rational Living

2.1 **Evolution of Reason** leads to a material life but with growing questions about a "behind-the-scenes" bigger picture.

2.2 **Use of Reason** leads to active search for a larger meaning and an element of control over the material plane.

2.3 **Awareness of a Higher Power** intensifies the search for meaning and leads to religion and sciences like astrology.

2.4 **Awareness of Higher Influences** brings in religious belief systems and worship of native and conceptual idols, but with no true understanding yet of their significance.

2.5 **Belief in Higher Power and Superstition** refines religious beliefs but still yields limited understanding of creation. (Most of humanity is at this level.)

2.6 **Early Awareness of Spiritual Life**, involves healing, telepathy, and early attempts to use spiritual powers. (Most New Agers are at this level.)

2.7 **Development of Wisdom and Knowledge** leads to knowledge of what lies beyond material existence. (Metaphysicians and truly spiritual people are at this level.)

Phase 3: Life With Intelligence

3.1 **High Technology and Spiritual Insight** delivers the "spiritual person," adept in sacred geometry, energy devices, and primitive genetic experiments.

3.2 **Awareness of Knowledge and Wisdom** frees us from false thinking of the past.

3.3 **Use of Knowledge and Wisdom** for genetic engineering and energy manipulation.

3.4 **Use of Natural Laws** to gain wisdom of the universe around us and the forces of nature.

3.5 **Use of Spiritual Forces**, aided by spirit, to use non-physical means to address problems.

3.6 **Understanding Life** through knowledge of the spiritual realms and our role in creation.

3.7 **Awareness of the Real Meaning of Life**, and the laws of creation. Knowledge that gods are simply beings with arcane knowledge, developed over time, and not some supernatural deity.

Phase 4 extends our spiritual understanding of life, culminating with the abilities to create new life forms and travel interstellar distances. **Phase 5** masters advanced creation of organic lifeforms and begins preparation for nonphysical existence. **Phase 6** involves switching to pure spiritual existence, culminating in the end of independent human existence. We now fully understand and are one with creation. **Phase 7** is far removed from what we could understand as individuated consciousness.

The Pleiadian Blueprint is remarkable because out of the 49 steps, over countless billions of years, the average human is currently at step 12, and advanced metaphysicians are at step 14, so we've a ways to go. But then we have a little time left, too.

Within the vast picture painted by the Pleiadians, measured in billions of years, we are moving forward slowly and steadily, both as individuals and as a species. Slowly, we will realize that each of us is part of a whole, just as our species is one of many throughout our local universe, again all connected in one awesome "thought" of the universe. We all start as pure, non-physical spirit, then branch out into our myriad different forms and, ultimately, we merge back into Universal Consciousness.

The Pleiadians point out in *The Pleiadian Mission* that all separate life streams progress at different rates, some many millions of years ahead of others. I am reminded of the Hathors, the very advanced species that ascended long ago, and now in spirit form work with our planet. Even in the very brief history of Earth, our legends talk of the Anasazi and the Toltec peoples, both of whom apparently ascended once their work was done.

According to the Pleiadians, *we are all the same.* It's just that some are further along the path than others, and the wiser species have an obligation to guide the less wise. This is just as true within our species—the wiser guide the others, not through control or coercion, but through loving counsel.

Peace *will* come to Earth, the Pleiadians promise, when we all realize that we are spirit first and biological second, and that to judge the path of learning and experience chosen by another is meaningless and simply a waste of energy.

Even though we grow at our own pace, we are in a race against time due to our rapidly growing ability to destroy ourselves and the planet. If our wisdom can't keep pace with our weaponry, our evolution may come to a fork in the path. Some of us may choose the path of power, control, and alignment with service-to-self ETs, while others will take the path of spiritual growth. (This conflict has been played out so many times on Earth that you'd think we'd have gotten it by now.)

What can those who choose the spiritual path do to tilt the playing field? The Pleiadians have given us eight pointers, via Billy Meier and Randolph Winters, which are summarized below.

1. *Find your own truth.* The only real knowledge is that which you've earned through experience and reflection. So open your mind, set aside your ego, and learn to observe without prejudice. Now start over on your belief system.

2. *Promote Integrity.* Be honest with yourself and with others. Respect their truth even though it differs from yours. Give without concern for anything in return.
3. *Be a Role Model.* As a leader in the New Age community, exemplify wisdom, integrity, intelligence, and love.
4. *Practice Equality and Universal Love.* See all beings as spirit beings on a path of growth and learning. Share with others on a spirit-to-spirit basis rather than on a material barter basis. Do not impede the love that is innate to your spirit.
5. *Honor planet Earth.* Spend time enjoying the physical wonders the planet has to offer. Know that all are guided by elementals, or spirit beings, who work with natural phenomena and learn to communicate with them. Live *with* the planet, not *on* it.
6. *Study Spirit.* Learn all you can about your larger identity and share it with others. Although we may each walk alone, we can walk in the footprints of those who have gone before.
7. *Help Educate the Young.* We are the accumulated experiences of all our lifetimes and it behooves us to help those just setting out in life by sharing our wisdom. Considering that over 50 percent of children in the U.S. are mentally, emotionally, or physically abused, what kind of legacy are we leaving them? Children respond well to love and encouragement. Whatever legacy we leave them, it should serve both them and their future well.
8. *Be Creative.* Expressing creativity keeps you youthful and fulfilled. Set aside time for creative expression and surround yourself with the fruits of your creativity. Constantly stretch your faculties and challenge your limitations. Remember, life is a school. Have you signed up for a new class lately?

Personal Blueprints

In addition to whatever blueprint we glean from any major religion to which we've been exposed, we each have several personal blueprints that define who we are, how our bodies are constructed, what guides the hundreds of choices we make in daily life, and how we conduct our relationships with ourselves, each other, and the universe at large. When we come to our twilight years and look back over our lives, we can see the choices that worked well for us and those that didn't, the latter usually made when we stepped away from our blueprint.

The single most important thing is to know and *live* your personal blueprints. It is important to base your blueprint on truth, otherwise weird and strange things can happen.

The Chakra System: "Wheels of Fortune"

Another structural blueprint that defines your very being is the chakra system. If you accept that your primary identity is your Higher Self, spirit, or soul, where is it and how does it communicate with your ego? And for that matter, where does your ego live anyway?

Your spirit is an entity made up of energy of such an extremely high frequency that scientific instruments can't measure it. In fact, it's not even in the same dimension as those instruments. So how does your spirit energize your body and communicate with you?

Surrounding your body is an etheric "double" that is higher frequency than your physical body. It conducts the even higher frequency, subtle life-force energy of your spirit through meridians (nonphysical wiring) between energy centers called chakras. Each chakra works with an area of the body and certain physical organs.

The etheric double houses the astral body which holds energy associated with emotions, the mental body which carries your thoughts, and you can visualize your inner self living in the causal body. All these bodies coincide spatially with your physical body. They are all composed of energy vibrating at immeasurably high frequencies, each in its own range which is why they don't get mixed up. (Right now, thousands of radio and TV signals are flooding through your body, all kept separate because they all have different frequencies.) All these bodies are composed of the same energy "stuff" but of different frequencies. In fact, you are composed of the same "stuff" as the rest of the universe, including whatever you believe the supreme deity to be.

Your various energy bodies are connected by "transformers" called chakras (the Sanskrit word for "wheel"). These also store information, memories, and emotions encoded as energy. Hence, your chakras contain much of what is unique about you, just like your cell's DNA defines what is unique about you physically. Seven of the chakras are of particular interest because they lie within the boundary of the physical body and influence its operation. (The seven lower chakras are explained more thoroughly in Appendix B.)

Operating from Balance

We live in a first, second, fifth and sixth chakra society; many of us live by our intellect and ability to communicate externally while working through survival issues. If we feel threatened by the power and authority of others, our third chakra is shut down or blocked by fear. If we manage to quell our fears for a moment, what happens? Our mind is up there, chattering away like so many monkeys in the forest treetops and often making just as little sense. The task facing us is to enlarge our sense of who we are, and be able to respect and value others as individuals while acknowledging any shortcomings in their behavior. That would move us into a fourth and seventh chakra state of unconditional love.

Unconditional love is directed to everyone much like a radio station's signal. Its antenna transmits to the world at large, regardless of who, if anyone, is listening. It imposes no conditions and does not try to possess the listeners. It just swamps anyone listening with its signals regardless of who they are and how they feel about the station.

Because they are conduits for your higher self to express through your personality, your chakras define who you really are. And if they're not all open to the same degree and balanced, one or more dominates the others. For example, you may be operating from fear of some sort if the lower chakras are in charge and carrying negative childhood imprinting, or, if your sixth chakra is in charge, you may operate from the intellect and judge others without concern for their intrinsic worth as people. Any good psychic healer can read the state of your chakras, balance them, and open them up at a pace you can handle.

Shifting Paradigms

We are in the midst of a great Spiritual Revolution in which humanity is searching for the deeper truths on an unprecedented scale. For some, this means turning back to the major religions, while others strike out on new paths, as did the Beatles when they sought the truth in the East.

In the past, major religions such as Christianity and Islam believed that they held the copyright on the Truth. We saw the Spanish Conquistadors imposing their beliefs on the Aztecs at sword-point, and the Crusades, in which King Richard of England took on Islam in the Holy Wars. Still today, we see two factions of Christianity blowing each other to pieces in Northern Ireland, and Jews and Arabs venting millennia of religious intolerance with each other. But slowly, as a planet, we are becoming more tolerant of others' beliefs.

The Spiritual Revolution, dubbed the "New Age," is about gleaning the real wisdom from all the major teachings on this planet and beyond. The day will come when the teachings of the Pleiadians, Arcturans, Sirians, and so on, stand shoulder-to-shoulder with the more traditional religions, and are taught in schools. I, for one, will be there to applaud this momentous event.

Probably the most exciting event in our history is unfolding as the days of the old millennium draw to a close with the emergence of a new species within the very midst of *Homo sapiens*.

Since 1995, we are seeing what Art Bell calls "millennium children" who are genetically different from the rest of us. According to the Genome Project appointed by the World Health Organization to map our DNA, as of 1998, geneticists have identified the purposes and function of only about 30 percent of the genetic material in our cells, with the remainder still a mystery. Is it possible that this mysterious 70 percent is a "back-up" to allow us to evolve in response to environmental changes such as HIV?

In the spring of 1998, Gregg Braden reported on the Art Bell Show that in 1995 HIV research that was published in science journals claimed that the DNA of one in a hundred people had mutated so that it was thousands of times more resistant to HIV. Researchers were amazed to find that this mutation happened *within the individual's lifetime* rather than over several generations as with any other mutation.

Other researchers found that previously dormant areas of DNA were switching on to produce immunity to other diseases such as cancer. Is some part of us manifesting spontaneous DNA mutation in response to toxins and viruses in our bodies? In 1996, the *New England Journal of Medicine* reported that babies born HIV positive were found to be completely free of any trace of the virus within months.

If this is true, what's the mechanism that turns DNA sequences on and off? Many studies report that *emotion* and *belief* actually switches on sections of dormant DNA in recovery from incurable diseases. Researchers believe that these spontaneous genetic changes are significant enough to warrant calling these people a *whole new species* living among us.

As of 1998, the effects have been limited to measurable phenomena, such as enhanced immunity and increased intelligence. The pioneering work of Robert Gerard, author of *DNA Healing Techniques*, suggests that full DNA activation (the technique he describes in the book) will increase psychic powers, abolish susceptibility to disease, enhance contact with one's spirit, and even trigger rejuvenation.

Improved psychic powers will bring about increased awareness not only of our own soul and its mission, but of the entire Spiritual Hierarchy and *its* mission. This also includes the realms of the higher-dimensional ETs who make up a large part of the Spiritual Hierarchy.

A major limitation implicit in organized religions is that they deny individuality. Religious dogma is a one-size-fits-all set of beliefs that followers are expected to adopt, lumping themselves together as they worship their collective deity. Since we all hold our unique piece of the Divine Blueprint, such denial of individuality is a serious shortcoming.

Ideally, we will be best served by gleaning whatever truths from the major religions we most resonate with by blending them with our personal blueprint. There's a down-side to this, however; it's hard work. It means study, reading, talking, and thinking. Unfortunately, it's much easier to go to the church, mosque, temple, or synagogue and be told what to think.

Compare traveling on a freeway versus on the side roads. On the freeway, you can move quickly but you must go where the builders decided they want you to go. No decisions or judgments are needed; you go with the flow. But on the side streets, you must choose your own route, making decisions at every intersection—left, right or straight on. Hard work and possibly dangerous.

The beauty of the freeway approach to your belief system is that all of your thinking has been done for you, neatly packaged and ready for use. Quick, easy, and convenient. No challenge, no surprises, no neat little jewels waiting to be discovered. There's safety in numbers because every week, you get together with others who will parrot the blueprint along with you. Believing the same doctrine as millions of others is safe. You have an authority to fall back on if things get tough or you're challenged. And millions of others to tell you you're right. It's so important to feel right that you might even go to war to prove that what you believe is right and that all the others are wrong. Given that there are so many paths back to your deity, all of them can't be right, can they? So the others *must* be wrong.

Eight Steps to Transformation

Those brave (or foolhardy) enough to strike out on their own and carve their own path will need a sharp machete. I am indebted to Eri-Ka Schneider Morningstar for this particularly powerful tool to help us in the process of awakening to our higher destiny. The following outlines an eight-step process for self-transformation (to contact Eri-Ka, see Resources):

1. **Awareness: the awakening Call.** A vague sense of dissatisfaction begins to pervade your life and you begin to feel somehow incomplete. In your search for higher meaning, your soul puts people, knowledge and understanding in your path to awaken you to your true identity. You become aware of the unity of all that is, of your magnificent role in the unfolding process of creation. You have become an initiate in the mystery school.

2. **Acceptance: Owning your Power as creator.** As you become increasingly aware of your identity and power, you begin to accept it and integrate your power to create your own reality. At this stage, any place in your life that is out of balance or dysfunctional comes to the fore to be looked at so that you can see where you have given your power away. You form more empowering relationships and your vibratory rate rises, allowing you to live more in unconditional love. A sense of your mission is awakened.

3. **Activation: Expressing your Divine Blueprint.** Powerful shifts occur in all levels of your life and you work to have your life reflect your soul mission. Your physical appearance begins to glow with your inner power and your psychic powers increase. Life may become an emotional roller-coaster as deeply held patterns are released.

4. **Action: Using your Power to creative positive change.** You drop everything that is not in alignment with your Divine Blueprint: jobs, relationships, and activities. You begin to move out into the world with your power and divinity. You are a conscious reality creator and are always looking for the highest expression of who you are.

5. **Aligning: Being at one with Universal Truth and Unity.**

6. **Allowing: Becoming an Anchor of Love and Divine Will.** These two steps are intertwined. As you align with Universal Truth, you naturally anchor grace in your life. You allow your soul to work through you at all times, aligning yourself with the larger purpose of creation.

7. **Assisting: Helping others in the process of Transformation**. You are a conscious and unconscious transmitter of Divine Love to all those around you, and through resonance with your energy, others, too, begin their own journey.

8. **Ascending: Bridging into the fifth dimension as an individual and as a planet**. You have been anchoring the fifth-dimensional frequency of Divine Love on the physical plane, and now the song of your soul, the song of Creation, and the song of all humanity blends into a glorious symphony of the One.

Imagine these eight steps arranged at the points of an eight-pointed star. You can use this star as a mandala in meditation for raising your personal vibration so that you can contact the Spiritual Hierarchy and speed up your process of personal transformation.

I would like to share with you the amazing story of synchronicity regarding this eight-step process. First, let me tell you a little about Eri-Ka. For as long as she can remember, she has been a powerful psychic. As a little girl, she would talk to animals, fairies, and other elementals. Living on a farm, her favorite animals to communicate with were horses and her thirty cats. During her teenage years, just as with me, the powers and the psychic sight receded, resurfacing in her early twenties when she read *An Ascension Handbook* by Tony Stubbs.

I met Eri-Ka for the first time at the Star Knowledge Conference in July, 1996, where we took an immediate liking to each other, and found that our professional interests dovetailed perfectly. I met her again in October when I was a speaker at the Whole Life Expo in Denver. I invited her to stay at my house if ever she was in California, which she did, and our friendship continue to deepen. Eri-Ka's work was greatly enhanced when she became a channel for the Elohim, those high entities who work with the forces of creation (see Resources).

Early in 1998, Eri-Ka wrote a magazine article about the eight-step process and described a dream in which she met a bunch of extraterrestrials. The article was published on April 3, and Associated Press picked up the story and ran it nationally, as though Eri-Ka claimed that the dream encounter had actually happened in real life. Not only that, but the AP wire also gave her name and home phone number. Every radio station and newspaper in her home state as well as many other states contacted her and she became the butt of many radio talk show jokes.

On Saturday, April 4, Eri-Ka was at the end of her tether with all the crank calls. She meditated to ask her guides what to do. "Call Robert Perala," they told her.

"No, I can't bother him. It's been over a year since we've talked."

"CALL ROBERT PERALA," they repeated.

In some distress, she called me to ask what to do. Without mentioning his name, I passed her over to Tony Stubbs who just happened to be working with me at the time. He gave her the necessary professional advice, but imagine her surprise at finding that the source of the advice was none other than the author of the book that had changed her life years earlier!

The point of this story is that before we incarnate, we make a number of agreements with other souls in our soul family to meet up once we're on the planet and it's very important to recognize those agreements when they come to fruition. Through synchronicity and resonance, our souls make the agreement so obvious that it's hard to miss, but you do have to pay attention. If you feel a special liking for someone, or find a synergy between your work, you've probably found a soul agreement.

With all these blueprints for living, now can we know what's true. Limited by our puny brains and our linear languages, there's no way we can possibly comprehend the big Truth. But accepting that, let's take a closer look at the Divine Blueprint.

Chapter 16

The Divine Blueprint

Many years ago, Spirit or whatever dropped the idea of this book into my mind, along with the title, *The Divine Blueprint*. I was horrified at the enormity of the title, and the arrogance of anyone presumptuous enough to call a book with a title such as that. Delusions of grandeur are not my style so the idea sat on the shelf until 1997 when I took it down, dusted it off, and found that I actually liked the title. Smart work on the Masters' part.

One gentleman told me that we already have a Divine Blueprint—the Bible. He said that every single word comes directly from the lips of God and is true down to the tiniest detail. I didn't feel like pointing out that it has been translated many times, from Aramaic to Greek to English, and has suffered considerable distortion at each step.

In fact, in the fourth century, the Roman Emperor Constantine reportedly married a "lady of easy virtue" who was horrified that Christianity, her husband's new religion, taught reincarnation. She worried that she would have to come back to atone for the sins of her life. Constantine didn't care one way or the other, so to appease his wife, he told the bishops at Nicea to remove all Biblical references to reincarnation. They complied willingly because reincarnation was bad for business (i.e., church income) since congregations who believed they had a number of lifetimes to "get right with God" had little motivation to shape up and contribute to the church fund. Therefore, based on the whim of one woman and the greed of the church fathers, all references to the offending truth were removed. The bishops also took the opportunity to rewrite large parts of the New Testament in order to strengthen political, societal, and economic control over church members.

As we strike out and carve our own paths through the dense thicket of beliefs, what about the entrenched dogma we leave behind? Take with you what works and leave the rest behind. If organized religions find that they're no longer answering people's questions or providing a "big picture" framework for explaining life, they have a choice. They can go on with business as usual, or they can change and adapt to a more sophisticated set of seekers.

The Bible tells us that "in the last days, men shall have great visions, and the truth shall be set upon the earth." This is *exactly* what is happening in these closing days of the millennium. We find channels on every street corner, that metaphysical books account for the greatest increase in new books being published, and that new spiritual radio and TV shows air every week. All this adds fresher ingredients to the mix, and the Internet flashes them around the world within seconds.

Be selective in this avalanche of new information. Avoid those that claim to be the "Absolute Truth." There is no way we can possibly comprehend the big Truth with our puny brains, or speak them with our linear languages. But accepting that, let's take a closer look at the Divine Blueprint.

The Divine Blueprint

The Divine Blueprint has two major components: (1) the micro-plan, which guides our daily lives, and is rooted in our genetics, our belief system, our emotions, and our soul; and (2) the macro-plan that guides the evolution of our planet, our species, and the universe as a whole. Both are intimately related in man's search for identity because the individual search can only be viewed against the backdrop of the macro-plan. Your piece of the Divine Blueprint lies within you, in your heart center, and by getting in touch with it, you can use it to weigh events and make decisions in your life. Each of us has the task of accessing this blueprint and aligning ourselves with it.

If there is such a divine blueprint, how do you access it? If your soul is the architect, how do you bridge the gulf between your ego that is reading these words and your soul that exists beyond time and space? The first step is knowing that your soul, along with its blueprint, exists on the other side of the gulf. Now, I'm telling you that you have a soul. Can I prove to you that you have one? No. And even if I could, that would be too easy. Do you believe me? Do you have to believe me? Of course not. This is a free will planet. The greatest mysteries left to solve are, "Who are you before you are born, and who are you after you die? And what's the thread between incarnations?"

Now let's take a look at the scope of this Divine Blueprint. In its smallest scope, it records the reasons why you decided to incarnate in this lifetime, what you hoped to accomplish, what you wanted to learn, and what you wanted to teach to other people. Enlarging the scope a little, your soul has had maybe thousands of lifetimes, so what does your soul intend to accomplish in all these lifetimes? Getting larger again, accepting that, as a soul, you are part of a larger soul group, what does your soul group collectively intend to accomplish over the millions of lifetimes?

In the larger scope, your Divine Blueprint is the same as that of many other souls, but at the smallest scope, it is unique and personal to you in this lifetime, laying out your specific goals, hopes, and aspirations.

In discussing the Divine Blueprint, I am not trying to rewrite ancient scriptures that have guided humanity for centuries. Instead, we are transcending them, to arrive at what I call "pure spirituality," universal principles that span Creation. What happens when you begin to live more in alignment with your Divine Blueprint?

Once you open up to the wisdom locked within your Divine Blueprint, you will be flooded by a "download" of information into your conscious mind. Torrents of ideas and knowing will cascade into your awareness.

The next question is: How will I react when that happens? Confusion? Fear? Probably. As new truths challenge old ideas you've cherished all your life, you won't know what to believe. You'll feel vulnerable, like a hermit crab between shells. All of your life, you've felt secure on this planet. God's up there, and Hell's down there somewhere, and you're somewhere in the middle, trying to get to Heaven while avoiding Hell. And now, whole bunches of ETs and angels are appearing, telling you that's not how it is. Now you learn that you're one species on a tiny lump of rock circling a relatively small star, surrounded by ancient civilizations with very advanced technology, and that we're all moving rapidly to a higher dimension.

How on Earth do you process *that* based on your personal experience to date? How can you feel safe anymore when everything you believe to be true is torn up in an instant? What to do? Try and shut out the new truths? Deny them? Kill the messengers who brought them? It must be "the work of the devil" trying to confuse and undermine society. Right? Wrong, I'm afraid. Welcome to the New Age, the Age of Aquarius.

Do you have the courage to embrace this new information *and* the extraterrestrial messengers? We are fast approaching the fork in the road when you must choose—the new unsafe, unproven paradigm, or the old, worn-out security blanket you've huddled under all your life. Scary, isn't it?

Your ability to handle this will depend on how well you have tapped into the Divine Blueprint, or "the big picture." And *that* in turn depends on how much you're in touch with your heart center because your mental apparatus just ain't gonna cut it. The new truths go way beyond the power of the mind, of what you *know* to be true, to the realm of what you *feel* to be true.

Examining new truths, evaluating them, weighing them against truths received by others—all in a time of social upheaval and turmoil—will be a challenge. It may take years, even decades, for things to clarify but when they do, humanity will have reached "a place called Truth."

The world is very different compared with the last time something like this happened. Two thousand years ago, the only communication was from wandering preachers and storytellers. News of the day traveled slowly, told and retold orally, allowing distortion to creep in, both deliberate and accidental. Today, news flashes around the world in seconds, courtesy of CNN and the Internet. The entire world attended the funeral of Princess Diana and Mother Theresa, and we grieved as a planet. We truly live in a global village, thanks to the awesome power of modern communications. This same power will be harnessed to spread the word and bring the planet to this place called Truth. When the entire planet hears the same words at the same time, there will be no room for distortion, "spin doctoring," or hidden agendas. Popes and bishops will not be able to rewrite the truth about reincarnation as they did in 325 AD.

Planetary communications doesn't mean that it will be easy, however. Conflict is inevitable and modern communications intensifies it. Today, anyone with a computer can reach millions of people to spread love, or fear and separation. Too many of us are too vested in the Old Age and its partial truths to give them up without a struggle; they may die defending the Old Age against the New. But slowly, truth will prevail as a new generation is birthed with full access to the Divine Blueprint. Truth will eventually be hammered out in the crucible of conflict.

As the old blueprints fall away because they fail to explain the events around us and what we're feeling, we will slowly (or quickly, in many cases) embrace the new, larger truths Within a decade or so, our bejeweled planet will, indeed, be a *place called Truth.*

Fulfilling the Divine Blueprint

Deep in our hearts, we each harbor a vision of what life would ideally be like. Many people have had visions of a future exalted humanity, a world beyond conflict and war, a world where the planet's resources are shared equitably among its inhabitants, human, animal, and plant. A world in which forgiveness is natural and following spirit is second nature, where loving compassion flows freely, and colors all our interactions, where we feel unity and connectedness.

The best way to evaluate a belief system is to look at what is created from it—in this case, our daily lives. What will life be like once we are living the Divine Blueprint?

The first major difference occurs at birth. The veil of forgetfulness is lifted. This means that you come will into this life with full memory of your last sojourn on the higher dimensions where you planned this life. You know who you are in spirit and your mission. Imagine remembering *all* your past lives, what you learned, the skills you picked up, and every role you've ever played. Imagine being fully telepathic from birth and communicating with your loved ones without having to learn the language. They remember you and have been eagerly awaiting your arrival. The joy you feel at reuniting with members of your soul family is matched only by theirs. Your birth is a time of great celebration as you telepathically compare notes about your lifetimes together.

Imagine free and easy access to *all* knowledge, both of this planet and of our cosmic brothers and sisters from other planets.

Imagine a world in which love flows beyond your wildest dreams, a love for all creation based on the deep realization that we are all one. A world of profound love that colors all your relationships with gentleness, kindness, compassion, and selflessness.

Imagine a world free from the fear of death because we all know death is but a transition back to our true spiritual nature, that which we call "life" is just a short sojourn in flesh.

Imagine a world in which doing any kind of harm to anyone or anything simply could not happen because everyone is fully aware of their spirit connection. This includes not doing harm to the planet, which sparkles like a jewel in the heavens with clear, blue skies, pristine land and glorious forests, sparkling, clean rivers and oceans teeming with abundant life.

Imagine a world in which the mysteries are unveiled, where we play in universal truths like innocent children in a sandbox. There are no secrets and no hidden agendas, for nothing can be kept "secret." Everyone dwells in a profound sense of connectedness and belonging to All That Is.

Above all, imagine that you know you are intimately a part of the Creator, a part of the Divine Blueprint. You will find this out through your heart, when you come home to that place deep within you, *a place called Truth.*

The Divine *You*

And now to the most important part of the Divine Blueprint—*you.* In all of creation, there is no other you. You are unique and one of a kind. While this is not news to you, it's something we tend to forget. The careful, calculated plan that you put together before your birth is now moving through you and becoming more evident than ever.

That blueprint, that life-path, your soul's purpose is becoming more evident to you as it awakens you to your true nature. It is also activating your conscious and subconscious minds to remind you of your soul mission, the reason you came here. All my research into the esoteric has led to one thing: when all said and done, it still comes down to the self—your original plan, what you came here to learn, and what you intended to accomplish with your life.

When you sense your own divinity, you feel many things, especially your true nature and the creator God. You are a particular point of the Creator itself. You and God are one and the same. To think that you are in any way separate is only an illusion that you agreed to hold, backed up by the misinformation handed down to you by those who thought they knew life's universal truths. What you deliberately agreed to forget at birth was the intimate knowledge that you and God are one together. Letting go of this illusion now would allow you to walk in so much more joy and harmony, knowing that you are truly living your Divine Blueprint within the Creator.

The Earth is in constant change and there are so many distractions that pull you away from your divine self. I give a very heartfelt salute to those of you who have spent years in research, reading hundreds of books, and attending countless workshops and lectures, because I know you are truly committed to bettering yourself and the planet. In doing this, you do it for all of us since we are all one in the end.

Living the Divine Blueprint is not easy, and you have probably been told that being divine or "supremely good" is simply unrealistic. It's not so much that people want to be bad, but that they don't know how to be good, and you *are* fundamentally good. The only difference between your successes and failures is the awareness and wisdom in between. And any so called failures in your life happened simply because you needed to acquire some piece of information. Each choice and decision you make during your day is an opportunity to fulfill your personal blueprint. It's comforting to know that even if you made a choice that did not appear to serve you at the time, it turned out to be a stepping stone to the success you so yearn for.

When in doubt, call on your divine higher self, knowing that you are divine and have the divine right to be great. You are a way-shower and a pioneer here with a mission at the greatest time in the history of mankind. Do you dare to be great? And do you dare *not* to be great? Are you ready to play your part in service to those who will need to know what you know over the years leading to ascension?

Your blueprint, or the game-plan you mapped out for this life, is becoming increasing evident to you as well as to others, due largely to the energies that are now coming into the planet. And those people with interlocking blueprints are coming together via stunning synchronicities to form teams, for be in no doubt, ascension is a team effort. No one person can "do it all." We all have pieces of the whole puzzle, and to be effective, those pieces must be joined together, just like in a jigsaw puzzle. Only then will we see "The Big Picture."

The energies flooding onto the planet magnify our subtle and conscious bodies and amplify the cause-and-effect templates within each of us. They also have a quickening effect on our individual blueprint as well as that of the planet herself. This vast scenario points to the universe preparing Earth and her people to be birthed into The Big Picture. The cause-and-effect quickening focuses our values and priorities on what we hold important as individuals and as a species, and we are quickly confronted by the consequences of our choices as everything seems to be speeding up.

Everyone seems to agree that the very fabric of our reality is shifting very quickly, that humanity is at a crossroads, and that ahead lies the New Millennium. Theologians, Bible scholars, and researchers of various spiritual doctrines strive to solve parts of this grand puzzle, and many retrofit the interpretations to suit their agendas. But the truth is bigger than that. While each religion plays a very important part in this conscious evolution and holds particles of truth, no one religion has a handle on the absolute, on the Divine Blueprint.

You carry a very special piece of the Divine Blueprint, built up carefully over many incarnations, not only on Earth but in many other realities. The question is, what are you going to do with all this knowledge?

The Divine Messenger

As a way-shower, you have one of the greatest opportunities in the course of human history right in front of you—the chance to step forward with some of the most significant information this planet has ever known. All your experiences, the books you've read, and the lectures and workshops you've attended add up to a huge body of wisdom. How well you own and use that wisdom is up to you.

During my out-of-body experience in Egypt, I saw the tremendous impact of each word we utter to everyone we meet. I saw that it's not a valiant push to "save the planet" that's needed as much as your daily words and deeds of kindness that, through the "ripple effect," spread out and affect thousands.

While many have dubbed me "a messenger," we are, in fact, all messengers. As conscious beings, we all transmit messages that will either improve a situation or make it worse, heal or harm another person, and spread love or fear. The oldest message of all is eternal: love, compassion, forgiveness, service, and integrity … the list goes on. What message are you spreading? Love or fear?

You Are Not Alone

Every channeled message I have ever heard, plus my guided fieldtrips into the astral plane, have all shown me that you are constantly surrounded by help from beings on the other dimensions. The love that these beings have for you in your struggle to pierce the veil would bring tears to your eyes if only you could feel it. But do not consider those beings the exalted ones and you the student—they have the easy job. It was *you* that bravely incarnated in this hostile environment, and *you* who are determined to shine your divinity into the darkness and ignorance. *You* are the exalted one who sacrificed awareness of your own divinity in order to incarnate and experience duality, knowing that your message will make a difference. Every waking moment, rejoice at the wonderful opportunty your spirit has created in incarnating as you, here and now, at the dawn of the Golden Age.

The Spiritual Hierarchy holds *YOU* as the exalted one for what you are doing, and they pledge their love and support to your efforts. Go forth with your message knowing that you are loved by the very highest archangel and ascended master. Call out to them and receive the help and assistance they promised to you before you came here. It is your birthright.

Tell the world that you are an emissary of the Creator and that you bring a message of the greatest love and hope that this planet has ever heard. All of creation is watching as we birth a glorious, golden future from the Divine Blueprint. Let us join together with other lightworkers and way showers, and manifest Heaven on Earth in our time. Let us move swiftly to new heights of love and divine service as we find the Divine Blueprint in our hearts, join with others, embrace the Christ Light, and manifest our divinity.

May the divinity in you see and honor the divinity in all those you meet, and let your light be a beacon to others searching in the darkness. Speak your truth quietly, for the truth has no need to shout, but speak it from your heart, knowing that *you* are a Divine Messenger, here to co-create a glorious new reality based on the Divine Blueprint, on Truth, and on Love.

Appendix A

Religious Blueprints

Christianity

The central element of Christianity, as expressed in the Gospels of the New Testament, is Jesus Christ, also known as the "Son of God" and the "Savior." Another major component is the love of God for his followers. Other attributes include God's dominion over heaven and on earth, and the judgment of good and evil.

Two primary issues to Christians are the love of God and the love of neighbor. But underpinning Christianity is the goal of resurrection, leading to everlasting life spent in the kingdom of God, where one's good deeds will be rewarded.

Judaism

One of the world's oldest religions, Judaism is an integrated cultural system encompassing both individual and communal existence, out of which sprang Christianity and Islam. Its central aspect is that of a single, transcendent God who created the universe and continues to govern it. The mind of God is evident in both the natural order of things (through creation) and a social-historical aspect (received through revelation, most notably at Mount Sinai when the blueprint was revealed and encoded in the Torah as a set of commandments on which members are to base their lives in interaction with one another and with God).

Also very important is the covenant, or contractual agreement, between God and the Jewish people, in which the latter acknowledge God as their sole deity, agreeing to obey his laws. In return, God acknowledges Israel as his chosen people and protect them. Thus the fortunes of Israel depend on obedience to God's commandments in a direct causal relationship between behavior and destiny.

The covenant promises that obedience will ultimately be rewarded and sin punished by judgment after death. At this time, the inequities suffered by the Jewish people would also be redressed by the coming of the Messiah to redeem the Jews and restore them to sovereignty in their land.

Islam

With almost a billion followers worldwide, Islam is based on the teachings of the Prophet, or Muhammad. The word "Islam" means "to surrender to the will or law of God," but this is to be done with free will rather than blind obedience to God's commandments. The blueprint is recorded in the Koran, believed to be dictated by God directly to Muhammad, and widely regarded as the least changed of all the major blueprints.

Islam stresses belief in one omnipotent God. God created nature, and then provided each component with its own laws to govern its conduct, resulting in a structured, harmonious universe in which everything has its proper place, presided over by God. According to Islam, God has four fundamental functions with respect to the universe and to humanity in particular: creation, sustenance, guidance, and judgment.

As with Christianity and Judaism, the blueprint includes a Day of Judgment, during which all humanity will be gathered and individuals will be judged solely according to the kindness or otherwise of their deeds. Those that "pass" will go to the Garden (heaven), and the "losers" will go to hell.

Hinduism

Originating in India, Hinduism has spread to many other parts of the world. The word "Hindu" comes from the Sanskrit word for river and the Indus). It is defined more by what its followers *do* rather than what they *think*, leading to a uniformity in behavior. Most Hindus worship Shiva, Vishnu, and the Goddess Devi, plus many lesser deities. Behavior includes reverence for cows, a ban on eating meat, and a caste system. Although there is no priesthood in Hinduism, the fact that the social system is inseparable from the religion gives each person a sense of responsibility.

The Hindu blueprint is contained in the Vedas, a set of four revealed teachings consisting of lengthy stories that tell the philosophy, law, geography, political science, and astronomy of the religion. Hindus believe that the universe is a great, enclosed sphere within which are numerous concentric heavens, hells, oceans, and continents, with India at the center. In vast cycles, the universe is believed destroyed by fire and flood, only to be followed by a new age. They also believe in reincarnation, with the soul being reborn in the body of another person, animal, vegetable, or mineral, depending on the actions, or karma, committed in past lives.

Buddhism

Buddhism, a major world religion, was founded in northeastern India and based on the teachings of Siddhartha Gautama, born in 563 BC, who challenged the authority of the Hindu hierarchy, denied the validity of the Vedas, and opened his movement to all castes on the basis that a person's spiritual worth was not a matter of birth.

Renouncing all attachments at the age of 29, he sought peace and enlightenment, and release from the cycle of rebirths. After many years of meditation, he attained the enlightenment he sought. He became a wandering preacher, gathering a body of disciples around him, some of whom committed his words to paper.

The Buddhist blueprint he devised rested on the Four Noble Truths:
1. Life is suffering, and human existence is one of pain from the moment of birth
2. All suffering is caused by ignorance of the nature of reality and the cravings that result from that ignorance
3. Suffering can be overcome by dispelling ignorance and attachment
4. The way to suppress suffering is by the Noble Eightfold Path, which consists of right views, right intention, right speech, right action, right livelihood, right effort, right-mindedness, and right contemplation.

Confucianism

Confucianism developed from the teachings of the philosopher Confucius, whose blueprint emphasized good conduct, practical wisdom, and proper social relationships. More an ideology than a religion, its principles are contained in nine ancient Chinese works by Confucius, the most famous of which in the West is probably the *I Ching*, or Book of Changes.

Central to the Confucian blueprint are love, goodness, and humanity in relationships, as typified in the Confucian golden rule, "Do not do to others what you do not want done to yourself." The teachings also govern the right conduct of politics, commerce, and business.

Taoism

About six thousand years old, Taoism, is based on the *Tao-te Ching* (The Way and Its Power), written by Lao-Tzu. In a departure from Confucianism, Taoism urges its adherents to ignore the dictates of society and seek only to conform with the underlying pattern of the Tao, or the way of the universe. In this blueprint, one has to do nothing strained, artificial, or unnatural. Through avoiding doctrines and knowledge, one can achieve unity with the Tao and enjoy its mystical and transcendent power.

Shintoism

Shinto is Japanese for "the way of the gods." It is an ancient Japanese religion and occupies an important national position. It has no fixed system of dogma or sacred writings, and worships a vast panoply of spirits, or nature divinities, such as the sky, the earth, the sun and moon, and storms. Ritual involves thanksgiving by means of offerings of valuables.

Overshadowed by the spread of Buddhism around the 6th century, the ancient practice of Shinto almost disappeared until the 18th century when it was revived as an important national religion in which the emperor ruled by divine right.

Appendix B

The Chakra System

The chakras (the Sanskrit word for "wheel") are actually frequency transformers that connect your energy bodies, stepping energy frequencies up and down between them as necessary. The chakras store information, memories, and emotions encoded as energy. Hence, your chakras contain much of what is unique about you, just like your cell's DNA defines what is unique about you physically. Seven of the chakras are of particular interest because they lie within the boundary of the physical body and influence its operation.

#1: Root Chakra, or Survival Center, is located at the base of the spine and coincides with the perineum. It is related to your ability to

PHYSICAL ORGANS & GLANDS

#7: CROWN
Pineal, Brain, Central nervous system

#6: BROW
Pituitary, Eyes, Hypothalmus

#5: THROAT
Thyroid, Neck, Ears, Respiratory system

#4: HEART
Thymus, Lungs, Heart, Blood pressure, Lymphs

#3: SOLAR PLEX
Pancreas, Stomach, Liver, Digestion

#2: SACRAL
Spleen, Ovaries, Adrenals, Kidneys

#1: BASE/ROOT
Genitalia, Legs, Feet, Lower spine

MENTAL/ EMOTIONAL/ SPIRITUAL

#7: SPIRITUAL
Compassion, Selflessness Spiritual connection

#6: INNER SIGHT
Clairvoyance, Service, Psychic awareness

#5: COMMUNICATION
Clarity, Creativity, Speaking feelings

#4: LOVE/HEALING
Harmony, Love, Trust, Giving, Growth, Flexibility,

#3: POWER
Will-power, Control over Self and Others,

#2: SEXUAL/CREATIVITY
Emotional needs, Boundaries, Sexual energy, Creativity

#1: SURVIVAL
Basic body needs, Safety, Sex, Groundedness

survive and operate effectively at the material level. It houses the vital life-force that energizes your body at its lowest level. It is also where survival issues such as the need for sex, food, and safety are stored. If open and operating correctly, you are comfortably grounded and relate well to those around you, have a realistic self-image, and are generally in good health with plenty of vitality. If it is not functioning correctly, you will be plagued by aches and pains, and feel ungrounded and not connected.

#2: Sacral Chakra, or Emotional Center, is located about three inches below your navel, and Eastern sources associate it with the spleen, ovaries, adrenal glands and kidneys. It also pumps energy from the first chakra into the various energy bodies. It houses your deepest emotions, your basic sense of self-worth, your connectedness with the world around you, your creativity, and your sexuality (as opposed to the raw need for sex). Signs of a healthy second are feelings of optimism, friendship, courage, sensitivity, belongingness, value to society, personal validity and worth, trust in yourself and in dealing with others, creativity, and a high degree of regard for yourself and your emotions. An unhealthy second manifests pessimism, guilt, difficult relations with others, lack of being in touch with your own emotions resulting in ill temper and unpredictability in emotions because of repression. Being the pivotal point between first and third chakras, a blocked or closed second chakra will trigger unhealthy survival instincts in the first and power-hungry tactics in the third.

#3: Solar Plexus Chakra, or Power Center, located about three inches above the navel, governs your personal power and capacity for operating in groups. If operating well, you have high vitality and resilience, self control, and respect for yourself and others. You will lead by coordination, encouragement and motivation, and are obviously in charge of your life without trying to take charge of the lives of others. If it is blocked, your dealings with others are hindered by feelings of inadequacy, indecisiveness, and anxiety about what others think about you.

#4: Heart Chakra, or Love Center, is the pivot between the lower three and the upper three chakras. It governs your compassion for yourself and others, the quality of your joy and sorrow, and your ability to give and receive unconditional love. If it's open, you feel at one with life and other people based on everyone's right to be here, equal fitness, and validity. You will be profoundly serene regardless of the turmoil around you, and will appreciate life with open, unconditional love. If

it's closed, you will experience tension, shallow emotions, supercilious behavior, judging based on trivial comparisons, meanness and conditional love. You will deny yourself life's treats and joys, hoard whatever wealth you have, and will lie to yourself and others.

This chakra draws in energy from the back, mixes it with your own personal energy running up and down the spine, and radiates it forwards to other beings and the planet. Being associated with the thymus gland, this chakra governs the immune system and, if closed, impairs your resistance to disease and prevents your personal growth.

#5: Throat Chakra, or Communication Center, just below the Adam's Apple, governs speech and all the senses except touch. If open, your senses are sharp, perception accurate, and your verbal communication is clear and sincere. It also aids clairaudience, contact with non-physical entities and with your own inner wisdom. With a closed fifth, you have problems with expressing yourself, not trusting yourself to speak, discrepancies between your words and deeds, clumsy and inappropriate comments, and a reliance on clichés.

#6: Brow Chakra, or Third Eye, located between and just above the eyes, is the prime channel for intuition, inspiration and access to the inner self. A clear, open sixth chakra is essential for contacting and working with your inner self, so develop it and protect it. Through it, you can access a wealth of wisdom and information that is available beyond the senses. A blocked sixth leaves you feeling cut off, without intuitive hunches, and relying only on what you have learned and sensed.

#7: Crown Chakra, located at the top of the head, is the channel for direct contact with higher energy and understanding your connection with the universe. (The appearance of an open seventh is the reason why artists paint a halo around the head of an enlightened subject.) An open seventh shows as a strong yet gentle personality, comfortably balanced between both earthly life and spiritual life, detachment from focus on the self, a compassion for others, and a total awareness of the transitory nature of death. A closed seventh results in being stuck in a no-growth pattern, reluctance or denial of any greater meaning in life, even to the point of a fear of life and certainly a fear of death.

The vast majority of humans have a blocked seventh. Opening it requires courage because it means going beyond the self and conventional materialistic goals, on a path of no return in which selfishness will be replaced by unconditional love. If you are holding any fear at all, your feelings towards your fellow humans are conditional because you are imposing an expectation of their behavior. Letting go of fear is the single greatest and most difficult task facing us, and because fear is so ingrained and such a habit, the first problem is just recognizing that you are trapped in it.

Reading List

Andrews, Colin, *Circular Evidence*, Bloomsbury, London, 1989

Braden, Gregg, *Awakening to Zero Point*, Sacred Space / Ancient Wisdom, Questa, NM, (1993, 1994)

—— *Walking Between the Worlds: The Science of Compassion*, Radio Bookstore Press, Bellevue, WA, (1997)

Brinkley, Dannion, *Saved by the Light*, Harper Collins, New York, NY, (1995)

Carroll, Lee, *The Kryon Books I – VI*, The Kryon Writings, 1155 Camino Del Mar #422, Del Mar, CA 92014, phone: (800) 352-6657

Clow, Barbara Hand, *The Pleiadian Agenda: A New Cosmology for the Age of Light*, Bear & Company, Santa Fe, NM, (1995)

Dyer, Wayne W., *You'll See It When You Believe It*, Avon Books, New York, NY, (1989)

Eadie, Betty J., *Embraced by the Light*, Gold Leaf Press, Placerville, CA, (1992)

Essene, Virginia and Nidle, Sheldan, *You Are Becoming a Galactic Human*, SEE Publishing Company, Santa Clara, CA, (1994)

Gerard, Robert V., DNA Healing Techniques, Oughten House Foundation, Livermore, CA, (1998)

Holes in Heaven (HAARP video), Heaven Project, PO Box 91655, Pasadena, CA 91101

Hunter, Larry, and Knott, Alex, *Project Gateway to Orion*, AARF, 1997 (see Resources)

Hynek, J. Allen, and Vallee, Jacques, *The Edge of Reality: A progress report on unidentified Flying Objects*, Henry Regnery Company, Chicago, IL, (1975)

Lake, Gina, *The Extraterrestrial Vision*, Oughten House Publications, Livermore, CA (1993)

—— *ET Contact*, Oughten House, Livermore, CA (1996)

Manning, Jeane, and Begich, Dr. Nick, *Angels Don't Play This HAARP*. Call (907) 249-9111

McCannon, Tricia, *Dialogues With the Angels*, Horizons Unlimited, Inc., Atlanta, GA, (1996)

—— *Beings of Light, Worlds in Transition (tape-set)* (Resources)

Milanovich, Norma Dr., *We, The Arcturians*, Athena Press, Albuquerque, NM, (1990)

Sitchin, Zecharia, *The 12th Planet*, Bear & Company, Santa Fe, NM, (1991)

Sterling, Fred, *Kirael: The Great Shift*, Oughten House Publications, Livermore, CA, (1998)

Stevens, Wendelle, UFO - *Contact from the Pleiades, an Investigative Report,* Genesis III Publishing, Munds Park, AZ

———— *Messages from the Pleiades, UFO Photo Archives*, Tuscon, AZ

Strieber, Whitley, *Communion: A True Story*, Avon Books, New York, (1987)

———— *Transformation: The Breakthrough,* Avon Books, New York, (1987)

———— Majestic: The Government Lied, Putnam's Sons, (1989) & Berkley Books, New York, (1990)

Stubbs, Tony, *An Ascension Handbook*, Oughten House Publications, Livermore, CA, (1992)

West, John Anthony, *The Mystery of the Sphinx*, video, (1995), The Sphinx Project (see Resources)

———— *Serpent in the Sky: The High Wisdom of Ancient Egypt*, Quest Books, (1993)

Winters, Randolph, *The Pleiadian Mission*,(1994), The Pleiades Project (see Resources)

Resources

Angela Browne-Miller, Metaterra, 98 Main St. #315, Tiburon, CA 94920

Art Bell (Coast-to-Coast radio), PO Box 4755, Pahrump, NV 89041, fax: (702) 727-8499

Art Martin, 8300 Rock Springs Road, Penryn, CA 95663, (916) 663-3910, Toll-free order line (800) OK-LET-GO

Betty Eadie, PO Box 25490, Seattle, WA 98125

Center of Attention Newsletter, 2221 Bowers Avenue, Santa Clara, CA 95051, phone/fax: (408) 241-7981. $52/Year (U.S.), $65/year (foreign), or $44/year (online edition).

Circle Phenomenon Research. (Colin Andrews), PO Box 3378, Branford, CT 06405. (For the CPR International newsletter.)

Compassion-In-Action, PO Box 84013, Los Angeles, CA 90073, phone: (213) 931-7315, fax: (213) 931-2514, email: CIAdmin@aol.com, website: www.twilightbrigade.com

Courtney Brown, The Farsight Institute, PO Box 49243, Atlanta, GA 30359

DROP-IN (Determined to Restore Our Planet), Louise Harrison, We Care Global Family, Inc., PO Box 340, Benton, IL 62812

Drunvalo Melchizedek (Flower of Life), Humming Bird Trust, PO Box 4904, Cave Creek, AZ 85327, phone: (602) 488-1195, fax: (602) 488-8572, email: humming@primenet.com

Eri-Ka Schneider Morningstar, PO Box 1745, Raymore, MO 64083, phone: (806) 497-0336, email: melchizedek@cheerful.com

Gina Lake (astrological consultations and workshops), email: ginnlake@msn.com

Gregg Braden, Sacred Spaces/Ancient Wisdom, PO Box 5182, Santa Fe, NM 87502, phone: (615) 773-7691

International Tesla Society, PO Box 17697, Colorado Springs, CO 80935, phone: (719) 475-0918. Membership of $39/year includes the *Tesla Journal of Modern Science* and the *Afterhours* newsletter. Internet: www.tesla.org.

Jane Hofstetter, artist, 308 Dawson Dr., Santa Clara, CA 95051

Jeanne Johnson , astrologer, Second Sight Solutions, 850 S. Oneida, Denver CO 80224, phone: (303) 322-1619, email: secondsightsolutions@juno.com

Jim Downey (exorcist, spiritual therapist, healer, and psychic),
    PO Box 11249, Piedmont, CA 94611, phone: 1-800-266-LOVE
Larry Hunter (Project Gateway to Orion), 4440 Richard Drive, Los
    Angeles, CA, 90032, phone: (213) 223-0198
Melinda Connor, intuitive, 6113 Manteca Ct., San Jose, CA 95123
Oughten House Foundation (DNA Activation), PO Box 3728,
    Livermore, CA 94551, phone: (925) 447-2372,
    email: oughtenhouse@rest.com
Paula Peterson (clairvoyant empath), Earth Code & Inner Light
    Network, PO Box 3395, Santa Cruz, CA 95063, (408) 454-1440,
    email: earthcode@cruzers.com
Pleiades Project and Randolph Winters, PO Box 1270, Rancho
    Mirage, CA 92270
Power Places Tours, 24532 Del Prado, Dana Point, CA 92629,
    phone: (714) 487-3450, fax: (714) 487-3456
Richard Boylan, Ph.D. (consultant and researcher), 2826 O St. #2,
    Sacramento, CA 95816, phone: (916) 455-0120
Ruben Uriate, Asst. State Director, MUFON; Circle Phenomenon
    Research International, California Coordinator, 25200 Carlos Bee
    Rd., #34, Hayward, CA 94542, phone: (510) 247-1968
Sheldan Nidle, PO Box 277-332, Kihei, HI 96753
Sphinx Project, PO Box 2249, Livonia, MI 48151, (1-800-508-0558)
Stephen Alexander (crop circle photographer), 27 St. Francis Rd.,
    Gosport, Hampshire, England PO12 2UG, phone/fax: 01705-352867
Tony Stubbs, 29164 Pinecone Ct., Menifee, CA 92584,
    phone/fax: (909) 672-6115, email: tjpublish@aol.com
Tricia McCannon, phone: (888) 873-6682 or (404) 873-3070,
    website: members.AOL.com/TMcCannon
United Light Publishing, PO Box 112467, Campbell, CA 95011,
    voice mail: (408) 792-3333, fax: (408) 370-3818,
    email: rperala @unitedlight.com, website: www.unitedlight.com

About Robert Perala

Born in 1955, Robert was visited by apparitions for most of his early life. After a close encounter with extraterrestrials in 1977, he devoted the rest of his life to the study of metaphysics, spirituality, the teachings of the mystery schools, and the Bible. His quest has taken him over all the world, including expeditions to Egypt and England.

In 1992, Robert was approached by Pleiadian emissaries and asked to be a messenger to humanity and convey the truths that remarkable shifts are already happening on this planet; and will continue to happen, as we enter the new millennium and approach the Biblical "end-times." The Pleiadians were also explicit about what we can and must do to prepare for the changes.

Robert's professional background includes marketing, advertising, and concept and design in the fashion industry.

Today, Robert uses every means at his disposal to get his message out. He is the founder of United Light Publishing, and is a sought after guest on TV and radio shows. He even hosts his own radio show out of San Francisco (KEST 1450 AM) and co-hosts the television show, "Space Cities (KMVT, Mountain View, CA).

In honor of Robert's contribution to society, The American Biographical Institute bestowed on him their prestigious Distinguished Leadership Award.

The Divine Blueprint: Roadmap for the New Millennium is the next logical outlet for this cosmic messenger and his enthralling message. He can be reached at www.unitedlight.com.

About Tony Stubbs

Tony was born in England in 1947, and after graduating in electronics, worked in the British telecommunications industry. He emigrated to the U.S. in 1979 to continue working with computers. In 1980, he woke up to the world of spirit and immersed himself in metaphysics while continuing a career in computers and desktop publishing.

Tony began channeling and in 1989, the Ascended Master Serapis announced that they were to write a book together: *An Ascension Handbook*, published by Oughten House Publications. Providing a clear and concise explanation of the ascension process, it has enjoyed five printings and is a metaphysical best-seller.

After a period of living in Mexico where he was the editor of an English daily newspaper, Tony moved to Denver, Colorado, and started a computer school. He continued with his desktop publishing business while teaching at universities and computer schools in Denver.

Tony then moved to California to join Oughten House Publications as Editor-in-Chief and Director of Operations, and is now an independent consultant to authors and small publishers on writing, editing, self-publishing and book production. He can be reached at tjpublish@aol.com.